Buried Alive

Essays on Our Endangered Republic

WALTER KARP

Buried Alive

Essays on Our Endangered Republic

FRANKLIN
SQUARE
PRESS

NEW YORK

Published by Franklin Square Press, a division of Harper's Magazine,
666 Broadway, New York, N.Y. 10012.

First edition.

First printing 1992. Second printing 2004.

Library of Congress Cataloging-in-Publication Data
    Karp, Walter.
        Buried alive : essays on our endangered republic / Walter Karp.
            p. cm.
        Includes index.
    ISBN 1-879957-02-7
    ISBN 1-879957-04-3 (pbk.)
    1. United States—Politics and government—1981–1989.
    I. Title.
    E876.K37 1992
    973.927—dc20 92-6414 CIP

Buried Alive: Essays on Our Endangered Republic, by Walter Karp, edited by Lewis H. Lapham
and Ellen Rosenbush. Preface by Lewis H. Lapham.

Designed by Deborah Thomas.

Manufactured in the United States of America.

CONTENTS

Preface

"The world is given to those whom the world can trust."
—Walter Bagehot

When Walter Karp died on July 19, 1989, at the age of fifty-five, the American republic lost one of its most vigilant and resourceful advocates. Over the span of a quarter of a century in the pages of the country's leading political journals he waged an unrelenting war of words against what he called "the official version of things." I know of no other collection of recent political writing that presents so clear a statement of the American promise. To read Karp is to read the blueprint on which the country raises up the architecture of its politics.

Both as journalist and historian Karp was loyal to his convictions and faithful to the rigor of his own thought and observation. Because he didn't court the grace and favor of those in office, he didn't depend for his opinions on the whispers and rumors current among the best people on the Sunday morning talk shows. He had the courage to think for himself, a writer cut in the American grain who could count among his antecedents spirits as troublesome as Ambrose Bierce, Albert J. Nock, and H. L. Mencken.

I was lucky enough to know Walter Karp for almost twenty years, and I noticed that whenever I was in his company I found myself improved. Karp's was a voice not only of dissent but also of conscience—restless, uncompromising, uncowed, prodding me to eschew

1

cant, to remember the uses as well as the right of free speech, to do better. He was a stormy petrel of a man, small and excitable, delighting in the rush of his words and the energy of his ideas, indifferent to his material circumstances, trembling with a furious intensity that was both moral and intellectual, remorseless in his pursuit of what he thought was the truth. I remember him as being somehow constantly in motion, barely able to contain himself, quick to doubt and to question.

His passion was politics, and his precepts were simple and few. He believed that in America it is the people who have rights, not the state, and that the working of a democratic republic requires a raucous assembly of citizens unafraid to speak their minds. He thought that if only enough people had the courage to say what they meant, then all would be well. His reading of American history (especially the writings of Jefferson and Lincoln) taught him that the boon of liberty never could be taken lightly or for granted, and that the American Constitution assumed a ceaseless and bitter struggle between the interests of the few and the hopes of the many, between those who would limit and those who would extend the authority of the people.

Karp made a clear distinction between the American republic and the American nation, and it was to the first and more fundamental of these two Americas that he professed his allegiance. The republic, he once said, is what Americans founded when they founded America. He construed it as "the great central fact of American life—the constitution of liberty and self-government, the frame and arena of all American politics."

The republic in Karp's understanding of it was more a creed or an idea than a set of rules or a system of laws, a common spirit shared by a people whom Lincoln knew to be conceived in liberty and dedicated to a proposition. The nation, by comparison, Karp thought a "poor, dim thing" assembled as a corporate entity, sustained by "an artificial patriotism," and given the semblance of life and meaning only when inflated with the excitement of foreign wars. He detested the jingoism of what he called the "money power and its hired politicians" who cried up the hollow and bloodless sham of the nation-state.

It was the implacable conflict between the American republic and the American nation ("deadly rivals for the love and loyalty of the American people") that Karp recognized as the great drama of American politics. He knew full well that the odds always favored the oligarchs and would-be despots who aligned themselves with the presumptions of the state. He knew that it was always more convenient to submit to the rule of the few rather than keep up the endless struggle for self-rule, that servility was easier than freedom. The long odds didn't intimidate him, and he never abandoned his delight in "the energizing principle" of the American republic that inspired its citizens to love their country not because it was their own but because it was free.

Karp enlisted himself in the ranks of the many (i.e., among those who would extend, not limit, the authority of the people), and his writing mostly had to do with what he called "the wanton abuse of power" on the part of government officials, both elected and appointed, who minted the currency of the public trust into the base coin of their own petty ambitions. Following Madison, Karp believed that popular government without adequate information, or the means to acquire it, was "prologue to a farce," and he was habitually wary of official attempts to stifle or suppress the informed debate on which a democratic republic relies for the knowledge of itself.

His method was one of investigative reading, and he approached his study of politics as a historian less interested in the news of scandal (which he accepted as a constant) than in what John Adams once called "that most dreaded and envied kind of knowledge" about the character and conduct of the nation's rulers. Karp thought that the meaning of political events revealed itself more plainly in the reading room of a public library than in a White House press conference or in private conversations with well-placed government officials, who, as Karp well knew, entertained their respondents with welcome and self-serving lies. Once embarked on a line of inquiry, he read everything pertinent to the composition of a reliable record—newspapers, documents, journals, congressional testimony—and then, with his facts firmly in hand, he measured the distance between what politicians said and what they did. He described his method as "simply a matter of paying attention to public deeds that have been largely ignored or made light of."

The essay "Liberty Under Siege" that appears on page 227 of the present volume offers an especially fine demonstration of Karp's virtues as journalist, historian, and polemicist. During President Ronald Reagan's two terms in office, the government mounted a systematic assault on precisely those habits of free expression that Karp deemed inestimably precious, and in defense of the republic Karp wrote his essay as a grand remonstrance.

He began, as always, with a summary of the facts, setting forth the record of an administration that over a period of five short years (in the name of efficiency, thrift, or national security) had asserted the government's "right to confidentiality"; authorized the CIA to question American citizens; withheld documents from Congress under the rubric of "executive privilege"; subjected academic and scientific research to the government's "review and oversight"; attempted to eliminate postal subsidies for schools, libraries, and the blind; obliged government functionaries with access to "sensitive information" to sign agreements saying that they never would write or speak about what they had heard or seen without prior permission; restricted the circulation of published books and journals; excluded the press from the invasion of Grenada; defined reporters (in the words of Secretary of State George Shultz) as being "always against us"; construed press leaks (in the words of Assistant Attorney General Richard Willard) as "consensual crimes"; set up an Official Secrets Act; attacked not only the accuracy but also the legitimacy of the press.

At the end of his essay Karp allowed himself a peroration, which I ask the reader's pardon to quote at length because it so well expresses the spirit of the man:

> Imagine a venerable republic, the hope of the world, where the habits of freedom are besieged, where self-government is assailed, where the vigilant are blinded, the well-informed gagged, the press hounded, the courts weakened, the government exalted, the electorate degraded, the Constitution mocked, and laws reduced to a sham so that, in the fullness

of time, corporate enterprise may regain the paltry commercial freedom to endanger the well-being of the populace. Imagine a base-hearted political establishment, "liberal" as well as "conservative," Democratic as well as Republican, watching with silent, protective approval this lunatic assault on popular government. Imagine a soft-spoken demagogue, faithful to nothing except his own faction, being given a free hand to turn Americans into the enemies of their own ancient liberties.

Karp's methods and convictions, to say nothing of his language, put him at odds with the rules of deportment and the canons of taste that regulate the tone of contemporary American journalism. He liked the old and straightforward words that were synonymous with American political writing in the late eighteenth century—"oligarchy," "tyranny," "elective despotism"—and he wrote his essays in a prose bright with fierce eloquence. The dismantling of the grandiose fictions behind which "the lying pantaloons" in Washington concealed their shabby cowardice moved him to wild and derisive outbursts of sardonic glee.

He published eight books and more than two hundred magazine articles, but he was never generally acknowledged as an important writer; he never earned more than $30,000 in any one year, and he received few of the ornamental honors, subsidies, and flattering reviews that the journalistic profession bestows upon the virtues of solemn orthodoxy. Karp's enemies, who were many and envious, dismissed him as "cranky," "old-fashioned," "too literary," "too historical."

The world didn't trust Walter Karp and rewarded him with nothing in its gift. I doubt that he expected otherwise. I think he would have been insulted if he had been offered a Pulitzer Prize. He would have thought that he had said something too easy, too obvious, too polite. Mainstream American journalism was a profession that he held in contempt because he understood that the press, by and large, takes its prompts from the government, that it repeats what it is told by official sources (the Congress, the White House, the Defense Department), that it is in the business of defending the interests of the few against the hopes of the many. To Karp's mind the media were passive by nature and subservient by habit, accepting "leaks" and "handouts" as if they were gratuities offered to a butler or a gamekeeper.

If Karp thought the republic betrayed by a lying and servile press, he thought it even more poorly served by the schools. As always, he began with Jefferson, who had urged the teaching of political history so that Americans might "know ambition under all its shapes and be prompted to exert their natural powers to defeat its purposes." Without a useful course of study (i.e., one that instilled in the student the habit of independent thought), how could the American people acquire, again in Jefferson's words, the general education enabling "every man to judge for himself what will secure or endanger his freedom"? Or, in Karp's words, how would they learn to detect the would-be despot wearing the cloak of the popular tribune, or the oligarchy masquerading as the enlightened and the elect?

Karp remembered, as the educational bureaucracies did not, that the purpose of an American education was the training of an American citizenry, and he was quick to recognize in the academic fashions of the day (whether John Dewey's doctrine of "industrial cooperation" or the more recent theories of "multiculturalism") a concerted effort on the part of the managers of the state to impose on the American people a condition of docile ignorance. Karp deplored the "grinding of American history into sociological mush," and of all the false lessons taught in the schools the one he thought the most corrupt was the one that encouraged people to think that politics didn't matter.

Karp had little use for the customary reduction of political discourse into the vocabulary of decorous abstraction. He understood politics as a series of not very difficult answers to the not very difficult questions of who does what to whom, for how long, and at what cost to the common good. Nothing so moved him to mockery and scorn as the assumption that the sequence of historical events could be assigned to the "unseen workings of indeterminate forces" or that the art of political chicane could be attributed to the paltry desire of money.

I remember arguing the point with him on more than one afternoon in a downtown café, and I can still see him glaring at me across the table and denouncing me as a fool too easily caught in the net of facile cant. "The hardest way to make a million dollars," he said, "is to become a United States senator. Any vicious, impudent, brazen, shrewd, gifted person can think of an infinite number of better ways to become rich than to become a crooked politician."

Not that Karp didn't think that most politicians weren't brazen or impudent or crooked, but he understood that they savored the sweet and palpable pleasures of exercising authority, and I can still hear him laughing at the "absurd notion—very popular in the news media and the universities"—that somehow political power was of no interest to the people who held and enjoyed that power.

Despite his mocking pessimism he was never cynical, and he retained his faith in the energy and imagination of the American people. Confronted with another proof of mindless folly in the day's newspapers, he was fond of citing Jefferson's dictum that "we are never permitted to despair of the commonwealth."

Even so, I think Karp was surprised by the lack of public objection to the Reagan Administration's assault on his beloved habits of freedom, an assault that continues unabated and uncontested under the Bush Administration. The government effectively stuffed the mouths of any and all public officials who had tasted of the forbidden fruit of sensitive information, and yet, except for a few squeaks of ceremonial alarm in the nominally liberal sectors of the Congress and the news media, the decree was received as amiably as the report of yesterday's stock prices.

Across the whole spectrum of the political debate the silence has become almost audible, and I sorely miss Walter Karp's passionate dissent, just as I miss his sardonic wit and his antic improvisations on the themes of oligarchy and elective despotism. He was a historian of the best kind—an excited amateur who didn't allow the weight of footnotes or the fear of a faculty committee to impede the line of his argument or the energy of his thought. The essays contained in this book still teach, as they did when they first were published, the lessons of liberty. Such was Karp's purpose in the writing of political history. He knew that the lessons were never easy and never could be well enough learned. "A republic," said Jefferson, "if you can keep it," and left the defense to posterity and citizens as fierce and as eloquent as Walter Karp.

Lewis H. Lapham
New York
April 1, 1992

PART I
REPUBLICAN
PRINCIPLES

The Two Americas

E ven as a schoolboy reciting the Pledge of Allegiance, I thought America an odd sort of place. It was not one country, apparently, but two. It said so in the flag oath. "I pledge allegiance to the flag of the United States of America," we chirped in unison, and then concluded triumphantly that it was "one nation indivisible, with liberty and justice for all." That was one America, the "nation," whose "alabaster cities gleam," we piped at other times, "undimmed by human tears." But the flag hanging limply in the corner represented something else as well. There was "the republic for which it stands," an extra-added America, the "republic" whose nature and purport proved a puzzle too deep for the schoolboy mind to solve. Solve it, however, we must, because there are two distinct Americas, two separate objects of a patriot's devotion, two distinct foundations of two contrary codes of political virtue. One is the American nation, the other is the American republic. At every important juncture of our public life these two Americas conflict with each other.

On a famous occasion some years ago, the President of the United States secured an injunction against *The New York Times* ordering it to cease publishing certain classified government documents, known collectively as "the Pentagon Papers." Faced with an unprecedented attempt at press censorship, the *Times* promptly called on the aid of a distinguished law firm that it had been retaining for several decades. The distinguished law firm flatly refused to defend the *Times* against the violation of its constitutional liberties. To publish the documents in wartime, a senior partner said, was shameful, disgraceful, and unpatriotic. It would weaken the nation's resolve and give aid and comfort to its enemies. As its patriotic duty to the country, the distinguished law firm willingly sacrificed its most prestigious client. But which America did the law firm so patriotically serve? It served the corporate entity known as the nation. What it did not serve was the American republic. To defend the infringement of liberty, to refuse to uphold the Constitution in a crisis, to support the alien methods of despotism—surely that in a republic is shameful, disgraceful, and unpatriotic. The nation pulls one way, the republic another. They are today deadly rivals for the love and loyalty of the American people.

It is an odd sort of rivalry, one that the republic, on the face of it, ought to win hands down. The republic is the great central fact of American life. It is the constitution of liberty and self-government, the frame and arena of all American politics. It gives laws their legitimacy and cloaks public office with public authority. The republic is what Americans founded when they founded America. The nation, by comparison, is a poor, dim thing, for the nation is merely America conceived as a corporate unit, a hollow shell. The flag is its emblem, "Uncle Sam" is its nickname; yet there is virtually nothing in the internal life of America that can bring that abstract entity to life.

It is not the people writ large, the way it is, say, in France or Iran. Americans are not fellow nationals, we are fellow citizens. As G. K. Chesterton rightly remarked after paying a visit, America is more a creed than a country, and the creed is republicanism. The ties of a common nationality do not bind Americans together and never did. Even when the overwhelming majority of Americans were of English descent the very act that created America was a solemn declaration of independence from mere ties of nationality. Spurning nationality is our deepest political experience as Americans. I used to wonder as a child why the Boston Tea Party rebels dressed up as red Indians. It seemed a queer thing to do, since the rebels, by and large, were not fond of Indians. Now I see what they meant. The tea dumpers were rebelling not only against English rule but also against English nationality. They were either free citizens or rude savages, but "true-born Englishmen" they were insisting they were not. Love of the nation, mistakenly called nationalism, does not spring from nationality in America. It is not the flame that once burned in the hearts of stateless Poles and colonized Irishmen, that once fired Italians with a dream of political unity. We were citizens of the republic long before we ever saw ourselves as members of a nation. In the early days of the republic, the very word *nation,* innocuous in itself, actually offended fastidious republicans. They detected an aroma of despotism about it, and they were not, it turns out, all that far wrong.

We have traveled a long way since then, but devotion to the nation in America is still, inherently, devotion to an abstract entity. Orators at American Legion conventions call the sentiment "old-fashioned patriotism," but American memories are short. Devotion to the nation—"nationism," I will call it—is not very old in America. In 1852 Abraham Lincoln lauded his hero Henry Clay for being a patriot in two sorts of ways. Clay loved his country, Lincoln said, "partly because it was his own country, but mostly because it was a free country." To love America because you cherish the constitution of liberty is republican patriotism—what the distinguished law firm cared nothing about. To love America because America helped rear you Lincoln took to be merely natural; but nationism is not even patriotism of this natural kind. Natural patriotism is personal and concrete. It is love not of an entity but of things familiar and formative. During World War II a much-repeated story went around about the GI slogging through Italy's mud who was asked what he thought he was fighting for. He was fighting, he said, for Mom's apple pie, hot dogs, and the right to cheer the Brooklyn Dodgers. It sounded childish at the time, and it was. Natural patriotism *is* childlike. At bottom it is scarcely more than love of one's own childhood. There is nothing childlike about nationism, however, and nothing natural about it. We were a patriotic people long before nationism existed.

That would be hard to prove in a paragraph, but occasionally history recovers from the past a forgotten voice that reveals with wonderful economy the historical novelty of the new. One such voice was an angry editorial published by the New York *Journal of Commerce* in the year 1895. What aroused the ire of the newspaper was what it called "the artificial patriotism being worked up at the present time." And how was it being "worked up," this fabricated patriotism that was neither natural nor republican? Through the new and, to the *Journal of Commerce,* repugnant "fashion of hanging the flag from every schoolhouse and giving the boys military drill." America was well into its second century before those in authority thought patriotism required flagpoles on schools.

For that matter we were well into our second century before anyone thought patriotism required schoolchildren to pledge allegiance to the flag. The first time the pledge was ever recited in a classroom was in 1892. Until then the only civilian American required to swear fealty to the country was the President of the United States, but he pledged himself to "preserve, protect, and defend" not the nation, which has no legal existence, but the Constitution.

The paraphernalia of nationism is quite new. Even flag-worship is new. In the late nineteenth century "Old Glory" was indeed a popular emblem, so popular that merchants used it to hawk corsets, cough drops, and player pianos. There was nothing sacred then about the flag, precisely because the cult of the nation did not yet exist. The elaborate etiquette that now surrounds the national regalia was not concocted until 1923, the handiwork of the War Department and the newly formed American Legion. The object of the flag code was to transform the country's banner into a semi-holy talisman and so give the abstraction called the nation a semblance of life. No doubt the War Department half succeeded. When certain anti–Vietnam War protesters wanted to enrage their fellow citizens they burned American flags, proving how caught up in the flag cult, one way or another, most Americans had become.

I can still remember my own terrifying introduction to the more recondite aspects of twentieth-century flag-worship. It occurred at a Boy Scout meeting in April 1946, when the scoutmaster asked the assembled tenderfoots what we were supposed to do when the family's flag had grown tattered and unseemly. Throw it in the garbage, yelled one young heathen with no future in scouting. If you did that, the scoutmaster replied in hushed and portentous tones, you would be arrested and sent to prison. Fear and awe swept over us at the thought that an ordinary little flag—*private property* your father might have bought at a Woolworth's—could bring down upon you the majestic wrath of the all-seeing American Government, a thunderbolt, as it were, from Mount Olympus. The scoutmaster was exaggerating, but not by much. What he did not tell us, however, was that the law you broke by rudely disposing of a tattered flag did not originate in the misty, immemorial past. It had been enacted by Congress just four years before, in 1942.

In creating the cult of the nation—the "artificial patriotism" of 1895—the mummery of flag-worship played its part, but the part is minor. It took far more than sacred bunting and schoolroom pledges to transform a lifeless abstraction—rooted in nothing, springing from nothing, legally nonexistent—into the powerful rival of the venerable American republic. What it took was the whole weight and force of American foreign policy since the late nineteenth century. The reason for this is quite simple. The American nation, which has no life at home beyond what bunting will impart, comes to life internationally, for only in active dealings with other countries does the abstract entity, the nation, genuinely act as an entity. The republic exists for its own sake. The American nation lives abroad, and nationism in America is always a species of internationalism.

Once, on a radio discussion show, the moderator, vexed with me for "tearing down America," began delivering a long harangue about the horrors of dictatorship in Yugoslavia, a country he had recently visited. How then, he asked in conclusion, could anyone really criticize American politics when you compare our freedom with Tito's repressions? That is the true international voice of the nationist. He extols liberty in America by comparing it with despotism abroad. The republican, by contrast, compares liberty in America with one standard only, the one established in the principles and promise of the American republic itself. To the nationist, new-fashioned patriot of the twentieth century, America is always a nation among nations.

It is most fully a nation, most intensely alive as an entity, when it wages war against other nations. Even in peacetime it is the memory of past wars and the menace of future wars that keep the idea of the nation alive in America. War and the cult of the nation are virtually one and the same. That is why the "artificial patriotism" of 1895 included "giving the boys military drill"; why it was the War Department that promoted the flag code; why "patriotic" parades are almost invariably military displays; why the veterans' organizations are the most strenuous guardians of nationism—America, to the Legionnaire, is America at war, the war in which he himself served. Therein lies the radical distinction between patriotism and the cult of the nation. Americans needed no wars to love their country because it was their own; still less did they need war to love their country because it was free. It is the artificial patriotism of the nation that requires war, for without war the nation is but a shade wrapped in bunting.

Not many Americans love war for its own sake. Indeed, the only genuinely popular war we ever fought was the Spanish-American War, partly because it lasted only a few months. In America the cult of the nation does not exalt military glory. What it exalts are the repressive virtues of wartime. What it cloaks with patriotic ardor is hostility toward the virtues of a republic at peace.

During the two years preceding America's entry into World War I—a war that the overwhelming majority of Americans were desperately determined to stay out of—those who favored intervention actually set forth in a fierce pamphleteering agitation the virtues they hoped war would instill in postwar America. Mindful that nationism was still in its infancy (whipping a fifth-rate power in 1898 had helped, but not much), the pamphleteers wanted war to "forge a national soul" for America, which apparently had no "soul" since it was just a venerated republic. They hoped war would give birth to "a new religion of vital patriotism—that is, of consecration to the State," a consecration sadly lacking in the republic, like the very concept of America as a "State." Mindful that the nation can only live abroad, they hoped an overseas war would permanently imbue Americans with "a strong sense of international duty." Otherwise the nation would fade from our minds. Above all, they wanted war to bring about a "change in the whole attitude of the people toward government." It would teach the rising generations, seared by memories of a great foreign war, to think more of what they "owed" to their rulers and less about what they could "get" from them. It would teach them, too, a "wholesome respect" for the powerful. The result would be a postwar America that would enjoy, the interventionists said, the blessings of "complete internal peace."

The interventionists of 1916 wanted war to bring forth a new America—the second America—conceived in trench warfare and dedicated to the proposition that a few should rule and the rest should serve. Citizens of the republic would be transformed into docile agents of the American "State." A people taught for 150 years to guard and cherish its liberties would learn, instead, to guard and cherish the "national soul." An exacting and troublesome citizenry (which Americans had been during the years between 1890 and 1916) would henceforth ask no more of its governors than the humble opportunity to serve their international objectives. A "new religion" of nationism would eclipse and even supplant the old republican patriotism. That, in truth, was the point, the Archimedean point, of the interventionist enterprise. Among liberal intellectuals a few years ago, it was fashionable to deride the popular American "cult of the Constitution." They thought it a bulwark of "reaction," and the American people, by implication, the dupes of the rich. The interventionists of 1916 knew better. It was the cult of the Constitution that they wished to obliterate and the cult of the nation that they hoped to erect in its place, through a titanic foreign war—the only possible way of doing it. As Bertolt Brecht once said, If the rulers cannot get along with the people they will just have to elect a new people.

The virtues of the citizen-turned-nationist would be simple, logical, and straightforward. For the sake of the nation, whose strength abroad demands "complete internal peace," he would do all that "internal peace" requires. He would forgo the exercise of his liberties—to speak, to act, to voice independent judgments—and urge his fellow citizens to do likewise, for the sea of liberty is turbulent and weakens the nation in the performance of its "international duties." For the sake of internal peace he would rest content with his lot and cease dividing the counsels of the powerful with selfish demands upon his government. In domestic affairs he would mind his own business and ask for nothing. In foreign affairs he would mind everyone else's business and call hotly for action. Eternal vigilance, liberty's steep price, he would willingly abandon because only a people that shows "confidence" in its rulers can provide them with the power to act forcefully abroad. Mutual respect, which citizens pay to one another simply because they are fellow citizens, he would replace with the patriotism of mutual suspicion—"positive polarization," as a presidential administration was to call it fifty-five years later. His own "vital patriotism" he would display by condemning as "disloyal" and "un-American" those who still cherished the republic and still fought to preserve and perfect it. Sedition, the crime of weakening the nation by critical words, he would undertake to root out among his neighbors ("America—Love it or leave it!"), although officially no such crime exists in America. Such was the new-modeled citizen envisioned by the warmongers of 1916 and extolled ever since by the promoters of nationism.

The agitators of 1916 did not go unanswered, for the republic had not yet been eclipsed. We had not yet reached the stage, for example, at which a respected political commentator describing "America as a civilization" could call the Constitution "at most" a "symbol" of national unity, a flag made of parchment. Despite the agitators' fine talk about fighting in Europe for "democracy against autocracy," their critics (who spoke for the great majority of Americans) were not deceived. They understood quite clearly that the interventionists wanted to establish a deadly rival to the American republic and a fount of new virtues that snuffed out republican virtues. The war agitation itself, said one antiwar senator, James Vardaman of Mississippi, was "a colossal blood-stained monument marking the turning point in the life of this Government." And he was right. If we enter the

European war, said another antiwar senator, William J. Stone of Missouri, "we will never again have this same old republic." And he, too, was right. What the interventionists wanted, their critics said, was a "Prussianized" America, an America whose citizens no longer loved their country because it was free but merely because it was feared. The critics' voices have long been forgotten, but like the angry editorial in the *Journal of Commerce* they reveal in their quaint, out-of-date language the historical novelty of the way we live now.

The novelty has long since worn off. In 1916 only a handful of Americans dared call openly for a "change in the whole attitude of the people toward government." Forty-five years and three foreign wars later, it was an American President, freshly sworn in, who was hailed for telling his fellow citizens to "ask not" what their country could do for them but to ask what they could do for their country while it paid "any price," bore "any burden," met "any hardship" to defend liberty abroad. Sixty-one years after 1916 another President, newly inaugurated, warned his fellow citizens that the chief "crisis" facing America was their lack of "confidence" in their betters. In the corridors of power the promoters of nationism are triumphant. Understandably they trust and advance only their own kind.

When the Nixon Administration was shopping around for a new legal counsel to the President, a bright young attorney working for the House Judiciary Committee caught the eye of the White House. Searching scrutiny certified him as a loyal, unblemished patriot who met the stringent requirements of the highest level of security clearance (something not required for any government service until World War II). And what did this eminently trustworthy young patriot believe? That an American President had the right to do whatever he could get away with. Had the young attorney shown signs of doubting that truly subversive proposition, would the FBI have "cleared" him? I doubt it. For the past twenty-five years the FBI, which, like the nation, first blossomed in World War I, has kept a secret file on the American Civil Liberties Union in Chicago, an allegedly "disloyal" organization. That assessment reveals much about the two Americas. Disloyal to the republic the ACLU certainly is not, since its chief activity is providing legal aid to citizens whose constitutional rights have been violated. Is it disloyal to the nation? Of course it is. Citizens active enough to require government infringement of their rights obviously disrupt the nation's "internal peace." Who but the disloyal would think it a duty to defend them? There is nothing illogical about nationism. Much of its strength in the country derives from its simple logic.

What confounds and unnerves the nationist is the indestructible fact of the American republic. He lives in enemy territory among a people still only half-conquered. That is one reason why J. Edgar Hoover strained every resource of his organization to provide Americans with a reassuring image—efficient yet politically innocuous—of the FBI. He didn't do so because he thought Americans would inevitably admire his G-men. Nobody labors to achieve the inevitable. On the contrary, Hoover feared that citizens-turned-nationists just might revert back again. So long as the republic endures, nothing can wholly prevent that reversion. The great historian of ancient Rome Theodor Mommsen once observed that a republic founded by popular consent exerts an authority over its citizens so strong, so pervasive, so intimately entwined with their lives that the citizenry cannot even imagine a life outside its sway. So it is with the American republic. If nationism runs strong in the country—and it does—the hearts of Americans are nonetheless divided, like the country in which we now live.

Until 1965 the division of our hearts, part nationist, part republican, lay concealed under the crushing weight of a quarter-century of war and continual foreign crisis. Then something happened. The nationists in power overreached themselves. A President who promised a war against poverty and no wider war in Asia launched a massive war in Asia and left the poor as poor as ever. To his shock and dismay, divided American hearts did not "rally to the flag." There was no outpouring of nationist sentiment. A magazine writer visiting Kansas in 1967 described the strange war temper in what was soon to be called "Middle America." On the one hand, not a single Kansas town had played host to an antiwar demonstration. On the other, local draft boards were cheerfully deferring every youth who offered any plausible grounds for deferment. Angry moral arguments against the war played little part in producing that surprisingly tepid response—a response that no contemporary poll could detect. What lay behind it was a profound sense of political betrayal. A President had promised peace and given us war, had committed a gross breach of faith and treated his countrymen with sovereign contempt. We were not nationists enough to cheer the fruits of a betrayal so deep; we were still republican enough to resent the contempt of the mighty. Loathed from coast to coast, the faithless President was peacefully driven from power. Six years later, another President, as lawless as his predecessor had been faithless, discovered, too, that Americans were not nationist enough to "stand by" a President for the sake of the nation, that we were still republican enough to resent the lawlessness of the mighty. He, too, was peacefully driven from power.

A half-conquered people had asserted, if only in a negative way, their old republican patriotism. There were still limits to what even citizens-turned-nationists would tolerate, and they were republican limits, so deeply American that Europeans, nationists to their marrow, could not even begin to fathom the events of that riotous decade. In those events the profound antagonism between nation and republic at last stood fully revealed.

That Americans would not tolerate faithless or lawless Presidents should have been grounds for modest rejoicing. I think the American people did rejoice—in private. I think we did take quiet pride in acting, for once, as a free people should. I think we felt a measure of public happiness in seeing the ponderous machinery of the Constitution set in motion for a republican end. What else can explain the extraordinary outpouring of good feeling on July 4, 1976, a celebration of the birth of the republic that turned the strife-torn streets of New York into a scene of tumultuous goodwill and mutual respect so palpable it seemed for a few sweet hours that republican patriotism had had a rebirth?

In the corridors of power where nationists congregate, there was no rejoicing whatever. That the "religion of vital patriotism" had not entirely snuffed out republican sentiment in America brought only wringing of hands, gnashing of teeth, and dire warnings of imminent disaster. Americans had refused to rally behind a war treacherously begun and dubiously justified. What was that, the nationists say, but proof of the people's lack of "will" and "resolve" to fulfill their "international duty"—as if only the powerful were licensed to define our duties. Americans had refused to let two successive Presidents abuse power and betray their trust. What was that, the nationists say, but a dangerous "weakening of the presidency"—as if presidential despotism alone kept America intact. Americans had shaken off their political torpor and participated in public affairs. What was that, a future aide of President Carter wrote in 1975, but a perilous want of "deference" in the American people—as if servility (pronounced "civility" by so-called neo-conservatives) could possibly be a virtue in a republic con-stituted for self-government. Americans had exercised keen vigilance over the powerful. What was that, the nationists say, but a national "crisis of confidence"—as if the powerful enjoyed a divine right to our trust. To impugn the republican virtue of vigilance, the nationists even coined a new name for it. They called it "post-Watergate morality," as if submission to corrupt power and blind faith in one's leaders were the old, the hallowed morality, like the "old-fashioned patriotism" of the American Legion. Every republican virtue that surfaced so surpris-ingly in the tumultuous decade the nationists, citing the rival virtues of wartime, have by now obliquely condemned. They are still trying to elect a new people.

Offspring of war, the cult of the nation is itself a weapon of politi-cal warfare, the undeclared war waged by the powerful few against the political vitality of the American republic. It is the only popular weapon they have. The republic cannot be destroyed—its collapse would bring ruin to all. Its legitimacy cannot be subverted—it is the source of all legitimacy in America. Even today the elementary max-ims of the republic cannot be defied with impunity, as President Nixon learned to his regret. The moment he claimed to stand above the laws his political doom was in sight. Too many Americans still remembered the copybook rule: "We are a government of laws, not of men." Americans, I think, can even distinguish in a general way the few genuine heroes of the republic from the common herd of famous leaders. In Washington, D.C., a city crammed with memorials to the undeserving—think of the Sam Rayburn Building and the John F. Kennedy Center for the Performing Arts—Congress has not yet dared to create more than three major monuments: to Washington, to Jefferson, and to Lincoln, the two great founders and the one great savior of the American republic.

Still, that does not add up to much. The republic is more than the form of our government plus a few rudimentary maxims and memories. It embodies a profound principle of political action—an "energizing" principle, as Jefferson called it. It is supposed to operate at all times and under all conditions against oligarchy, special privilege, and arbitrary power. The energizing principle is the preservation and perfecting of self-government, the securing to each citizen of an equal voice in his own government. That grand object, as Lincoln once said, we must as republicans constantly strive for, constantly try to "approximate" even if we can never perfectly achieve it. Without its energizing principle a republic becomes a hollow form or, still worse, a ponderous hindrance. Yet it is a truly burdensome principle to live by. It is easier to be servile than free, easier to submit to the rule of a few than to keep up the endless struggle for self-rule. It is easier to fight enemies abroad than to fight for the republic at home. That is why the virtue of virtues in a republic, as Montesquieu long ago observed, is the citizens' love of the republic—"to be jealous of naught save the republican character of their country," as the Workingmen's Party put it 150 years ago when it campaigned for free public schools in America. That is why the enemies of popular self-government have striven to erect and strengthen the rival cult of the nation, by war if possible, by the menace of war when there is a perilous lull in the fighting. It is the only way to undermine the people's love of the republic and subvert among the citizenry themselves its energizing principle.

In the name of the nation, that undermining goes on unceasingly. It is the reason why the one thing never taught in our free public schools is "to be jealous of naught save the republican character" of our country. In my own school days we learned more about Betsy Ross and the wonders of the Panama Canal than we did about Abraham Lincoln, whose birthday is no longer celebrated in a dozen states that once paid his memory that homage. Above all, it is the reason why what old Henry Cabot Lodge called the "large" foreign policy—the policy of having a busy foreign policy—has governed our foreign affairs for so many long years. It is precisely the "large" policy that keeps the nation alive and the republic in twilight.

After forty consecutive years of war and rumor of war—one-fifth the republic's entire span of existence—it is a wonder, perhaps, that republican virtues survive at all. That they do bears witness to the awesome authority of our republican foundations, since almost nothing else in contemporary America keeps them alive. What has not survived is honest political utterance. In the two Americas everything gets mislabeled. Subverters of the republic hunt down "subversives," and enemies of the republican principle decide who is and who is not "un-American." We describe as "old-fashioned patriots" those who warn us that American liberties endanger the nation, and the "religion of vital patriotism—that is, of consecration to the State," nonexistent in 1916, is the "neo-conservatism" of 1979.

The Radical Republic

B y any reasonable definition, a conservative ought to be a philo-sophical friend to things as they are, someone who can detect the subtle uses of apparently obsolete customs, uncover the hidden virtues that redeem apparent abuses, who can trace with a cherishing intelligence the complex links that bind society into a workable whole. In any commonwealth a true conservative would be an eminently useful voice. Yet in its entire history as a country, America has failed to produce a single important political writer or statesman who meets the commonsense definition of a conservative.

Historically, the typical American "conservative" has been someone determined to overthrow something fundamental to the common life of the country. We have had conservatives who wanted voters disenfranchised and "mass democracy" curbed; conservatives who pined for a parliamentary system of government; conservatives who wanted America ruled by a council of corporate magnates; conservatives who yearned for established churches and fixed social classes. Today we have conservatives who would dismantle the federal government in order to restore "the free-market economy" and conservatives who would have us wage holy war against Russia though the very heavens might fall. So far from cherishing things as they are, the conservative in America is almost invariably a malcontent. Britain has its Burke, Coleridge, and Dr. Johnson, its Pitt, Disraeli, and Churchill. American conservatives cannot lay firm claim to a single American hero. Alexander Hamilton is often regarded as the archetypal American conservative, and in a certain sense he was. At one point in his career Hamilton talked of overthrowing the republic and making himself First Consul.

That America produces no genuine conservatives is not a trivial quirk of the American character. The truth is, it is impossible to be a genuine conservative in America. The moment you set about defending the American system of things as they are, the horns of an American dilemma will impale your efforts. The dilemma is simply this: that part of things as they are in America is the awesome fact of our republican form of government and its radical assertion of the sovereignty of the people. There is no getting around that fact. The conservative, for example, rightly prizes political legitimacy, knowing as he does that illicit power—power without authority—cannot afford to rest, to stop, to conserve. It can tear a commonwealth to shreds. In America, however, all legitimate power rests on republican foundations; nothing is legitimate in America merely because it is old or customary. If you cherish legitimate power in America, how are you going to cherish and defend the existing fact of usurped and illicit power—the power, say, of great corporations and political-party syndicates? The conservative must either set himself against such power or set himself against the foundations, which define what is rightful and what usurped in the political realm. The American system of things as they are will not let itself be cherished as a whole. Prize one fundamental aspect of our common life and you must call for the reformation of some other fundamental aspect of our common life. There is no middle ground in America, and consequently no true conservatism in America. Of this there is no better proof than the elaborate attempt by Garry Wills, one of the country's most intelligent, erudite, and resourceful political writers, to propound a truly conservative creed [*Confessions of a Conservative*, Doubleday, 1979].

Wills's effort began, he tells us, when, back in 1957, fresh out of a Jesuit seminary, he joined up with William Buckley and the *National Review*. It did not take him long to realize that there was nothing very "conservative" about his *National Review* colleagues. The "libertarian" element in the circle consisted of semi-anarchists who pleaded for untrammeled individualism; the "authoritarian" faction, at the other pole, dreamed neomedieval dreams of state-enforced virtue and discipline. Instead of cherishing the American system of things as they are, both factions were vehemently opposed to most of it. "They were rebels against the present order—which is not a bad thing in itself," Wills says, "though it is an odd position for those calling themselves conservatives." What Wills wanted to devise, on the contrary, was an "ideology" that would make it possible for him to "admire" things as they are. That sounds like a cold-blooded, not to say cynical, objective. After all, Edmund Burke did not need an "ideology" in order to love the crazy patchwork of British politics. He loved it first and thought about it after. What inspired Wills, however, was not cynicism but a profoundly religious intention. Like his great mentor, St. Augustine, he wanted to humble the spiritual pretensions of the political realm. He wanted, and still wants, to admire the American system of things as they are—"to settle for less," in his phrase—so that politics in America might lose its terrible power to captivate our souls.

He soon concocted a political theory he thought might do the job. He called it "the convenient state," and it contains, he says, "the germ of everything else I have had to say or explore in the area" of politics. According to Wills, the state must be regarded as a mere worldly convenience, a coming together of people so that they might live in "temporal peace." To ask more of the state would be fatal to peace itself. Against this "convenient ideal," the American state, unfortunately, offered a competing and far from modest ideal, what Wills calls in a telling phrase "the Lincolnian ideal of a state 'dedicated to a proposition.' " This, he realized, was a "kind of masked theocracy." The vaunting propositions propounded at Gettysburg ("conceived in liberty," "all men are created equal," "government of the people, by the people, for the people") arrogated to the secular realm what properly belongs to divinity. Whatever the merits of the argument, Wills had grasped quite early in his career the essential dilemma of American conservatism. To cherish things as they are in America—to "settle for less"—you must somehow snuff out the vaunting propositions embedded in the American republic.

That was as far as Wills had gotten as of 1961 or thereabouts. Plainly he had not gotten very far. Determined to admire things as they are in America, what, after all, did he actually admire? Very little, apparently. He cherished an ideal that did not exist, namely an American state that ought to confine itself to holding "people together in peace." What he opposed was "dedication to a proposition" that, throughout our history, has demonstrably disturbed mere "temporal peace" and that perpetually prevents America from "settling for less" with Old World resignation. As Tocqueville long ago observed, it was because of our high democratic expectations that in America men's "hopes are sooner blasted and care itself is more keen."

The turbulent events of the 1960s had a curious effect on Wills's conservatism. During those years a grass-roots civil-rights movement fought its way to victory—a practical triumph for "dedication to a proposition." Popular opposition to a dubious military intervention shattered the ironclad dogmas of the Cold War—and Wills's own adherence to them. On prime-time television Democratic Party bosses acted like a band of thugs in their eagerness to crush a rank-and-file rebellion at the party convention. Angry blacks demanded "power to the people" and community control of the schools and police. Americans in all walks of life began demanding more control over their lives. For the first time in a half-century, a putatively self-governing people had begun to complain openly about the state of self-government itself, a topic that our politicians do not much care to discuss. After a fifty-year hiatus they did not do it consistently or eloquently or effectively. The democratic upsurge of the Sixties did not come within miles of curbing private power or abating corrupt privilege. The "political class," in the British phrase, remained firmly, if nervously, in charge. For that very reason, Wills, who wrote about many of the events of the Sixties for *Esquire,* drew the fundamental conclusion that America is *in fact* the "convenient state" of his 1961 "ideal": a state devoted merely to holding "people together in peace," a state whose republican propositions *in fact* play no serious part. He is pleased that such is the case, but that, he rightly insists, is beside the point. He believes it is true "empirically," true because he can demonstrate that this is "the way our society actually works." What he tries to demonstrate, in short, is that our republican foundations, principles, and propositions are not an active part of the American system of things as they are. The attempt is bold and ingenious, yet all Wills succeeds in demonstrating is that if you omit "dedication to a proposition" you cannot explain "the way our society actually works."

According to Wills, the chief bulwark of the American "convenient state" is what he calls our "meaningless elections." When Americans choose a President, says Wills, we never actually vote for a well-defined policy. No candidate in his right mind would offer one. In order to win a candidate must mute, muffle, and dodge, soften rather than sharpen, blur rather than define. Even in the epoch-making election of 1932, as Wills rightly points out, the voters decided nothing except that they wanted a Democrat in the White House. During the campaign Roosevelt never revealed his New Deal plans. Our elections do not and cannot "stimulate, encourage, or direct change," for "our election system is simply not an instrument for making decisions."

The only thing they really do—and this, Wills says, they do admirably well—is to "hold people together in peace." They realize the "convenient ideal." For one thing, elections successfully confer legitimacy on our Presidents: every American agrees that the man who wins by the rules is the rightful occupant of the White House, which, as Wills and others have pointed out, is no mean achievement given the bloody political history of mankind. For another, they ensure, as far as human wit can ensure anything in politics, that the occupant of our highest office will be a "safe" man. "Elections sift men in order to find the safest, least original man—the man minimally objectionable to a maximum number of people." Because they are without serious content, sharply defined conflict, or even sharply defined candidates, our meaningless elections keep a diverse and divided people from leaping at each other's throats. "The voting process succeeds—it expresses a consensus, but only by stripping away the debatable, the new, the risky, the difficult. It returns people to the few safe things they agree upon."

Such, according to Wills, is how our elections "actually work," and to some extent he is right. It is certainly difficult to imagine American presidential campaigns pitting two clearly defined "programs" against each other, debating them with logical rigor, and then leaving a clear-cut decision to the verdict of the voters. To yearn for that kind of "good election" Wills rightly regards as futile. Nonetheless, Wills's "empirical" account of elections is much too shallow to cope with the subject, since presidential elections are but a part of the political system. Consider his assertion that elections "return people to the few safe things they agree upon." The political depths lying below that statement are immense, for if Americans agree on just a few things, those things are anything but "safe." Americans believe we ought to enjoy equality of opportunity—a Square Deal, a New Deal, a Fair Deal, that is what these slogans promised: a new beginning, a fresh and fairer start. Americans believe and have never ceased believing in their right to an effective voice in their own government. The politician who assailed these propositions in public would be committing suicide. The presidential candidate who spoke in favor of both, who promised, if elected, to further both goals, would not be "unsafe" to the voters. He would be unsafe to the politicians who groom and nominate men for high office. It is they, not the voters, who do the really decisive "sifting" of candidates, and what they invariably sift out are men, quite "unoriginal" men, who might, if elected, endanger *their* political power.

In Wills's home state of Wisconsin, Senator Robert La Follette was a "safe" man to the voters for a quarter of a century. Wisconsinites judged him "safe" (despite a national campaign of vilification against him) because he fought all his life, with admirable courage and tenacity, against the private power of corporations and political-party bosses. And how did La Follette get a chance to prove to the voters that he was "safe"? By overthrowing a Republican state machine that had kept him off the ballot for years precisely because what made him "safe" to the voters—his "dedication to a proposition"—made him a menace to the party managers.

Sifting village Hampdens and township Lincolns out of the political arena is the first rule of party politics in America. In a chapter on what he calls "normal politics," Wills describes our politicians as a breed admirably adapted to peacekeeping compromise, but on that rule they rarely compromise. Challenge a local party syndicate in a mere state legislative district and you will find your ballot petitions falsely voided, your district lines redrawn, your votes miscounted, your supporters bribed, threatened, or beaten—not in some benighted backwoods but in a middle-class neighborhood in New York City in this very year of grace. The sifting process never ceases, and there is nothing peaceful about it. In the words of Mr. Dooley, a far more "empirical" political observer than Wills, "Politics ain't beanbag."

It is not our "meaningless" elections that Wills admires, but a party system—normal politics—that strives unceasingly to drive "dedication to a proposition" out of the political arena. Admiring that is his privilege, but it is a far cry from proving empirically that republican principles play no role in how our society actually works. Simply as a menace to be scotched, they are the shaping force of our normal politics.

After reading Wills's account of the voting process, I began to suspect that his empiricism was seriously warped by his "convenient ideal." As it turns out, even when "dedication to a proposition" bears positive fruit, Wills manages to shut his eyes to it. He does so by what can best be described as an ingenious system of misattributions. According to Wills, the basic institutions of modern America are potentially brutalizing and despotic: our society is "plutocratic"; our economy is a bureaucratized "state capitalism" operating through collusion between government and big business; we are ruled, for all practical purposes, by "the managerial elite." Fortunately, Wills says, America has found a way to "ameliorate the impact of state capitalism." What he cannot explain is why we enjoy such "ameliorations" at all.

What ameliorates bureaucracy in America, Wills says, is the fact that American bureaucracy remains accountable to the people. It must explain itself in public; it can be stopped in its tracks by lawsuits, appeals, and political pressures. It is not the rule of caprice and ruthless fiat that it so often is elsewhere in the modern world of state capitalism—in Sweden, for example, whose constitution expressly forbids citizens from suing the government and whose welfare bureaucrats can tear children out of their homes without the slightest fear of their parents. To the accountability of bureaucracy in America, Wills says, we owe much of our freedom. That is true and well-observed. The important question is why it is true. According to Wills, bureaucracy in America bestows the blessings of accountability on us by a sort of noblesse oblige. The truth is, however, that no bureaucracy, here or anywhere, voluntarily surrenders power to its clients, as bureaucrats refer to the citizens under their control. Accountability must be beaten out of them with a stick. If our bureaucracies are accountable at all, it is because the American people, children of the American republic, still cannot tolerate openly arbitrary rule. They will not abide bureaucratic fiat unless it is softened by formal systems of appeal and the possibility, however remote, of legal reprisal. Wills misattributes to bureaucracy what "dedication to a proposition" has wrested (none too successfully) from bureaucracy.

According to Wills, our state capitalism is also ameliorated by the modern development of a property right in "services," as distinct from the traditional property right in land. These services include the right to an old-age pension, which Americans enjoy by federal statute, and the "right to an education," which Americans enjoy by the statutes of every state in the Union. Such rights, Wills points out, have become the functional equivalent of a property right in a homestead—fifty acres and a mule—that Jefferson deemed essential to the personal independence of the citizenry. They do "much to disperse governmental power and spread the tools of modern living." This is an important, indeed republican, observation. A citizenry worn down by economic fears, kept down by gross ignorance, and dependent on the capricious goodwill of philanthropists will not for long maintain more than a semblance of government of the people, by the people, for the people.

Again the question arises: To what do we owe this amelioration of modern life? According to Wills, it is a blessing bestowed on us by the managerial elite, which apparently takes time out from arrogating governmental power in order to disperse it to the peasantry. Yet no managerial elite gave us the Social Security Act of 1935. It was pried out of a grudging Roosevelt Administration by the Depression-born demands of a people who had finally got fed up with the soul-shrinking terrors of the business cycle. What the "elite" provided was the regressive tax, as Wills himself notes, that finances our pensions, a tax intentionally designed to discourage the poorer half of the citizenry from demanding more "property rights in services" under the Social Security system.

Nor were our free common schools the gift of any managerial elite. Americans long ago demanded them, and precisely because they were "dedicated to a proposition." Citing Jefferson, they demanded free schools that would teach future citizens how to judge for themselves what secured or endangered their freedom. Knowing that such a *republican* education perpetually endangers would-be elites, they insisted that the common schools be separated from the apparatus of government and placed under the democratic control of the local community. What the managerial elite has given us are our corrupted and bureaucratized common schools, which never teach future citizens what secures or endangers their freedom, which teach future citizens that they are merely future workers who go to school, in the immortal words of Lyndon Johnson, "to get a better job." America's free, locally controlled common schools were one of the finest achievements of a republican citizenry, and Wills would give credit for that achievement to the very managerial elite that has done so much for so long to debase it.

For the most pervasive amelioration of state capitalism we owe our greatest debt, Wills says, to "normal politics" in America. Normal politics works to soften harsh conflict and to pave the way for necessary changes. It represents the electorate by balancing "elites against each other." It is operated by what Wills appears to regard as a human type, the subspecies "politician," an inherently mediocre, shallow-minded glad-hander who represents, in Wills's view, the "convenient ideal" incarnate. By perfecting the small arts of compromise, by telling everybody what he wants to hear, by persuading voters to "settle for less," the politician keeps our politics admirably modest. Indifferent to "the Lincolnian ideal of a state 'dedicated to a proposition,' " our politicians "give cohesion to society, ease frictions, promote mutual deference." Their "gift" to us is peace.

Such, according to Wills, is the way our politics "actually works," and here, too, he makes an observation of the greatest importance: "normal politics" in America is indisputably *not* dedicated to realizing republican propositions. Because it is not, however, "normal politics" is almost the reverse of what Wills says it is. Our politicians "promote mutual deference" except when their stock-in-trade is setting whites against blacks, Protestants against Catholics, ethnics against WASPs, city dwellers against upstate farmers, patriots against "pinkos," and Middle America against everybody else. *Divide et empera* is a far more important rule of normal politics than easing frictions and promoting cohesion. There is no better way to keep free men from acting together than to set them at each other's throats, and that is what our "normal politics" does. As Tocqueville observed, a despot does not need to be loved by his subjects as long as they loathe one another. If "mutual deference" exists in America, it is because we can still dimly recognize a fellow citizen beneath the racial, religious, and social divisions that our "normal politics" so adroitly exploits.

"Normal politics," Wills says, gives us "peace," except when it gives us war, war preparations, and what Wills himself condemns as our "Cold War grandiosity" and self-righteousness. Just why our normal politics should be so admirably modest at home and so murderously self-righteous abroad Wills cannot even begin to explain. He appears to regard our Cold War excesses as a sort of mysterious moral aberration in our leaders. Yet the explanation for this glaring contradiction is by no means obscure. Our shallow-minded, compromising politicians simply know how our society "actually works" better than Wills does. They have grasped, as he has not, that they can only practice a "modest" politics at home because of their "grandiosity" abroad. There is no better way to drive "dedication to a proposition" out of the American political arena than to export it across broad oceans. At home it menaces normal politics; overseas it can only kill soldiers and foreigners.

Wills's final misattribution is perhaps the most revealing of all. According to him, the most admirable feature of the American system of things as they are lies in the fact that the compromising politician meets a "challenging" force in the uncompromising zealot. These "martyrs and prophets," as Wills calls them, form America's "spiritual elite" and include in their number such historical figures as William Lloyd Garrison, Jane Addams, and Martin Luther King, Jr. They play their beneficial part in the system of things by "calling for moral renewal and difficult change." If "politicians maintain our country," Wills says, "the prophets make it worth saving." These secular saints maintain the purity of their purpose and the nobility of their souls because, Wills says, they operate "outside the essentially compromising political arena." This is a strange statement in itself, one that suggests that for Wills the "politician" and the "prophet" are not really citizens in conflict but contrasting human types. In any case, the statement is plainly untrue. King was as much of a public man—a politician—as Senator Everett Dirksen. It was precisely because he entered the political arena, because he was not a hole-in-corner prophet, that he helped win civil rights for black people and undying glory for himself. He fought for those rights because he was dedicated to a proposition, and he triumphed because he spoke to Americans who could not find it in their hearts, bigoted though they might be, to deny the validity of the proposition. If Americans actually believed in Wills's "convenient state," few people outside the Montgomery ghetto would have any reason to remember King's name.

So much is obvious, but there is a deeper question involved. What makes it possible for people like King to enter politics in the first place? Why, in other words, does the American political arena remain free? According to Wills, it is our "modest politics" that makes room for the prophets and martyrs. That, Wills says, is the chief blessing of modest politics. Yet it is not our modest politics that made room for King; all our modest politics did was create the need for King by immodestly oppressing black people for a hundred years. What made room for King was the Bill of Rights and, less obviously, a decentralized federal system that creates little public arenas in every city and town—spaces of freedom where citizens can begin to act and speak on their own despite the dominion of "normal politics." Determined to prove that republican propositions and principles play no part in the way things actually work, Wills ends by attributing what freedom we enjoy to the goodwill of "the politician" and the noblesse of "the managerial elite."

His empiricism ends in fantasy, for the truth, I fear, is almost exactly the opposite. If America were merely a "convenient state," if our people ceased to respect the Constitution of liberty and self-government, if they lost every vestige of "dedication to a proposition," we would have precious few liberties, precious few "ameliorations," and precious few "prophets" to thank our leaders for. If we enjoy such blessings at all, it is because the "masked theocracy" of the American republic is as much a part of things as they are in America as "state capitalism," "normal politics," and "the managerial elite." Some struggle to realize our republican propositions, others struggle to nullify them, and politics in America is no more than that struggle itself under a hundred guises, including the Willsian guise of politicians versus prophets. We Americans, James Madison said, are either friends or enemies to republican government. Garry Wills would prefer to be neither, but the choice is not his to make. In the end, one side or the other must claim him and everyone else in this republic.

Reflections
(After Watergate)
On History

Historians have not—as I write this—gotten around to explaining the Watergate affair after their usual fashion. They have not yet told us, that is, that the scandalous deeds were really due to powerful trends and historical forces lying deep below the surface of events. What all concerned have been eager to learn, what the various official investigators have tried to find out, what truth and justice demand, is something very different from the explanations that historians will surely provide. It is this difference rather than the Watergate scandal itself that deserves some mention before the memories fade.

What we all have been trying to learn, quite simply, is what happened—who were the men involved in certain crimes and their criminal concealment; what did they do and why did they do it; what did Mr. A say to Mr. B and was it an order or only a guarded suggestion; did Mr. C, on hearing from B, act with full knowledge or only through purblind loyalty. And so on. What those concerned with the truth of Watergate have tried to discover is the *story* of the Watergate affair, a historical narrative, framed chronologically, of the interrelated deeds and intentions of many men. When that story is fully told, it will be like—in kind, if not in substance—any other historical narrative: Thucydides' account of the Peloponnesian War, Gibbon's account of Rome's fall, Lincoln's account, in great speeches, of a concerted effort to legalize the extension of slavery. All these are *stories*, narratives of men's deeds and their intentions, and the consequences of those deeds. When the Watergate story is finally told, it will reveal no historical trends, no social processes, none of those "deeper" causes that modern historians invoke to account for what actually happened. These agents of history will simply not be found on the stage where the action took place. Doubtless, everyone will tell the Watergate story somewhat differently, but insofar as each tells a story the narrative will disclose no agents of history other than the actions and purposes of men.

We have come to assume of late that historical narratives of this kind—stories of what happened—are inherently superficial. We expect to hear, eventually, about those underlying causes that have become the mainstay of the modern understanding of history. There is nothing strange about that expectation, for we have been trained— quite rigorously trained—to conceive of history as the outcome of causes more potent than men's deeds. Remember one's school quizzes? Name the five underlying causes of World War I. Discuss the six basic reasons for the decline of the Roman Empire. Scan almost any modern history text and you will find the same general conception of history. It will speak of "trends" toward centralization, of the economic "processes" that have caused the near-disappearance of the farmer. It will discuss the "growth" of imperialism, nationalism, capitalism, and then lay down the general causes of these general historical results.

Since the ancients saw in history no reality apart from men's deeds, they would say to the modern historian: Do not tell us about the alleged basic causes of America's emergence as a world power; tell us, instead, what men did that made it emerge. Should the modern historian reply that the story is all very well but the real causes (let us say) are the closing of the frontier, the increasing wealth of the nation, and the growing nationalism of the citizenry, the ancients would still cling to their conception of history. Do you really believe, they would ask, that the closing frontier compelled Dewey to seize the Philippine

40

Islands and that the gross national product in 1899 forced President McKinley to assume a protectorship of China? It may be, the ancients might argue, that the closing frontier created social problems that American leaders chose to solve through a new, outgoing foreign policy. But that still does not make the closing frontier an underlying cause of anything. Had America's leaders chosen a different solution, the story would have been different, though the frontier would still have been closed. The ancient mind, in a word, construed history in the active voice—who did what and why—for it saw nothing in history except active men acting. Nobody has put the ancients' case more succinctly than that most ancient of moderns, G. K. Chesterton. "The question for brave men," he said, "is not whether something is increasing but what we have done to increase it."

The modern mind construes history in the passive voice, for it sees history as the result of general agencies more compelling than the actions of individuals. It barely concedes that men act at all, for to speak of a historical fact—America's emergence as a world power, say—as the general result of general causes is to say that those whose actions produced it could not have acted otherwise, that for all practical purposes they were the pawns of history and circumstance. The modern mind shrinks from the reality of action with an almost audible shudder. American involvement in the Vietnam War, for example, began in deadly earnest when an American President decided to bomb North Vietnam. That is what actually happened, but it runs counter to the modern ideology, and so a number of historians and commentators have now informed us that the war was the result of a "decision-making process," as if only a general trend could initiate anything.

Between the ancient and the modern viewpoints lies an unbridgeable chasm, because the two views have nothing in common. Each, philosophically, is entire unto itself; each refutes and blots out the other. To the question which view do we choose, no abstract answer is possible. It is like asking which is better in the abstract, a hamburger or a rose. There are times, however, when we know beyond any doubt which view we prefer. When something important happens in public affairs, when something arouses in us our dormant love of truth and justice, then everybody understands implicitly that the modern ideology is irrelevant, that the truth is in the story, and that only the old, brave questions are worth asking.

Suppose a Senate Watergate Committee member tried out the modern ideology and sought from one of the witnesses some deeper, historic explanations. Did you feel, he might ask, that historic forces were working upon you when you entered into the conspiracy? Did you feel yourself in the grip of the growing modern trend toward lawlessness? If the witness replied that he had, we would know at once he was lying under oath. No abstract argument could persuade us for one second that when the witness entered the plot he was pushed into it by history. Suppose the entire Senate Watergate Committee adhered to modern ideology and declared that it had no interest in the superficial story of what happened and cared only about the deeper historical forces that produced the Watergate affair. We would conclude, we could scarcely help but conclude, that the senators were also involved in a cover-up.

There is a deeper moral to this, however, that is far from easy to draw. In the Watergate affair, we have not been passive spectators. It is our very desire for truth that set the inquiry in motion and long sustained its momentum. We have not been a mere audience watching political "theatre." We have been members of a national grand jury sifting fact from fiction in a sordid tale of official misdeeds. We have become, willy-nilly, active participants in grave affairs of state. Whenever that occurs, the concept of history as something that happens to men evaporates like fog.

The ancient view of history was discovered by the Greeks through no accidental stroke of genius. It arose with Herodotus after the Greeks created the polis and discovered, in the new freedom of the city, that men were not by nature mere creatures of habit and circumstance. They could come together and freely act together and by their common actions make things happen that otherwise would never have happened. They discovered in the new experience of political freedom that history is the story of men acting. It was not some murky

Babylonian scheme of universal and invariant cycles, a conception suited for barbarians who, enchained by immemorial custom and lacking experience of freedom and action, could well believe that history was the result of superhuman forces. The Greek discovery, the ancient view of history, has been almost eclipsed in our time. Yet it is always being rediscovered through the same experience that led to its original discovery—the experience of being citizens, of participating in great affairs, of sharing, through our love of truth and justice, in the making of historic events. At such times we regain something of the ancient public virtue and understanding, and grasp anew the brave, ancient truth that history is the story, endlessly ramified, of the diverse deeds of many men.

Thucydides in the Cold War

Around the time Republicans were vowing to "roll back Communism," a wise old college professor of mine suggested that his Humanities I class might get more out of Thucydides if it compared the Peloponnesian War to the ongoing struggle between America and Russia, then only recently named the Cold War. This, he assured us (quite needlessly), would not do violence to the great Athenian historian, since Thucydides himself believed that "human nature being what it is, events now past will recur in similar or analogous forms." Of the profundity of that remark Humanities I had not the slightest inkling. Nonetheless, analogies fell at our feet like ripe apples.

The combatants we identified readily. Authoritarian Sparta, ruling over a mass of terrified helots, was plainly the Soviet Union. Democratic Athens was America, of course. There were even neat correspondences between the two sets of foes. Sparta, as Thucydides tells us, was an insulated, agricultural, and sluggish state, rather like Russia. Athens, like America, was commercial, fast-moving, and far-ranging. "They are never at home," complained a Corinthian envoy to the Spartans, "and you are never away from it." In Athens and America, commerce and democracy seemed, 2,300 years apart, to have nurtured the very same kind of citizen. "I doubt if the world can produce a man," said the great Pericles, "who, where he has only himself to depend upon, is equal to so many emergencies and graced by so happy a versatility as the Athenian." What the Athenians possessed, concluded Humanities I, was Yankee ingenuity.

More striking than the analogies between past and present combatants were the resemblances between the two conflicts. In neither struggle do the enemies fight alone. Like America and the Soviet Union, Athens and Sparta are leaders of great confederations of inferior and subordinate allies. Similarly, they represent hostile political principles: Athens championing democracy; Sparta, a traditional oligarchy. In the Peloponnesian War, as in the Cold War, the enemies are "ideological" foes. And neither is physically capable of winning. Sparta, with its invincible infantry, is so superior by land that Athens avoids pitched battles at all costs. Athens is so superior by sea that Spartan ships flee her peerless navy on sight. As a result, the Peloponnesian War, like the Cold War, is fought indirectly, peripherally, and spasmodically.

That was about as far as Humanities I got in its hunt for analogies between the ancient struggle for supremacy in Hellas and the ongoing struggle for supremacy in the modern world. Youth and ignorance doubtless limited our inquiry, but a greater handicap was the fact that the Peloponnesian War lasted twenty-seven years while the Cold War had not yet survived six.

That was nearly three decades ago, decades in which the struggle for supremacy between America and Russia did not cease for a single day. When I decided to reread Thucydides, the struggle was about to enter a new and more vigorous phase, under a newly elected President and a political faction that Thucydides would have unhesitatingly described as the war party. Two things struck me as I read: that the Cold War, now so long protracted, had come to resemble the Peloponnesian War more than ever; and that in this resemblance lay a wholly unexpected vindication of political history, created by Thucydides, despised by the modern *eruditi,* and barely kept alive today by Grub Street hacks and doting amateurs.

The grounds for vindication are clear enough. Ancient Hellas and the modern world have nothing in common technologically, economically, or socially, none of those "factors" so dear to the hearts of the modern historian. If the ancient war and the modern war bear strong and essential resemblances, only political causes could have produced them: precisely those political causes that Thucydides' titanic genius found operating in the Peloponnesian War.

"Of the gods we believe, and of men we know," an Athenian envoy tells an ally of Sparta's, "that by a necessary law of their nature they rule wherever they can." Our nature as *political* beings is what Thucydides describes. Nothing compels men to enter the bright, dangerous arena of political action, but what lures them there—love of fame, power, glory, fortune, distinction—makes it fairly certain, a "law," that they will strive to rule over others. According to Pericles, Athenians, out of a love of splendid deeds and for the glory of their city, "forced every sea and land to be the highway of [their] daring." In doing so they also forged a far-flung empire, which they had to struggle continuously to maintain; for if men strive for dominion, others strive to resist it. "You risk so much to retain your empire," the Athenian envoy is told, "and your subjects so much to get rid of it."

In the striving to gain dominion and in the inevitable struggle to maintain it, men produce one thing with certainty—they "make" history. Such was Thucydides' great discovery. History is the story woven by men's deeds, and the political nature of man provides a completely intelligible account of the story. That is why the great Athenian dared to predict that the tragic events of the Peloponnesian War would one day recur in similar forms.

Consider the origins of the Peloponnesian War. Thucydides describes the petty squabbles that poison relations between certain allies of mighty Sparta and those of upstart Athens. The squabbles set in motion the great train of events, but, like Soviet-American squabbles over the Yalta accords, they are not, says Thucydides, the "real cause" of the war. "The growth of the power of Athens and the alarm which this inspired in Lacedaemon [Sparta] made war inevitable."

In 432 B.C. the Hellenic world reached a political condition that the modern world was to duplicate in 1945 A.D.—and with much the same result. Two superpowers, Athens and Sparta, have so completely absorbed all the available power in Hellas that any further gain by one appears a menacing loss to the other. Under such conditions no real peace is possible. Of course, if men and states accepted the diminution of their power there would have been no Peloponnesian War (and precious little human history), but that is just what men and states do not accept.

War with Sparta is unavoidable, Pericles tells the Athenian assembly (it is pondering whether to accede to a Spartan fiat), because "we must attempt to hand down our power to our posterity unimpaired." Moral scruple has nothing to do with it. The Athenian empire "is, to speak somewhat plainly, a tyranny," says Pericles, referring to Athens' crushing subjugation of her nominal allies. "To take it [the empire] perhaps was wrong, but to let it go is unsafe." With respect to its unwilling allies, Athens resembles the Soviet Union and, like it, must expend a great deal of her strength keeping her "allies" down.

Because such tyranny is inherently unstable, Pericles urges his countrymen to fight a strategically defensive war and seek no "fresh conquests" in the course of it. The result of the Periclean policy reveals the extraordinary, history-making dynamism released by merely trying to hang on to one's own. Framed by a statesman of the highest genius, the policy scores a brilliant success and then leads Athens to its ultimate ruin.

To the astonishment of the Hellenic world, the newfangled Athenian navy, as Pericles foresaw, proves tactically superior to Sparta's great infantry, which the Athenians, safely walled up in their city, can avoid with impunity. Facing a foe so swift, so daring, so immune to injury, Sparta, after seven years of war, becomes deeply unnerved. "Being new to the experience of adversity," observes Thucydides, "they had lost all confidence in themselves."

Buoyed up by their unexpected triumphs over the traditional leader of Hellas, however, the Athenians fall prey to the fateful temptation inherent in all political action—rashness. Success "made them confuse their strength with their hopes," says Thucydides, providing, at least, a definition of political rashness that cannot be improved upon. After a Spartan garrison surrenders without a fight, something unprecedented in Spartan history, the Athenians are ripe for any daring folly; just as President Truman, blinded by General MacArthur's sweeping victory at Inchon, rashly attempted to conquer North Korea; and just as President Kennedy, puffed up by his Cuban missile triumph, was ripe for the Vietnam War—a confusion of strength and hope that drained the country of both.

The Peloponnesian War, like the Cold War, brings civil war and revolution in its wake. The political causes are the same in both cases. When states are at peace, hostile factions and classes within countries are willing to rub along together. But when the great powers are desperately competing for allies, domestic rivals are no longer willing to preserve internal peace. Popular leaders can call on the opposing power to put their domestic enemies to the sword; oligarchic factions, to set their own cities aflame.

Love of dominion, the desire for "the first place in the city" (never far from the surface in peacetime), convulses all Hellas in wartime. Men betray their own cities without scruple and cheer foreigners for killing their own countrymen. Political exiles, aided by foreign powers, wage ceaseless war against their own cities. The Peloponnesian War, which spawns a half dozen analogues of the Bay of Pigs and of Moscow-trained revolutionary brigades, blights the integrity of the city-state, just as the Cold War now erodes the integrity of the nation-state.

Athens is by no means immune to the war's corrupting effects on domestic politics. At one point Athenians undergo a spasm of political paranoia that duplicates with remarkable fidelity the American McCarthy era. The causes here, too, are the same, as the sequence of events clearly shows. Shortly after the Spartan garrison's stunning surrender, Sparta humbly sues for peace, and the Athenians, a little out of breath themselves, reluctantly and ruefully accept. Thucydides regards the peace, which lasts six years, as a mere incident in a continuous war. It was, says Thucydides, "an unstable armistice [that] did not prevent either party doing the other the most effectual injury."

The chief reason for the instability is the emergence in Athens of a self-serving war party. Ten years have passed since the outbreak of war. Great Pericles is dead; new men have arisen with ambitions of their own, Pericles' own ward Alcibiades among them. The Periclean policy of deadlock, based on the determination to preserve past glories, does not content them. They want to win fresh glory for themselves, and with it, says Thucydides, "the undisturbed direction of the people." Their real complaint about the peace with Sparta is that it is an unambitious use of Athenian power (which is exactly what the American foes of détente believe).

Confusing strength with hope, the leaders of the war party think Athens can do far more than merely hold Sparta at bay; it can destroy Spartan pretensions forever. Like the Republicans of 1951–52, the war party will accept, in effect, "no substitute for victory." Like millions of Americans in 1951–52, the Athenian people, "persuaded that nothing could withstand them," find deadlock exasperating. Why must irresistible Athens suffer the endless tensions of the unstable armistice? Is it possible that there are oligarchy-loving pro-Spartans in their midst?

A shocking act of impiety, analogous to the Alger Hiss trial, turns baseless suspicion into angry conviction: "oligarchical and monarchical" Athenians are conspiring to subvert the democratic constitution. The enraged citizenry demands arrests; blatant perjurers supply the evidence; nonconformists, including Alcibiades, fall prey to the mania. At the war's outset Pericles had proudly noted the extraordinary personal freedom enjoyed by Athenians, who "do not feel called upon to be angry with our neighbor for doing what he likes." Now those who live differently from their neighbors fall under suspicion of treason. A war begun to safeguard the power of a democracy profoundly corrupts democracy.

Firmly in control of a rapidly degenerating polity, the war party launches its grandiose plan to tilt the balance of power once and for all against the Spartans. Beyond the little world of Hellas, across the Ionian Sea, lie the broad island of Sicily and a dozen Greek colonial city-states. The Athenians, as Thucydides icily remarks, do not even know Sicily's size; they are ignorantly contemptuous of the island's colonial "rabble." Nonetheless, the self-vaunting, overconfident Athenians intend to conquer it and use that huge accession of imperial power to throw down Sparta itself. When an opponent of the enterprise warns Athenians of the enormous costs and hazards of a war so far from home, enthusiasm for the expedition grows even warmer.

In the seventeenth year of the Peloponnesian War, "by far the most costly and splendid Hellenic force that had ever been sent out by a single city" sets sail for faraway Sicily. Vietnam is but a pale analogy to what fortune inflicts on the great armada. Thucydides' account of its hideous, heartbreaking fate—how its leaders blundered, how its strength drained away, how its dauntless Athenian oarsmen, the backbone of the democracy, lost their nerve and their courage—is one of the great feats of historical writing. On the hostile shores of a distant island, before the walls of an underestimated enemy, the power of Athens crumbles away forever.

Since the Cold War continues with no end in sight, its story remains incomplete. Still, it seems fairly certain even now that the same principle that makes the Peloponnesian War intelligible, 2,300 years after its end, will make the Cold War intelligible to posterity: "Of the gods we believe, and of men we know, that by a necessary law of their nature they rule wherever they can."

Why Johnny Can't Think

U ntil very recently, remarkably little was known about what actually goes on in America's public schools. There were no reliable answers to even the most obvious questions. How many children are taught to read in overcrowded classrooms? How prevalent is rote learning and how common are classroom discussions? Do most schools set off gongs to mark the change of "periods"? Is it a common practice to bark commands over public address systems in the manner of army camps, prisons, and banana republics? Public schooling provides the only intense experience of a public realm that most Americans will ever know. Are school buildings designed with the dignity appropriate to a great republican institution, or are most of them as crummy-looking as one's own?

The darkness enveloping America's public schools is truly extraordinary considering that 38.9 million students attend them, that we spend nearly $134 billion a year on them, and that foundations ladle out generous sums for the study of everything about schooling— except what really occurs in the schools. John I. Goodlad's eight-year investigation of a mere thirty-eight of America's 80,000 public schools—the result of which, *A Place Called School* [McGraw-Hill, 1984], was published last year—is the most comprehensive study ever undertaken. Hailed as a "landmark in American educational research," it was financed with great difficulty. The darkness, it seems, has its guardians.

Happily, the example of Goodlad, a former dean of UCLA's Graduate School of Education, has proven contagious. A flurry of new books sheds considerable light on the practice of public education in America. In *The Good High School* [Basic Books, 1985], Sara Lawrence Lightfoot offers vivid "portraits" of six distinctive American secondary schools. In *Horace's Compromise* [Houghton Mifflin, 1985], Theodore R. Sizer, a former dean of Harvard's Graduate School of Education, reports on his two-year odyssey through public high schools around the country. Even *High School* [Harper & Row, 1985], a white paper issued by Ernest L. Boyer and the Carnegie Foundation for the Advancement of Teaching, is supported by a close investigation of the institutional life of a number of schools. Of the books under review, only *A Nation at Risk* [U.S. Government Printing Office, 1984], the report of the Reagan Administration's National Commission on Excellence in Education, adheres to the established practice of crass special pleading in the dark.

Thanks to Goodlad et al., it is now clear what the great educational darkness has so long concealed: the depth and pervasiveness of political hypocrisy in the common schools of the country. The great ambition professed by public school managers is, of course, education for citizenship and self-government, which harks back to Jefferson's historic call for "general education to enable every man to judge for himself what will secure or endanger his freedom." What the public schools practice with remorseless proficiency, however, is the prevention of citizenship and the stifling of self-government. When 58 percent of the thirteen-year-olds tested by the National Assessment for Educational Progress think it is against the law to start a third party in America, we are dealing not with a sad educational failure but with a remarkably subtle success.

Consider how effectively America's future citizens are trained not to judge for themselves about anything. From the first grade to the twelfth, from one coast to the other, instruction in America's classrooms is almost entirely dogmatic. Answers are "right" and answers are "wrong," but mostly answers are short. "At all levels, [teacher-made] tests called almost exclusively for short answers and recall of information," reports Goodlad. In more than a thousand classrooms visited by his researchers, "only *rarely*" was there "evidence to suggest instruction likely to go much beyond mere possession of information to a level of understanding its implications." Goodlad goes on to note that "the intellectual terrain is laid out by the teacher. The paths for walking through it are largely predetermined by the teacher." The give-and-take of genuine discussion is conspicuously absent. "Not even 1%" of institutional time, he found, was devoted to discussions that "required some kind of open response involving reasoning or perhaps an opinion from students. . . . The extraordinary degree of student passivity stands out."

Sizer's research substantiates Goodlad's. "No more important finding has emerged from the inquiries of our study than that the American high school student, *as student,* is all too often docile, compliant, and without initiative." There is good reason for this. On the one hand, notes Sizer, "there are too few rewards for being inquisitive." On the other, the heavy emphasis on "the right answer . . . smothers the student's efforts to become an effective intuitive thinker."

Yet smothered minds are looked on with the utmost complacency by the educational establishment—by the Reagan Department of Education, state boards of regents, university education departments, local administrators, and even many so-called educational reformers. Teachers are neither urged to combat the tyranny of the short right answer nor trained to do so. "Most teachers simply do not know how to teach for higher levels of thinking," says Goodlad. Indeed, they are actively discouraged from trying to do so.

The discouragement can be quite subtle. In their orientation talks to new, inexperienced teachers, for example, school administrators often indicate that they do not much care what happens in class so long as no noise can be heard in the hallway. This thinly veiled threat virtually ensures the prevalence of short-answer drills, workbook exercises, and the copying of long extracts from the blackboard. These may smother young minds, but they keep the classroom quiet.

Discouragement even calls itself reform. Consider the current cry for greater use of standardized student tests to judge the "merit" of teachers and raise "academic standards." If this fake reform is foisted on the schools, dogma and docility will become even more prevalent. This point is well made by Linda Darling-Hammond of the Rand Corporation in an essay in *The Great School Debate* [Simon & Schuster, 1985]. Where "important decisions are based on test scores," she notes, "teachers are more likely to teach to the tests" and less likely to bother with "nontested activities, such as writing, speaking, problem-solving or real reading of books." The most influential promoter of standardized tests is the "excellence" brigade in the Department of Education; so clearly one important meaning of "educational excellence" is greater proficiency in smothering students' efforts to think for themselves.

Probably the greatest single discouragement to better instruction is the overcrowded classroom. The Carnegie report points out that English teachers cannot teach their students how to write when they must read and criticize the papers of as many as 175 students. As Sizer observes, genuine discussion is possible only in small seminars. In crowded classrooms, teachers have difficulty imparting even the most basic intellectual skills, since they have no time to give students personal attention. The overcrowded classroom inevitably debases instruction, yet it is the rule in America's public schools. In the first three grades of elementary school, Goodlad notes, the average class has twenty-seven students. High school classes range from twenty-five to forty students, according to the Carnegie report.

What makes these conditions appalling is that they are quite unnecessary. The public schools are top-heavy with administrators and rife with sinecures. Large numbers of teachers scarcely ever set foot in a classroom, being occupied instead as grade advisers, career counselors, "coordinators," and supervisors. "Schools, if simply organized," Sizer writes, "can have well-paid faculty and fewer than eighty students per teacher [sixteen students per class] without increasing current per-pupil expenditure." Yet no serious effort is being made to reduce class size. As Sizer notes, "Reducing teacher load is, when all the negotiating is over, a low agenda item for the unions and school boards." Overcrowded classrooms virtually guarantee smothered minds, yet the subject is not even mentioned in *A Nation at Risk,* for all its well-publicized braying about a "rising tide of mediocrity."

Do the nation's educators really want to teach almost 40 million students how to "think critically," in the Carnegie report's phrase, and "how to judge for themselves," in Jefferson's? The answer is, if you can believe that you will believe anything. The educational establishment is not even content to produce passive minds. It seeks passive spirits as well. One effective agency for producing these is the overly populous school. The larger schools are, the more prison-like they tend to be. In such schools, guards man the stairwells and exits. ID cards and "passes" are examined at checkpoints. Bells set off spasms of anarchy and bells quell the student mob. PA systems interrupt regularly with trivial fiats and frivolous announcements. This "malevolent intruder," in Sizer's apt phrase, is truly ill willed, for the PA system is actually an educational tool. It teaches the huge student mass to respect the authority of disembodied voices and the rule of remote and invisible agencies. Sixty-three percent of all high school students in America attend schools with enrollments of five thousand or more. The common excuse for these mobbed schools is economy, but in fact they cannot be shown to save taxpayers a penny. Large schools "tend to create passive and compliant students," notes Robert B. Hawkins, Jr., in an essay in *The Challenge to American Schools* [Oxford University Press, 1987]. That is their chief reason for being.

"How can the relatively passive and docile roles of students prepare them to participate as informed, active and questioning citizens?" asks the Carnegie report, in discussing the "hidden curriculum" of passivity in the schools. The answer is, they were not meant to. Public schools introduce future citizens to the public world, but no introduction could be more disheartening. Architecturally, public school buildings range from drab to repellent. They are often disfigured by demoralizing neglect—"cracked sidewalks, a shabby lawn, and peeling paint on every window sash," to quote the Carnegie report. Many big-city elementary schools have numbers instead of names, making them as coldly dispiriting as possible.

Public schools stamp out republican sentiment by habituating their students to unfairness, inequality, and special privilege. These arise inevitably from the educational establishment's long-standing policy (well described by Diane Ravitch in *The Troubled Crusade* [Basic Books, 1985]) of maintaining "the correlation between social class and educational achievement." In order to preserve that factitious "correlation," public schooling is rigged to favor middle-class students and to ensure that working-class students do poorly enough to convince them that they fully merit the lowly station that will one day be theirs. "Our goal is to get these kids to be like their parents," one teacher, more candid than most, remarked to a Carnegie researcher.

For more than three decades, elementary schools across the country practiced a "progressive," non-phonetic method of teaching reading that had nothing much to recommend it save its inherent social bias. According to Ravitch, this method favored "children who were already motivated and prepared to begin reading" before entering school, while making learning to read more difficult for precisely those children whose parents were ill read or ignorant. The advantages enjoyed by the well-bred were thus artificially multiplied tenfold, and 23 million adult Americans are today "functional illiterates." America's educators, notes Ravitch, have "never actually accepted full responsibility for making all children literate."

That describes a malicious intent a trifle too mildly. Reading is the key to everything else in school. Children who struggle with it in the first grade will be "grouped" with the slow readers in the second grade and will fall hopelessly behind in all subjects by the sixth. The schools hasten this process of falling behind, report Goodlad and others, by giving the best students the best teachers and struggling students the worst ones. "It is ironic," observes the Carnegie report, "that those who need the most help get the least." Such students are commonly diagnosed as "culturally deprived" and so are blamed for the failures inflicted on them. Thus they are taught to despise themselves even as they are inured to their inferior station.

The whole system of unfairness, inequality, and privilege comes to fruition in high school. There, some 15.7 million youngsters are formally divided into the favored few and the ill-favored many by the practice of "tracking." About 35 percent of America's public secondary-school students are enrolled in academic programs (often subdivided into "gifted" and "non-gifted" tracks); the rest are relegated to some variety of non-academic schooling. Thus the tracking system, as intended, reproduces the divisions of the class system. "The honors programs," notes Sizer, "serve the wealthier youngsters, and the general tracks (whatever their titles) serve the working class. Vocational programs are often a cruel social dumping ground." The bottom-dogs are trained for jobs as auto mechanics, cosmeticians, and institutional cooks, but they rarely get the jobs they are trained for. Pumping gasoline, according to the Carnegie report, is as close as an auto-mechanics major is likely to get to repairing a car. "Vocational education in the schools is virtually irrelevant to job fate," asserts Goodlad. It is merely the final hoax that the school bureaucracy plays on the neediest, one that the federal government has been promoting for seventy years.

The tracking system makes privilege and inequality blatantly visible to everyone. It creates under one roof "two worlds of schooling," to quote Goodlad. Students in academic programs read Shakespeare's plays. The commonality, notes the Carnegie report, are allowed virtually no contact with serious literature. In their English classes they practice filling out job applications. "Gifted" students alone are encouraged to think for themselves. The rest are subjected to sanctimonious wind, chiefly about "work habits" and "career opportunities."

"If you are a child of low-income parents," reports Sizer, "the chances are good that you will receive limited and often careless attention from adults in your high school. If you are the child of upper-middle-income parents, the chances are good that you will receive substantial and careful attention." In Brookline High School in Massachusetts, one of Lightfoot's "good" schools, a few fortunate students enjoy special treatment in their Advanced Placement classes. Meanwhile, students tracked into "career education" learn about "institutional cooking and clean-up" in a four-term Food Service course that requires them to mop up after their betters in the school cafeteria.

This wretched arrangement expresses the true spirit of public education in America and discloses the real aim of its hidden curriculum. A favored few, pampered and smiled upon, are taught to cherish privilege and despise the disfavored. The favorless many, who have majored in failure for years, are taught to think ill of themselves. Youthful spirits are broken to the world and every impulse of citizenship is effectively stifled. John Goodlad's judgment is severe but just: "There is in the gap between our highly idealistic goals for schooling in our society and the differentiated opportunities condoned and supported in schools a monstrous hypocrisy."

The public schools of America have not been corrupted for trivial reasons. Much would be different in a republic composed of citizens who could judge for themselves what secured or endangered their freedom. Every wielder of illicit or undemocratic power, every possessor of undue influence, every beneficiary of corrupt special privilege would find his position and tenure at hazard. Republican education is a menace to powerful, privileged, and influential people, and they in turn are a menace to republican education. That is why the generation that founded the public schools took care to place them under the suffrage of local communities, and that is why the corrupters of public education have virtually destroyed that suffrage. In 1932 there were 127,531 school districts in America. Today there are approximately 15,840 and they are virtually impotent, their proper role having been usurped by state and federal authorities. Curriculum and textbooks, methods of instruction, the procedures of the classroom, the organization of the school day, the cant, the pettifogging, and the corruption are almost uniform from coast to coast. To put down the menace of republican education its shield of local self-government had to be smashed, and smashed it was.

The public schools we have today are what the powerful and the considerable have made of them. They will not be redeemed by trifling reforms. Merit pay, a longer school year, more homework, special schools for "the gifted," and more standardized tests will not even begin to turn our public schools into nurseries of "informed, active and questioning citizens." They are not meant to. When the authors of *A Nation at Risk* call upon the schools to create an "educated work force," they are merely sanctioning the prevailing corruption, which consists precisely in the reduction of citizens to credulous workers. The education of a free people will not come from federal bureaucrats crying up "excellence" for "economic growth," any more than it came from their predecessors who cried up schooling as a means to "get a better job."

Only ordinary citizens can rescue the schools from their stifling corruption, for nobody else wants ordinary children to become questioning citizens at all. If we wait for the mighty to teach America's youth what secures or endangers their freedom, we will wait until the crack of doom.

The New Social History

Writing American history is a harmless occupation, but teaching it to American schoolchildren is a political act with far-reaching consequences. The reason for this is clear. You cannot recount the past without making fundamental political judgments, and you cannot deliver those judgments in a classroom without impressing them deeply on the minds of future citizens. Children know a great deal about many things, but about public affairs they know virtually nothing. Most of us carry to our graves scarcely altered the political lessons we imbibed half-consciously from long-forgotten history textbooks. Professors of American history erect Gothic cathedrals of erudition on political axioms acquired from their fifth-grade "social studies" readers. To teach American history to a great mass of American schoolchildren is to exercise genuine political power. Yet of all forms of political power, the power to teach history to children is the only one Americans have handed over without a struggle to a remote and unaccountable few, commonly known as the educational establishment. *America Revised,* by Frances FitzGerald (subtitled "History Schoolbooks in the Twentieth Century," Atlantic/Little, Brown, 1979), is an attempt to describe what the educational establishment has done with that power through the years.

FitzGerald's main achievement is the scutwork. She has pored through the pages of hundreds of musty American history textbooks, something nobody, I believe, has ever done before. She describes their contents, delineates their overall "philosophy," and shows how they changed from generation to generation. About what it all signifies, however, she has only confused and contradictory notions. She never really understands that her subject is the education—and miseducation—of a self-governing people. Still, FitzGerald's material is invaluable; when cast into a political history of which FitzGerald seems blissfully ignorant, it reveals a great deal about the way we are currently ruled.

The history begins just before the turn of the century, when the first school managers powerful enough to impose their conception of history on a large number of children introduced the first American history text to the public schools. Until then what little history American schoolchildren learned they had direct from their schoolmarms by way of a sort of oral tradition. What they learned, however, they learned so well that historian Mark Sullivan blamed nineteenth-century schoolmarms for delaying our entry into the First World War. The only history they taught, Sullivan complained in his six-volume chronicle *Our Times,* was the American Revolution, and the way they taught it had made it impossible for most Americans to believe that England was fighting for "democracy against autocracy" in the trenches of France. The schoolmarms' American Revolution is readily reconstructed. On one side stood the tattered sons of liberty, whose forebears had come to an unknown continent in search of religious freedom. On the other side stood a tyrannical king and his arrogant Redcoats, foredoomed in their pride to a stunning defeat. What better way than this to inculcate love of liberty and hatred of tyranny in the future citizens of a free republic?

Since American educators always claimed they were providing "training for citizenship," the first history textbooks might have been expected to fortify the oral tradition of the schoolmarms. In fact, they did exactly the opposite. According to FitzGerald, the first history text taught children that the colonists had come to America for "commercial motives" and not for religious freedom at all. With that premise laid down, FitzGerald writes, the texts "looked on the American Revolution as a matter of practical politics more than anything else." Instead of the sons of liberty, the pioneer texts offered the sons of the dollar; instead of a revolt against arbitrary power, squalid maneuvering for economic advantage. The obvious lesson of these texts is that Americans who profess to fight against tyranny are probably hypocrites trying to make money, an excellent lesson if you happen to favor tyranny. Such was the "citizenship training" offered by the pioneer textbooks. Most American schoolchildren never read them, however, since they were used exclusively in a few big-city school systems "to Americanize" (as the phrase went) the children of immigrants. The first exercise of the power to teach history was an attempt to corrupt the utterly defenseless. It was also a harbinger of what was to come.

"Americanizing" native Americans was a far more delicate problem, and educational leaders were long reluctant to try it in any systematic way. The problem became inescapable, however, in the early years of the twentieth century, when, for the first time, Americans in large numbers began attending public secondary schools. This new turn of events, so far from being a source of pedagogical satisfaction, threw educators into a panic and set off the greatest crisis in the history of American education. The crisis was this: the public secondary schools, which had catered chiefly to the well-to-do and successful, adhered to a traditional liberal-arts curriculum of history, language, and literature—the "arts that liberate," as Montaigne has called them. With the children of ordinary people attending high school, American educators found themselves face to face with the specter that had haunted Europe for a century: the danger of educating people *beyond their station,* or, as the National Education Association preferred to put it, leading them "away from the pursuits for which they are adapted." The danger was largely political. By teaching the liberal arts to commoners, the new secondary schools might well become the spawning ground for popular tribunes, politically ambitious guttersnipes, and similar dangerous malcontents. As J. E. Russell, head of Columbia University Teachers College, put it in 1905: "How can we justify our practice in schooling the masses in precisely the same manner as we do those who are to be their leaders?"

Something had to be done quickly or democracy might one day break out. Educational leaders quickly worked out a solution. Let the secondary schools teach the children of workers what was fit only for workers. As Woodrow Wilson, president of Princeton, sternly advised the Federation of High School Teachers: "We want one class of persons to have a liberal education and we want another class of persons, a very much larger class of necessity in every society, to forgo the privilege of a liberal education and fit themselves to perform specific difficult manual tasks." Since there was no way to stop "the masses" from entering high school, the only way to meet the crisis, in short, was to prevent them from learning anything liberating when they got there. Instead, the educational leaders said, the new secondary schools should offer vocational training in particular and something called industrial education in general. This, the influential Douglas Commission said in 1905, was a "new idea" in education, and in truth it was. Until ordinary Americans began attending secondary school, no secondary school in the civilized world had ever seen fit to teach its students a trade. FitzGerald attributes this vulgar innovation to the supposed fact that lofty university presidents like Wilson and Russell had lost their influence over public education—a perfect example of thoughtless snobbery.

The "new idea" must have been somewhat perplexing to schoolmarms of the old-fashioned sort. The public schools were supposed to train citizens, yet here were the country's leading educators—"we"— insisting they regard their pupils not as future citizens but as future working hinds, whom Charles W. Eliot, president of Harvard, urged teachers to "sort" by their "evident or probable destinies." If the schoolmarms were troubled, however, a stalwart band of educational reformers stood ready to reassure them that training Americans for their industrial "destiny" was the heart and soul of "democratic" education. By far the most important of the reassurers was John Dewey.

Neither the subtle reasoning nor the ardent idealism of the famed educator mattered much in the history of American education. What proved important were a few of his salient principles. Suitably adapted, they have supplied educational leaders with the lasting framework for a pedagogical system designed to prevent "the masses" from ever learning in a classroom what a free people ought to know. For that purpose, Dewey's most important contribution was his conviction that democracy has little to do with politics and government. Democracy, according to Dewey, was "primarily a mode of associated living," which for most Americans meant working together in factories. Having stripped democracy of its political character, Dewey and his colleagues, who prided themselves on their "realism," went on to redefine it as "industrial cooperation." With this new, "realistic" definition, they effected a permanent pedagogical revolution. For one thing, it enabled the Deweyites (and more interested parties) to sever the venerable ties that bound the common schools to the needs and requirements of popular government. The schools were to be adapted instead, Dewey wrote in 1897, "to the circumstances, needs, and opportunities of industrial civilization." Instead of the American republic, the American economy would call the tune. The new "realistic" definition of democracy even stripped public education of its *theoretical* republican objective, which was, as Jefferson had said, to teach future citizens "how to judge for themselves what will secure or endanger their freedom." Such knowledge was unlikely to enhance, and might well impair, "industrial cooperation." The new object of "democratic" education, Dewey said, was to teach every child "to perceive the essential interdependence of an industrial society." Thus instructed, the future citizen (i.e., factory worker) would develop what Dewey called "a socialized disposition."

With economic "interdependence" as its subject and a "socialized" worker as its goal the new "democratic" curriculum had little place for history. For *political* history, which recounts the diverse deeds of men, there was to be no place at all. Jefferson had urged the schools to teach children political history so that Americans might "know ambition under all its shapes and [be] prompt to exert their natural powers to defeat its purposes." From the political past they would learn to detect the would-be despot wearing the cloak of the popular tribune and the oligarchy masquerading as the enlightened and the elect. How could free men protect their liberties if they never learned from political history that liberty, in fact, has ambitious enemies? To Dewey, on the other hand, political history was "undemocratic" (and FitzGerald wholeheartedly agrees with him) precisely because it deals with the deeds and intentions of ambitious men. The doings of the high and mighty, in Dewey's "realistic" view, were no business of American schoolchildren, who were to share in the public life of America by leading "a socialized life" in the American work force. Instead of political history they were to be given "social studies," which would teach them, among other industrial matters, about the modern division of labor ("how milk is brought to the city") and, in the loftier grades, about the "evolution" of American industry. Given such instruction, Jane Addams noted in her 1902 work *Democracy and Social Ethics,* American children would not only develop a cooperative disposition but would find their adult toil "much more exhilarating," realizing, as they did, the useful slot they were filling on the national industrial "team."

Stripping Deweyite "realism" of its idealistic trappings proved but the work of a moment to the educational leaders, who knew a good thing when they saw one. In 1911 a committee of the National Education Association, the largest and most influential of the teachers' organizations, urged the nation's high schools to drop history altogether, on the Deweyesque grounds that it failed to promote the "social efficiency" of the ill-bred. Social studies, history's fledgling rival, would be better able, said the committee quite correctly, to "accommodate youngsters to existing conditions." That was not what Dewey had in mind, but it was latent in his "cooperative" precepts, and the educational leaders were not the only ones to realize it. Revealingly enough, the first public-school system organized on Deweyesque lines was established in 1907 in Gary, Indiana, a one-year-old company town founded by, and largely in thrall to, the U.S. Steel Corporation. J. P. Morgan knew a good thing when he saw one, too. So did the United States Congress. Under President Wilson's leadership, it began funding "vocational education" in the public schools, the first serious federal attempt to shape the content of public education.

To the purblind Deweyites political history was elitist; to the powerful few it was politically dangerous—then and always. "Throughout history," as FitzGerald rightly notes (though, alas, only in a passing remark), "the managers of states have with remarkable consistency defined good citizenship as a rather small degree of, and participation in, public affairs." To replace political history with Deweyite social studies was the perfect means of meeting the educational requirements of the powerful. In social studies American youngsters would learn that America was chiefly an industrial system and not a republic at all, that a "good citizen" is a worker who gets up when the alarm clock rings and speeds to his job on time. In social studies, too, they would learn that the "real" history of America is the "development" of American industry—history without politics in it, which teaches the most corrupt of political lessons, that politics does not matter. Pedagogical wit could scarcely devise a better instrument for ensuring "a rather small degree of knowledge of, and participation in, public affairs." To replace political history with social studies has been the abiding goal of America's educational leaders since ordinary Americans began attending high school. Interestingly enough, it took them more than half a century to register a complete triumph.

FitzGerald does not try to explain why American parents, teachers, and local school boards resisted, circa 1911, what Americans since 1965 have accepted without demur. The general explanation, perhaps, is that corrupting a venerable republic is not the work of a day.

For one thing, the "new idea" of industrial education was a new idea seven decades ago. At the time, millions of Americans believed strongly that America was a democracy corrupted by industrial capitalism, alias "the money power." That America was nothing more than industrial capitalism—the essential axiom of social studies and Deweyism—had never crossed their minds. Indeed, it was still a fairly new idea even to advanced intellectuals. Americans were still a political people who thought in political terms. Samuel Gompers, the British-bred trade unionist, used to complain bitterly about the political proclivities of America's trade-union members. Instead of "bargaining at the workplace," as all good workers should, they insisted on contesting elections, backing insurgent candidates, and behaving for all the world as if they were citizens. Not surprisingly, Gompers was an ardent champion of "industrial education." Because Americans thought in political terms, they cared greatly about "the money power" but little about the division of labor. As for history, the only idea they had of it was political. In a history book you read about armies, wars, generals, rulers, heroes, and villains—George Washington on the one hand, George III on the other. What social studies was designed to root out of the popular mind had yet to be rooted out when the NEA urged the high schools to replace history with social studies.

The old habits of thought would no doubt have proved a flimsy barrier had the educational leaders enjoyed in 1911 the power to impose their will on America's decentralized public education. Today, a quite small number of educators have virtually unchecked sway over the curriculum of America's public schools, which have become, as one educator put it in 1962, "a monolith under oligarchic control." The "textbook philosophy" (FitzGerald's phrase) the educational oligarchy propounds is the "philosophy" the textbook publishers dispense—one that the large majority of school districts will buy and pass on to the overwhelming majority of students. In 1911 the educational elite had no such sweeping power. Local control of the common schools, though waning, had not yet become a sham. To a degree, it could still meet the purpose for which it was originally intended: preventing the "managers of states" from teaching a republic's children that "good citizenship" consists in "a rather small degree of knowledge of, and participation in, public affairs." The usurpation of local control in the years after World War I was to be an essential element in the corrupting of a venerable republic.

Events on the national political stage proved a still more formidable barrier to the designs of the educational leaders and almost derailed them completely. When "industrial education" was first concocted, Americans had seemed a thoroughly defeated people. A handful of finance capitalists controlled the economic arteries; a disciplined Republican Party held national politics in thrall. A powerful few seemed to reign supreme in virtually every career and profession.

America, as Henry Cabot Lodge said at the time, had at last become "an aristocratic republic." Then, quite suddenly, middle-class Americans awoke from their slumber and discovered that they were as powerless as everybody else. To the shock and dismay of Lodge—who thought it the end of civilization as he knew it—middle-class Americans, a complacent bourgeoisie for decades, began pouring into the public arena, determined to overthrow "the machine," to curb monopoly and bring the "money power" to heel. Just when the leading educators were urging the schools to look on America as an "industrial society," middle-class Americans—who did the teaching, served on the school boards, and voted in the school-board elections—had suddenly remembered that America was a republic, and an endangered one at that.

Traditional modes of thought, the absence of an educational oligarchy, and the middle-class political revolt combined to produce a surprising result. Although the new "industrial" pedagogy made rapid headway, America's schools, despite the united urging of big businessmen, trade unions, and leading politicians, refused to let go of history. Instead, they fortified the curriculum with the only American history texts ever used that were not intended to corrupt future citizens. These texts flourished in the years between 1910 and 1930, which FitzGerald terms the "Hundred Flowers" era of American history texts. Written by trained historians, representing diverse points of view, the new texts, born of the Progressive revolt, were intensely political and remarkably free of cant. Their virtues are well worth noting, because eliminating those virtues was to be the immediate task of the educational establishment, which had to put off for another generation the extinction of political history.

The most popular textbook of the period was *American History*, by David Saville Muzzey, first published in 1911. It was the antithesis of "industrial education" in every respect, since the grand lesson of Muzzey's text was that politics matters greatly, and matters to every citizen. Muzzey's readers learned, first and foremost, that the actions of people made American history and that the high and the mighty, in fact, have power—a liberating truth in itself. Moreover, the powerful bore constant watching, for villainy was not unknown in high places. In Muzzey's history President Polk, for one, was a bastard who instigated an unjust war with Mexico in order to grab some territory. Readers of Muzzey learned that democracy in America, too, bore watching. Indeed, Muzzey's history of America is largely the history of the vicissitudes of democracy. A Yankee Republican of the old school, Muzzey seems to have viewed all modern life as one giant menace to liberty and self-government. The major problem of the age, he warned young readers, was "the corruption of the government by the money power." American democracy needed defending, and it had nothing to do with industrial cooperation.

Muzzey's most successful rival was Willis Mason West, whose textbook *American History and Government,* published in 1913, seems to have been a rejoinder to Muzzey's. Whereas the latter thought democracy in America had gone from a Golden Age to the dogs, West, more a man of the left, commenced his history with the bold assertion that "democracy has as yet been tried only imperfectly among us." Politically divergent though they were, the two leading texts agreed on the main point. American history was essentially political history, and the dramatic theme of that history, the impulse of political life and the catalyst of action, was the struggle over democracy itself.

While texts such as these were circulating (often in watered-down revisions), the educational leaders seem to have bided their time until they were powerful enough to eliminate from the curriculum history lessons so inconducive to "social efficiency" and so unlikely to "accommodate youngsters to existing conditions." All through the post-Versailles years the nascent educational establishment, backed by state legislators, strengthened its hold on the public schools and on the schools that train public-school teachers. During those years the number of local school districts was cut from 120,000 to less than half that number. State educational commissions were established to reduce still further the formal autonomy of the remaining districts. By a dozen different devices—licensing laws, state guidelines, and so on—control of the curriculum passed completely out of the hands of citizens and into the grip of an increasingly tight-knit, ingrown professional oligarchy. All it needed to emasculate the lingering "Hundred Flowers" tradition was a sharp change in the political atmosphere. With the outbreak of World War II the oligarchy struck at once, and the tradition, FitzGerald says, came "abruptly" to an end. For the next twenty-five years every new textbook used in the schools was written on the assumption that its readers were potential subversives.

In the new textbooks, which soon swept the country, political history became a hollow and meaningless form. Politics was reduced to acts of government, and villainy in high places vanished from the past. All American wars were now righteous and all American Presidents virtuous men who did, FitzGerald writes, "as well as could be expected given difficult circumstances." Imperialism, a term freely applied in the earlier texts to America's seizure of the Philippines, was now reserved exclusively for overseas ne'er-do-wells. Jingo nationalism, refreshingly absent in the "Hundred Flowers" era, pulsated through every page of the new propaganda texts. "There is a fascination with patriotic symbols," FitzGerald reports, "the flag, Independence Hall, the Statue of Liberty." Readers were adjured to accept, admire, and adore virtually everything about America except its republican institutions. In the new propaganda texts—and this is the telltale of their calculated corruptness—democracy ceased to be the theme and catalyst of American history; it excited no strife, inspired no banners, and suffered no defeats. Instead, it became the fixed and unchanging attribute of the United States, like the spots on a leopard—"a Platonic form abstracted from history," as FitzGerald well puts it. Severed from history, democracy ceased to be menaced by anything except foreign enemies and their domestic agents, whose activities in the neighborhood, one textbook advised, should be promptly reported by "young people" to the FBI, "in line with American traditions."

Even as a "Platonic form," however, democracy was too dangerous to describe at length. From the new textbooks readers learned that democracy meant the right to vote and nothing more, a definition that does not distinguish America's republican institutions from the totalitarian politics of the Soviet Union. Even reduced to a nullity, democracy, to the educational establishment, was still too dangerous to praise too highly. The fear that citizenship might break out haunts the pages of the propaganda textbooks. Instead of lauding democracy, the textbooks found subtle ways to denigrate it. One of the major texts of the era, FitzGerald says, "concludes with an essay extolling the virtues of freedom not for its own sake but merely as the greatest asset in the world struggle." A more common technique of denigration was the textbooks' insistence that what was truly great about America was its enormous gross national product. The textbooks, FitzGerald says, were "far more enthusiastic" about the GNP than about the Bill of Rights. Without eliminating political history entirely, the textbooks, which devoted considerable space to "industrialization," were hearkening back to the corrupt basic tenet of Deweyism—that America was not a republican polity but, far more important, an industrial system. Times had changed, however. Whereas "cooperation" had been the dubious deity of the original industrial pedagogy, the new deity enshrined in the propaganda texts was productivity pure and simple. One prominent junior-high-school history text argued, for example, that slavery was not all that bad because it alleviated America's chronic shortage of labor. Whereas Lincoln had said that if slavery were not evil then nothing was evil, this modern school text, still in use ten years ago, taught children that nothing is evil if it enhances production—the common principle of the capitalist, the commissar, and the tyrant.

Such were the corrupt history textbooks the educational oligarchy inflicted on a republic's children, from the bombing of Pearl Harbor to the bombing of North Vietnam. Around 1965 that textbook era, too, came to an end with what FitzGerald calls "the most dramatic rewriting of history ever to take place" in America. The cause of this eludes her, but it was quite obviously the civil-rights movement that provided the main spur for revision. At a stroke it exposed the sham of the propaganda textbooks. American democracy could hardly remain "a Platonic form abstracted from history" while Americans were out in the streets and on the hustings fighting for political liberty. Moreover, insurgent blacks demanded a place in the history texts, which had ignored their very existence for decades. Thanks to the civil-rights movement, the time was peculiarly ripe for restoring to American classrooms a deeper and more exacting political history than even Muzzey and West had provided. Here was yet another educational crisis, almost comparable to the construction of high schools at the turn of the century. Educational reformers hit on a solution at once. If the corrupt political-history texts were doomed, what American schoolchildren should get in their stead was no political history at all.

One group of reformers, known as "The New Social Studies Movement," urged the educational establishment to teach sociology instead of history. Whereas the established social studies made do with crude notions such as the division of labor, the New Social Studies would teach budding scholars how to use such refined social-science concepts as "role," "status," and "culture." This, the reformers said, would sharpen their "cognitive skills," as it had so manifestly done for professors of sociology. The American past could remain in the curriculum, but only as a "laboratory for testing social-science concepts," to quote a New Social Studies manifesto. Grinding American history into sociological mush readily recommended itself to the educational bureaucrats in the Kennedy Administration, which supported the endeavor with the customary avalanche of grants.

A second group of reformers urged the school managers to offer textbooks that were "relevant" to the immediate problems of "disadvantaged" minorities. What these disadvantaged needed, their self-appointed spokesmen said, were history texts that enhanced their ethnic and racial "pride." Since no political history of America could possibly make anyone proud of being scorned, proscribed, betrayed, or enslaved, the new ethnicity, too, won rapid and pious approval. Through a judicious blend of "social-science concepts" and sops to ethnic pride, the educational establishment has found another way to secure "a rather small degree of knowledge of, or participation in, public affairs." It is not really new, however. It is simply the old industrial education dressed up in a new disguise.

As in the old industrial pedagogy, the first principle of the contemporary textbooks is that America is not a republican commonwealth.

It is merely a society like a dozen others, including outright tyrannies and totalitarian regimes. That, of course, is fundamental to any system of corrupt education in America, as educational leaders had realized more than half a century before. Over the years, however, industrialism had lost its savor. The new America of the textbooks is not an industrial society anymore. It is now, FitzGerald says, a "multiracial, multicultural society" composed of distinct ethnic groups and races, each with its own history, achievements, and heroes—César Chavez for Mexican-Americans, for example. This new textbook America, with its "multiple perspectives," FitzGerald regards as an intellectual advance over the "outdated" view of America as a nation-state. On the other hand, she notes, taking both sides of every issue from sheer inability to decide what is important and what is mere cant, this new textbook America is indistinguishable from Yugoslavia, or, for that matter, the Ottoman Empire. America's future citizens, previously taught to regard themselves as workers, are now taught to regard themselves as ethnic tribesmen—"We're family"—who must learn to live harmoniously with other tribes cohabiting on the North American continent and especially with American Indians, who, being the most tribal, are the most admired figures in the contemporary history texts. Millions of young Americans, for example, know more about Ishi, the last "wild Indian"—he was captured in 1911—than they do about the Founding Fathers. A number of contemporary history texts begin with glowing accounts of the Aztecs and the Mayans in line with the basic textbook principle that America is a lot of tribes living in North America. "Poor Columbus," FitzGerald writes. "He is a minor character now, a walk-on in the middle of American history." So, too, is the American republic.

Like the old social studies of "industrial development," the new history texts offer a past shorn of politics and virtually devoid of people. The educational leaders have at long last triumphed over the very idea of political history. In the new textbooks no man and no deed is responsible for anything. History, in the social-science "laboratory" of the textbooks, is now the product, FitzGerald says, of "impersonal institutions and faceless social forces," which she regards as more "democratic" than political history—exactly what it is not and can never be. On the other hand, she is dismayed to discover that "there is no known case of anyone's creating a problem for anyone else" in this wonderland of abstractions. It is impossible for anyone to do so. In the new sociologized history texts, no human being has ever enjoyed sufficient power to do anything for good or ill. Famous men, in this "democratic history," are loci of impotence with illustrious names attached. Watergate, in the latest texts, is something that *happened* to Richard Nixon, and history in general is a slew of forces, pressures, and disasters inflicted by fate on the high and the mighty, who appear as hapless men of goodwill. "There are," FitzGerald says, "no human agencies left."

To erase every trace of human action, the textbooks perform prodigies of verbal mendacity. In one typical textbook, FitzGerald says, the authors attribute the "problems" facing post-Reconstruction America to "the era of Reconstruction," as if an "era" can possibly cause anything. In the no-action history of the textbooks, abstractions do everything because humans are forbidden to do anything. At all costs the readers must never be allowed to suspect that people are capable of making a difference. Like the Stone Age tribes they are asked to admire, our children are now taught to regard the American past as an incomprehensible destiny as empty of human purpose as the landscape of the moon.

With the extinction of political history the educational oligarchy has finally resolved the grand crisis of twentieth-century education: how to prevent the masses from learning what is fit only for their leaders. From the new textbooks the children of the American republic will never gain knowledge of, or the slightest incentive to participate in, public affairs. Nor will they ever learn from their sociologized texts how to detect "ambition under all its shapes." What the new textbooks teach on every page and with every passive verb is that, for all practical purposes, there is no such human activity as public affairs and no such human motive as political ambition. How can there be when "faceless social forces" make our history and the high and the mighty appear only as the victims of fate? No reader of these degraded texts will ever learn from them how to "judge for themselves what will secure or endanger their freedom." The new textbooks have snuffed out the very idea of human freedom, for that freedom at bottom is precisely the human capacity for action that political history records and that the textbooks are at such pains to conceal. In the "multiracial, multicultural" America of the textbooks every citizen is a tribesman and every tribesman the hapless subject of powers and dominions he does not even know exist. Such is "good citizenship" in the corrupted common schools of contemporary America.

The educational establishment, FitzGerald concludes, has deprived Americans of their "birthright," a personal loss she sincerely laments, but the judgment scarcely covers the ground. What the *political* history of the textbooks reveals is that a powerful few, gaining control of public education, have been depriving the American republic of citizens, and popular government of a people to defend it. And the American history textbook, so innocent-seeming and inconsequential, has been their well-chosen instrument.

How Republics Die

It is one of the revealing curiosities of history that the founders of the American republic were none too sanguine about the viability of republican government. Some of them feared that the new republic might fall under the sway of a despot raised to power by the ignorant masses; others, that it might be subverted by an oligarchy of the privileged. These were, and still are, deeply considered and honorable, though contradictory, views. The citizens who hold one or the other might, in fact, be thought of as constituting the two real and enduring parties in any republic, whatever the official views of the official parties might be.

In the unending debate between these groups, those who fear mob-inspired despotism have always enjoyed one powerful intellectual advantage, for the history of classical antiquity bears out—indeed, has done much to inspire—their fear. In ancient Greece and republican Rome it was emphatically and repeatedly the patrician class that defended republican institutions and the mob, through its chosen tyrant, that subverted them. Republican Cato and imperious Caesar define the classic confrontation, but dozens of lesser Catos and lesser Caesars had played similar roles before them in the Greek city-states.

Yet there is another notable chapter in the annals of republics that tells a different tale, a tale in which the destroyers are not the mob but the privileged. That chapter narrates the complex and tragic history of the vanished city-states of medieval Italy.

They began to emerge, these tiny municipal upstarts, in northern and central Italy—Lombardy and Tuscany—during the eleventh century, when scarcely a trace of ancient republicanism was left in Western Christendom. Pisa was the first to establish a formal government, an executive commission of "consuls," appropriating the title of ancient Rome's most exalted officials. This usage, soon adopted by neighboring towns, represented a deliberate attempt to bestow authority on their precarious governments, for in theory feudal order ruled over all, and the towns, or "communes," as contemporary Italians called them, had no authority whatever.

Thus the communes were not only upstarts but also political usurpers. To the extent that a new commune won jurisdiction over the people of a diocese, it usurped the power of the local bishop; insofar as it pushed its rule into the countryside, it usurped the authority of some feudal magnate; when it engaged in war or diplomacy with its neighbors, it defied the Holy Roman Emperor—the supreme ruler, in theory, of every member of every commune. Like woodsmen felling trees, the men of the commune were clearing a space for municipal liberty in the vast forest of feudalism. By the middle of the twelfth century there were some three hundred such communes, energetically enlarging their jurisdictions, pinching the power of bishops, dukes, and marquises, and ignoring the Holy Roman Emperor the moment his armies left Italy. Their victory over the feudality astonished all who knew of it. A Jewish traveler reported in the twelfth century: "They possess neither king nor prince to govern them, but only the judges appointed by themselves."

Outwardly at least, communes were utterly new organisms and their inhabitants utterly new men. Between the surrounding feudal order and the civil society of a city-state there is scarcely a point of resemblance. In the former, all ties among people are personal; in the latter, men find their primary bond through living together in a common territory under a common law. Under feudalism, a crime is a personal affront to be avenged by the victim's family; in a city-state, it is an offense against the community, punishable only by its magistrates. In the feudal order, people rule because rule is their birthright; in communes, they rule by consent of their fellow inhabitants.

In establishing republican communities the men of the communes had to do more than merely triumph over the surrounding feudality; they also had to extirpate the feudal ethos itself. They never quite succeeded in doing this. If, as Aristotle said, a free city is one whose members are "able to rule and to obey in turn," then the fatal flaw in the Italian city-states was the refusal of those who ruled to take their turn at obeying.

Although from the earliest days the communes had popular institutions of government—usually large, elective councils—power rested for a long time with men of noble birth and knightly titles, the *maiores,* in the parlance of the commune, as distinct from the *populares,* the people. The knights of the communes were by no means great lords, and most of them were happy to make money in trade; they had, as a rule, joined their destinies to that of the new communes to escape from vassalage to the dukes and counts of the surrounding countryside.

Within the towns, however, knights expected—like any feudal lord—to rule by right of birth: escaping vassalage themselves, they did not scruple to reestablish vassalage in the towns and to walk the streets of their cities with armed retinues in their train. While the plain people strove to strengthen the city courts, the *maiores* held to the family law of revenge, as if the city's civil jurisdiction were fit only for the rabble. Civic patriotism and public spirit left them unmoved: they were as likely to betray as to further their own commune's ambitions vis-à-vis its rivals. Ensconced in fortified town houses, waging civil war in the streets among themselves like the gangs of Prohibition-era Chicago, the nobles of the communes looked upon the communal government either as an instrument for family advancement (when their own family controlled it) or as a sword to be blunted should a rival family hold it in its grasp.

The true "new men" of the communes were not its rulers but the people themselves. It was they who defended the common law and stood by the government, shedding their blood in its cause, when the feuding nobles were tearing it apart. As P. J. Jones, a leading modern authority on the Italian city-states, has noted, "it was the populares, despised and misruled by their betters, who understood the meaning of civic virtue and the true requirements of republican government and did so long before the humanists of Florence began studying republicanism in the texts of classical antiquity."

Though they were far from meek and hapless, there is genuine pathos in the *populares*' fidelity to law and in their faith in legalistic contrivances. When the internecine warfare among the nobles had all but destroyed the consulate, the people created a new municipal officer—the *podestà*—a sort of city manager chosen from another city for a fixed term of office in the hope that a paid official from a neutral quarter would administer municipal affairs in a professional manner and thereby overawe the nobility. But the ruling families were too strong and too contemptuous of law for such a feeble constitutional makeshift to have much of an effect.

The *populares,* however, were undaunted. If the civil government was too weak to curb the insolence of the "magnates," as they were now called, there was nothing to do, popular leaders decided, but organize the people themselves as the active arm of the government. In almost all the Italian city-states the *populares* formed groups known as *popolos,* each headed by an elected captain and council. Backed by its own militia drawn from all the wards of the city, the *popolo* of every commune dedicated itself to upholding the communal government— and to curbing the insolence of the magnates.

With that, the fates began to close in on the free city-states of Italy. In Lombardy, the resurgence of the people was more than the nobility could stomach, even though it was their own profound contempt for republican institutions that had brought that resurgence about. A choice was now put before them: to share power with the despised *populares* or to surrender their power to some feudal magnate who would rule the city as a despot but at least protect their privileges. The magnates chose the privileges—and political impotence. With that choice, municipal liberty in northern Italy was virtually snuffed out by the end of the thirteenth century. The powerful Visconti family became the despots of Milan. The counts of Montefeltro made Urbino their fiefdom. The D'Estes took over Ferrara and Mantua, the

Scaliger family came to dominate Verona. Soon the forest of feudalism had grown back over a good half of the little world of the Italian city-states.

Even where the *popolos* proved stronger than the nobility—in Pisa, Siena, and Florence, for example—the refusal of the mighty to "obey in turn" eventually did its work of ruination. Though technically members of the *popolo,* the great Tuscan merchants and bankers—"the fat people," their fellow citizens called them—proved as determined to rule as the older nobility had been, and as loath to share power. By subverting the constitution, rigging elections, and suppressing dissent, the new magnates turned the republican institutions of their cities into hollow and meaningless forms.

In the fifteenth century the city-states of Tuscany, like those of Lombardy before them, succumbed one by one to a tyranny scarcely distinguishable from the oligarchy it replaced. Finally, when Florence became the proprietary domain of a Medici "duke of Florence" in 1531, the Italian experiment in republican self-government came to its definitive end. It had hung on bravely for five centuries.

Is there a lesson in the story? One political observer thought so. The lesson for him was that it is the men of privilege and influence who are likely to harm, and the people who are surest to defend, republican institutions. "The demands of a free people," he noted, "are rarely pernicious to liberty." That is not the maxim of a sentimental American Jeffersonian. It is the somber conclusion of Niccolò Machiavelli as he looked back, in the bitterness of blighted republican hopes, on the "wasted world," as he called it, of vanquished republican Italy.

The Parliament of Fans I

E ven by the modest standards of network television, the afternoon soap operas are a pretty artless form of entertainment. This is because soap opera is the only form of drama with no beginning, no middle, and no end. It rolls along like the daily life of the species, without shape, without logic, and without any discernible point. "Soaps" are so artless and humble that when letter-writing fans complain about a character, the scriptwriters obligingly infect him with a fatal blood disease, and when the fans demand to see a good woman married, the writers whistle up a bridegroom. The advice and consent of the parliament of fans plays so large a part in shaping the stories that soaps amount to a folk art, the only one spawned by the electronic age.

Like many other thriving folk arts (which are commonly esteemed only after their demise), soap opera is thoroughly disreputable. When the beautiful and accomplished widow of Anwar Sadat remarked not long ago that one of her favorite diversions in America was watching the afternoon soaps, *The New York Times* thought it was newsworthy. And it *was* newsworthy. Although more than 25 million people can be found watching soap operas on weekday afternoons at 3:00, no distinguished member of the audience ever admits his fellowship with the kind of people who send wedding presents to soap opera brides. Many people would rather admit to stealing nickels from newsstands than confess to a fondness for *All My Children* or any of the twelve other programs that flow like a current of mush through the three major networks from noon to 4:00 P.M. Even the avowed fans seem half-ashamed of their habit. When interviewed by pollsters they commonly say they watch soap operas because it gives them something to discuss with their friends, which is more an alibi than a reason.

Soaps are appallingly goofy. That is one cause of their disrepute. Admit to enjoying them and you admit to extracting pleasure from a dramatic world where the prevalent ailment is amnesia, where the most common human activity next to sex is blackmail, and where the question most likely to be posed about murder is how to break the news to the murderer's child ("This will be very difficult for you to understand. Your mother is in jail."). Goofiness, however, is not the only reason for soap opera's bad name. After watching for several weeks not long ago I was struck by something else: soap opera is embarrassingly indiscreet. It seizes upon disreputable cravings and indulges them shamelessly.

This is well illustrated by a quality that strikes the new soap-viewer's eye right away; namely, soap opera's lavish display of remarkably attractive people. Whether the characters are young or old, rich or poor, vicious or virtuous, they are almost invariably a pleasure to look at. Soap opera conducts a kind of democracy of comeliness, where even sidekicks and underlings are handsome. In doing this, soap opera faithfully reflects America's grand passion for physical beauty, which the moviemakers found buried beneath the country's official puritanism many decades ago. It has been a thoroughly disreputable passion ever since, however, for though it was previously enjoyed by ancient Greeks and Renaissance Italians it is commonly condemned by Americans as proof of our culture's immaturity. Since soap opera is as indifferent to "mature values" as an organ-grinder's monkey, soaps indulge the popular delight in carnal beauty with unstinting largess.

Another shady craving indulged by soap opera is an unappeasable appetite for erotic romance. Roughly twice a day on any given network, for example, the soaps enact the feverish prelude to the first night of love. One afternoon last January, when the snow was falling heavily, three different couples could be seen on CBS, canoodling by firelight and saying such things as "You get all of me," and "I want you," and "I've waited for so long." The next afternoon the firelit couples of the previous day appeared in bright morning light exchanging blissful pillow talk—"There is a certain glow about you"—after which they went to the kitchen for hot mugs of coffee and scrambled eggs. Heavily bracketed by "before" and "after" scenes such as these, love's sweet (out-of-wedlock) consummations have a certain honeymoon quality on the soaps, a tribute, perhaps, to the undeniable fact that life provides us with few keener pleasures and none quite so perishable.

A considerably darker passion indulged by the soaps is a notable craving for revenge. Driven by hatred and resentment, a remarkably large number of soap opera characters devote their best energies to wreaking vengeance on Jezebels who broke up their marriages, on rich families who once snubbed them, on unscrupulous business magnates who drove beloved fathers to drink. Sometimes the avengers are evil, but soap opera is not pious: revenge is too sweet to be enjoyed only by the wicked. Kay Chancellor of *The Young and the Restless,* for example, is a more or less kindly person. To avenge herself against beautiful, sultry Jill Abbott, however, she is prepared to show Jill's wealthy, honorable husband photographs of his wife in bed with his son. This is only right because Jill Abbott is a vicious voluptuary who long ago stole Kay's husband and destroyed his life. Schemes of soap opera vengeance may take so many years to execute that only veteran viewers can remember why, for example, the infinitely slimy Carl Hutchins of *Another World* was so determined to ruin wealthy, honorable Mac Cory, whose wife he abducted the last time I tuned in.

Revenge, however, is also part of the daily routine of soap opera life. On *All My Children,* slinky, tigerish Cynthia Preston, newly married to wealthy, honorable Palmer Cortlandt, encounters an ex-husband at a swanky dress shop. In a furious slanging match Cynthia is bested and promptly vows revenge (and justly so, I thought). "I want the satisfaction of hurting that pig the way he hurt me," she says. No sooner has she completed the first step in her plan of vengeance—the re-seduction of the ex-husband—than she discovers that another avenger is loose in Pine Valley. Wolfish Zach Grayson has secretly photographed the re-seduction scene in order to get revenge on Cynthia, who treats him like dirt. It says much about the secret passions indulged by the soaps that the preferred victims of vengeance tend to be wicked beauties of wealth and position and the wealthy, honorable gentlemen who stupidly marry them.

What gives soap opera its unique and unmistakable character, however, is its unabashed indulgence of an insatiable craving for emotional scenes. In soap opera the characters are constantly having heart-to-heart talks ("I want you to tell me everything"), constantly baring their souls ("You have no idea what it is like to be alone in the world"), tendering dubious advice ("If you really love someone you stay together no matter what"), declaring their love ("I want to share my life with you"), and unleashing resentment ("Stay out of my life") in furious harangues. What commonly generates these scenes is the unique soap opera art of saponification, or the rendering of actions into soapsuds. In Oakdale, home of *As the World Turns*, a tough police detective is assigned night duty helping the FBI crack a bootlegging case. The question is (and only a soap would ask it): How will the detective find time to "make love" to his self-important wife, who works very long hours as an assistant district attorney? On *General Hospital* a murder investigation is stalled for a week in order to exploit more fully the hand-wringing anguish of the woman falsely accused of the crime. "Bobbi is going through hell," her friends keep saying. The real culprit is shown going through hell, too, as the police commissioner of Port Charles closes in on her with wonderful slowness of foot.

On *Days of Our Lives* the city of Salem is about to be blown to smithereens as the climax to a monstrous plot. A young man coerced into the plot strives to get his girlfriend safely out of town without revealing the secret. His stratagem is a proposal of immediate marriage, whereupon the story marks time for several days—with zero hour approaching—in order to explore the effects of a brusque marriage proposal on a proud spirit.

First, the girlfriend refuses to be "rushed" in such a way: "When I get married I want it to be the right time." Next, she complains about her lover's secretiveness: "I feel you have been shutting me out." Then she feels she is being taken too lightly: "I spent a lot of time building up my career," she says, refusing him this time on feminist principles (to which soap opera pays lip service while secretly portraying them as a major barrier to human happiness).

These personal reactions, it is worth noting, are entirely plausible, but only soap opera would make them an important aspect of a major crime. This is because soap opera cares little about crime except as grist for domestic grief. When "the top crime boss" in Genoa City, home of *The Young and the Restless,* flies into a rage that makes his goon squad quake, it is his daughter's desire for an apartment of her own that causes his fury.

The soaps care so little about human action in general that they scarcely bother to make it credible. On *All My Children* a young man leaves his beautiful, susceptible fiancée alone with a known Lothario because, incredibly, he feels "tired" and has to go home. One day on the same show a woman plots to drive a tycoon mad: "Of course I want revenge. Who wouldn't want revenge?" Yet a few days later she accepts his offer to edit a fashion magazine. On *As the World Turns* a handsome young English peer named Lord Cushing settles in Oakdale with his cockney chauffeur for the improbable purpose of opening a "sports center." This, however, is just a ruse. He is really in search of his long-lost mother.

Silly actions of this kind occur constantly on soap operas, although, interestingly enough, they seldom occur in evening television dramas. This is not because evening television is markedly superior to daytime soap opera but because it is so radically different. On prime-time television, action counts for nearly everything and feelings for very little. In soap opera, exactly the reverse is true: what matters are the feelings that action arouses. From the point of view of the soaps, ordinary television drama looks rather heartless.

It was just this question of a point of view that had me puzzled as I watched my afternoons wash away in a vast, indulgent tide of soap opera drivel. For some time I could find nothing in the soaps remotely resembling a coherent viewpoint. To the unaccustomed eye, soap opera seems hardly more than an endless procession of vicarious treats:

warm embraces and sweet revenge, happy reunions and dangerous alliances, not to mention the lively companionship abounding in the various swanky restaurants and supper clubs where soap opera society hangs out. Yet the soaps do have a point of view, and since it is both disreputable and indulgent it is perfectly consistent with the genre's general approach to its fans. The point of view derives from the soaps' daily assurance to viewers that the one truly unpardonable sin is coldness of heart.

It is the sin, preeminently, of the truly wicked, who are quite distinct from everybody else on the programs. In soap opera ordinary people often do bad things; what sets apart the truly wicked is that they plot to do those things. Their coldness enables them to be so successful at it. "A man like that can outwit everybody," says a victim of Stafano DiMera, the arch-villain of *Days of Our Lives.* "It's all a game to him. He's like a chess player." Treating life like a game, the wicked are farsighted, resourceful, and unshakably self-assured. They are conspicuously self-controlled in a crisis, like Jill Abbott of *The Young and the Restless,* who can lie with a brazen face to escape the exposure of her depravity. They are single-minded, tireless, and uncommonly resilient. In a word, the coldhearted villains of soap opera possess every quality that leads to success in real life.

The wicked are the successful in the real world, more or less thinly disguised. And soap opera makes it clear what relationship is likely to exist between the coldly calculating schemers of the world and ordinary bumbling humanity. It is the relation of oppressor to victim. Ordinary people have too much heart to treat life like a game. On the soaps they take life as it comes. If they are wealthy, honorable gentlemen—stock figures in soap opera—they are likely to be doting cuckolds. If they are women who occupy a humbler social station they get pregnant out of wedlock, throw away promising jobs, fall in love with louts, make the wrong friends, and altogether "get in over their heads." The wicked ferret out the sins of the bumblers and blackmail them into submission. Glib, scheming Kyle Sampson, the evil young oil speculator of *The Guiding Light,* forces a young reformed prostitute to spy on her employer, a good oil man whom Sampson is trying to ruin. Blackmail is so common in soap opera that it almost amounts to an obsession, but it makes its point: the warmhearted many are the natural prey of the coldhearted few, who plan ahead. When the wicked stumble in soap opera it is often because they, too, turn out to have hearts, much to the detriment of their plans.

Coldhearted planners thrive; the warmhearted stumble from pillar to post. This is not a particularly consoling message to the kind of people who plan ahead. It might even seem to them like a grievously false accusation. After all, if you want to see your newborn baby well placed in a top-notch law firm, isn't it just common sense to enroll it in a top-notch pre-nursery school? Maybe, but soap opera was not written for middle-class careerists. To a surprising extent it is written against them. In its shapeless, goofy way soap opera champions the point of view of people who find the careful management of ambitious careers more than a little repellent, if not downright incomprehensible. This is because the soaps are popular through and through. On behalf of its parliament of fans soap opera makes a daily plea for the dignity of foolish hearts and feckless lives. Nothing else in the mass media does. Perhaps this explains the enduring appeal of this bizarre electronic folk art.

The Parliament of Fans II

A ccording to a much-discussed book called *Post-Conservative America,* fascism will soon be menacing the United States, inflicted upon us by what author Kevin Phillips calls "populist lower-middle-class conservatism." This debased conservatism, he argues, manifests itself in hatred of the rich and the poor, in hunger for a Leader, in the belief that "it might be necessary to use force to restore the American way of life." This political force, as detected by Phillips, shows a marked proclivity for "cultural and moral traditional-ism" and a sharp appetite for "nationalist pride and grandeur." Its political triumph will produce, he says, "a peculiarly American author-itarianism, apple-pie authoritarianism"—the bitter fruit of lower-middle-class America's jingoism, its disillusion with Reagan, and its lawless moral bigotry.

My first thought on reading Kevin Phillips's prognostication was that American conservatives have been predicting rabble-inspired tyrannies since July 4, 1776. My second thought was the rueful admission that this, in truth, is no happy time in America. Popular frustration, disillusion, and "traditionalist" reaction are not merely the bogeys of a timid elitist. They are real enough, so real that I decided to do what I had not done since Uncle Miltie was the king of video: sit down and watch attentively the ten or so most popular prime-time television series (soaps, sitcoms, mysteries) of the 1981–1982 season. If there was such a thing as "populist lower-middle-class conser-vatism," it seemed to me that nothing would reveal its nature more clearly than *Dallas, M*A*S*H, The Dukes of Hazzard,* et al. This is true because you cannot tell popular stories, and maintain their popular rank against stiff competition, unless you affirm with dogged devotion and perfect pitch the moral and political sentiments of millions upon millions of viewers, the bulk of whom Kevin Phillips would surely describe as "lower-middle-class." What makes most of the top dozen television dramas almost unbearably insipid is also what makes them an opinion poll incomparably more subtle than the clumsy questionnaires of the professional pollsters.

Take the quite complex issue of "moral traditionalism" that, to give Kevin Phillips his due, runs rampant through almost every hit show that I watched. In *One Day at a Time,* Mrs. Romano's daughter elopes to Las Vegas; in due course she is persuaded to return home for a "real wedding" that will give joy to grandma. Matrimonial ritual triumphs over footloose romance. In *Alice,* Mel Sharples, owner of the diner, decides to have his nose surgically improved. Lying in the hospital, however, he suddenly recalls that his uncomely, banana-shaped nose is just like his late father's. "It's a Sharples nose," says Mel in a sudden surge of pride. Cosmetic surgery is canceled as filial piety triumphs over personal vanity.

Moral and cultural traditionalism are ever victorious, but the main point, the politically significant point, is that they are never shown triumphing over any particular enemy. They are pitted against no faction, group, creed, or individual bent on subverting old-fashioned morality. Moreover, on at least half a dozen hit shows the prevailing moral conservatism is cast in a strikingly genial mode. This is done by pitting old-fashioned ways and precepts against modern-day social novelties. The main novelty in prime time is the irregular household. Alice is a divorcée with a teenage son; Mrs. Romano is a divorcée who raises a college-age daughter and a young boy who is not even a kinsman. Archie in *Archie Bunker's Place* is an aged widower who lives with a teenage niece and her female cousin. The family in *Too Close for Comfort* lives in two separate apartments in the same two-story house: the parents upstairs, the two daughters and their cousin below. In *Three's Company,* the household is extremely irregular, consisting of two nubile young women and a young man, linked at the outset by no ties of family, friendship, or sexual intimacy.

The irregular household is obviously a way of epitomizing a whole slew of social novelties that America has experienced during the past twenty turbulent years. What are the consequences? The answer is, there aren't any. The divided family in *Too Close for Comfort* suffers no real division at all. When the father reads his will aloud to the assembled household, everyone starts complaining just like any old-time, old-fashioned family would. Alice renounces her "big break" as a touring singer in order to raise her son properly. The household relationship in *Three's Company,* which consists chiefly of suppressed desires and unavowed affections, forces the three roommates into an endless succession of fibs and white lies. That a false position breeds falsity is the traditionalist moral principle of the program and the source of what little humor it generates.

The theme running through all these irregular-household shows is that, despite social novelty, the old moral verities always triumph, which is another way of saying that novelty and change are not so threatening after all. A century's worth of social thinkers and historians have been trying their best to persuade us that nothing ever remains the same, but the plain people of America, invincibly anti-intellectual, still believe that nothing important ever really changes. In this they would agree with Rudyard Kipling, who once said, "The gods of the copybook maxims always return." That confident faith is not the sort of debased and frightened traditionalism that sweeps tyrants into power.

Traditional precepts, moreover, must stand the test of experience. They are not adhered to slavishly, for Americans still possess the old, bumptious habits of freedom. The essential comedy of Archie Bunker, for example, consists in his utter inability to distinguish between old-fashioned prejudice—"all boys is animals"—and old-fashioned common sense. Experience, come upon him unbidden, makes the distinction for him, or at any rate for the viewers. In one fine episode Archie persuades his good friend and neighbor to accept as a lodger an ailing man who is patently deranged. The man is a Republican, a businessman, and an Elk—so Archie, always blinded by hand-me-down doctrines, is certain he's sound as a bell. After turning everyone's life into a nightmare, the wretched man dies right before the two friends' eyes. In the final scene Archie's friend grows maudlin thinking about his late lodger's dying without any family at hand. Archie, however, will have none of that. Old-fashioned common sense tells him that his pal's mournful pity is but self-pity ill-disguised, although he had to learn the hard way that an Elk can be a madman ill-disguised.

Experience separates what is valuable and what is dross in the mishmash of verities and follies that make up the cultural and moral tradition. In *One Day at a Time,* Schneider, the aging, amorous janitor, takes up with a twenty-two-year-old girl, much to the Romano family's dismay. Hoping to placate them, he begins spouting a half-dozen variations on that most common of popular American delusions: that aging is largely an illusion. "You're only as old as you feel," insists Schneider. "It's not the clock on the wall that counts. It's the clock inside your heart." It will not take long before life with a twenty-two-year-old girl teaches Schneider the painful truth that growing old, alas, is no illusion.

Since experience distinguishes what is true from what is false in the moral tradition, bigotry—the refusal to learn from experience—is looked upon as the very prince of follies, or worse. It does not protect the cultural and moral traditions. It weakens them. In the moral order affirmed by the prime-time hit shows (an order that can safely be called "populist lower-middle-class conservatism"), bigotry and traditionalism do not work hand in glove, as Kevin Phillips assumed. They appear as antagonists.

An episode of *The Love Boat* gave sharp form to this moral precept in the story of the identical twin sisters who make the cruise on a single ticket, each of them taking turns appearing in public. One sister is looking for romance. The other is an avowed misanthrope determined to despise and repel all men. In a word, she is a bigot; by any traditional moral reckoning, she is a moral subversive as well, for humans, we all know, were born to mate. What cure her are the comical consequences flowing from the heated affair that develops between her sister and the ship's doctor. Whenever he sees the man-hating twin taking her share of the cruise, he rushes forth and woos her ardently. Icy stares, pursed lips, rigid posture, harsh words—none of the devices this young lady uses to repel men can repel the doctor. He is puzzled, but persistent beyond anything the man-hating twin has ever had to cope with. In due course she embraces the doctor and abandons her life-blighting creed. Experience rescues tradition by stamping out the subversive power of bigotry.

The separation of traditionalism and bigotry may not seem, at first glance, especially profound or significant. Neither does the larger moral code of which that separation forms a conspicuous part. Indeed, the moral virtues that the prime-time hit shows affirm and celebrate are singularly unheroic. Honor, glory, self-sacrifice, renunciation, devotion to harsh duty, adherence to unpopular principle—these play almost no part in the moral world of the prime-time shows. The Duke boys in *The Dukes of Hazzard* valiantly foil the greedy schemes of Boss Hogg, but only to protect their family. Beyond that they seem to have no more public spirit than the village idiot. Thomas Magnum of *Magnum P.I.* is one of the few figures in the noble private eye tradition who is not represented as a shopworn Galahad tackling the world's corruption single-handed. On the contrary, he is the friend of a man so rich and powerful that the very mention of his name opens doors Sam Spade would have had to pry loose with a jimmy and Jim Rockford with a complicated lie.

The chief moral virtues celebrated in the prime-time hits are sweetly modest ones: tolerance, forgiveness ("We all make mistakes, don't we?"), helpfulness ("What are friends for?"), and kindliness. One episode of *Alice,* quite typical, was spent showing Alice letting down a teenage admirer as painlessly as possible. Half the hit shows on television depend for their popularity on an audience in love with kindliness, thoughtfulness, and decency. Whatever threatens these virtues—arrogance and self-importance, for example—is always fair game on prime time. Much of the moral charm of *M*A*S*H* lies in its utterly convincing demonstration that even in a wartime army, candor and kindness need never yield an inch to military hypocrisy, martial cant, and the arrogance of rank—or even military obedience, if it comes to that. Of "nationalist pride and grandeur" there is no sign whatever on the prime-time shows I watched. There's no grandeur of any kind.

It would be easy enough to deride a moral code so limited and undemanding that it makes neighborliness the highest good. It would be a mistake to do so, however, for the real significance of that code is not moral but political. It is the moral code of liberty and democracy; its object is to protect democracy and liberty from harm. The neighborly virtues that form the prime-time moral code—the willingness to help, the willingness to forgive, the determination to consider the other person's feelings—stand as a popular bulwark against tyranny. This is because a tyrant, as Tocqueville long ago pointed out, does not care if his subjects hate him as long as they dislike one another. The great worth of the neighborly virtues is that they safeguard mutual respect, the thoughtful regard in which fellow citizens hold one another simply because they are fellow citizens. The great value of mutual respect is that it enables free people to act together in great public affairs and so foil the lawless designs of would-be tyrants and ruling cabals. Without such mutual respect, no constitution could safeguard our liberties.

That the televised moral code is deeply political the makers and viewers of prime-time television seem to understand clearly enough, though perhaps in a wordless, intuitive way. This is reflected in the two most striking features of the shows I watched: the determination to celebrate traditional morality without scoring off of a social enemy, and the emphatic insistence that bigotry is no friend of traditional morality. The explanation for this seems clear enough. We live in dark and frustrating times; we have lived through rapid and painful social changes. It is now, most of all, that mutual respect needs special protection. It is as if the great body of the American people were determined not to become the lawless bigots Kevin Phillips expects us to be. The moral code of prime-time television reflects the political determination not to lose the bulwark of our liberty.

Because it is a code of political morality, the prime-time moral code mirrors, too, the American people's enduring love of equality, which figured largely in almost every prime-time show I watched. Commonly it takes the form of equal relations between ostensible unequals: Mel and his waitresses; the Romanos and the janitor; the Harts and their factotum Max on *Hart to Hart;* the Duke boys and the Hazzard County powers; everyone on *M*A*S*H* regardless of rank. What levels the inequalities between employer and employee, master and servant, governor and governed, officer and enlisted man is, of course, the counterforce of equality deriving from citizenship.

In the moral code of prime time, egalitarianism is always a mark of goodness. The unforced, unfailing respect the Harts show to those poorer, weaker, and less lucky than they is clearly meant to be their signal virtue. To the viewers it gives welcome reassurance that the possession of every material blessing need not undercut the equality of citizens. To hate the rich as such forms no part of the prime-time moral code. Only when the very rich deny the fellowship of citizens do they bring moral odium on themselves. What marks Mrs. Channing of *Falcon Crest* as wicked is her arrogant assertion that family "tradition" takes precedence over mere, stupid "equality." To sneer at the Declaration of Independence is an act of intolerable impiety to the majority of "populist lower-middle-class conservatives"; such an attitude will never bring fascism in its train. The "neo-conservatives" who pretend that it will do not fear fascism, they merely hate equality. The same popular conservatism (as opposed to neo-conservatism) makes J. R. Ewing of *Dallas* America's favorite villain. He is inequality incarnate. Every time he unleashes his personal, lawless, and utterly irresponsible power, he dashes our ancient hopes for a republic of equals. Every time he destroys somebody's self-respect by reducing him to a hapless pawn, he does violence to the deepest meaning of equality in America.

That "all men are created equal" has never meant that all people are alike. The proposition is not refuted by noting that Mr. Jones is five inches taller than Mr. Smith. What it does mean, fundamentally, is that no one is ever entitled to reduce another to a mere means: no master can treat his servant as if he were only a servant; no government can treat the governed as if they merely performed social functions. How well Americans understand this (as the Reaganites are beginning to learn) is neatly attested by an episode of *The Love Boat* that offered three variants on the theme of equality violated by turning people into means. One subplot concerned a long-grieving widow who falls in love with an amiable professor the moment she sets foot on the ship. The second involves a penniless Lothario who persuades an oil heiress that he's a Riviera swell. The third concerns a young woman's determination to bear a genetically well-endowed child by seducing a handsome, healthy, intelligent pro football quarterback. The subplots thicken quickly. The heiress discovers that her glib suitor is a professional fortune hunter. The football star refuses to be reduced to a chromosome supplier. The professor discovers that the widow loves him because he resembles her late husband. All three have been reduced to means, their self-respect badly marred. Not until equality is established between each of the three pairs can happy endings ensue. Unless we recognize the requirements of equality, the whole system of mutual respect is menaced.

This is political understanding of no small order, although Americans possess it by the saving light of intuition, for on the face of it there is no reason why Americans should have any political understanding at all. We are systematically miseducated in our schools, taught that a citizen is a guy with a job, that the Gross National Product measures a republic's greatness. We are despised by our betters and viciously blamed for all that goes wrong. We are lied to by our leaders, day after day, decade after decade, without let or hindrance. We ought to be lost, cowed, utterly bewildered, but somehow we are not, at least not for long. As the prime-time shows prove, we always return to first principles—to liberty and equality and to the moral code of democracy, which preserves them and us from harm. Some day perhaps the light of intuition may flicker and fail, but not, I think, just yet.

The Cold War Decoded

Rumors of peace were rife last spring when I began poring over a ten-year accumulation of notes on the Cold War, which was said to be drawing to a close, bringing with it "the end of civilization as we know it," as Joseph Heller was said to have remarked. That wickedly cynical quip actually raised a momentous historical question: if the Cold War was really ending what would be done to replace it? For the global rivalry between the U.S. and the U.S.S.R. made possible one of the great turnings in American history—the postwar transformation of the old republican commonwealth into a globe-straddling imperial republic.

A kind of erudite misdirection has long distorted that great transformation. It is thought to be the mere unintended by-blow of deeper forces, fears, and ambitions. In the orthodox account of the great transformation, a modest, essentially passive America was compelled to spread eagle's wings in order to prevent communist-led Russia from taking over the world. In the "revisionist" alternative, America's capitalist rulers were compelled to spread eagle's wings in order to prevent Russian-led communism from taking over the world, which is merely the official orthodoxy in a "Marxist" garb, hotly accusing America's leaders of their own cherished alibi.

Two weaknesses propped together, said Da Vinci, make one strength, and so it is with the prevailing orthodoxy and its prop, the prevailing heterodoxy. Not until I had burrowed through the Cold War annals, not for the first or even the second time, did it finally dawn on me that the imperial republic was born not of the strife between capitalism and communism; that is the grand misdirection. It was born of the ineluctable republican struggle between those who would "limit," in Tocqueville's words, and those who would "extend the authority of the people." What will replace the waning Cold War is not only a momentous question; America's leaders are already supplying a momentous answer.

What follows is a history of the postwar imperial republic from its birth to its death to its current transmutation.

It is a history that begins during World War II when a vast, exultant ambition fired America's leaders. They were determined at war's end to bestride the world like a colossus, to punish aggression, to root out "spheres of influence," to ensure the independence of all nations great and small—in a word, to "make the world over," in the exuberant phrase of the exuberant hour.

There was nothing entirely new in all this. As far back as the 1890s, when the nation's leaders had cried up a "large" foreign policy—the policy of looming "large" in the world—imperial ambitions had been germinating in American politics. Breaking out on occasion, they had always met powerful resistance. America's continental traditions stood in the way. So, too, did the venerated maxims of the founders. The strongest barrier of all, perhaps, was the American people's deeply held suspicion that power abroad and democracy at home were ever and always at war. America might gain "an imperial Diadem, flashing in false and tarnished lustre the murky radiance of dominion and power," in John Quincy Adams's memorable words, but "she would be no longer the ruler of her own spirit." The American people were right, more right than they could possibly know at the time, but the bombs that fell on Pearl Harbor shattered their former self-assurance. Amid the fevers and excitements of World War II, the great ambition, so long germinating, burst into grandiose bloom.

American officials spoke ecstatically of the beckoning "job of world leadership with all its burdens and all its glory." Postwar America, armed and mobilized, the "trustee for civilization," bears "responsibility for maintenance of world peace," declared James V. Forrestal,

THE COLD WAR DECODED

Truman's secretary of war, in April 1945. As early as 1943, the State Department, grown giddy with newfound consequence, was already working up "a diplomacy which pretended that we were interested in every disputed region everywhere," as Walter Lippmann scornfully remarked at the time. In the British Embassy's weekly report from Washington, a young philosopher-diplomat named Isaiah Berlin noted in a February 1943 dispatch that "dreams of world domination are widespread and while they may yield to Mr. Hull's or the President's wiser counsels, their strength must not be discounted." Yet even the sharp-eyed Berlin underestimated the strength of the long-pent ambition to transform the old republic once and for all.

Thus, in the glory days of August 1945 his weekly embassy report noted that "America sees Soviet Russia as its only rival for world supremacy and at the same time has no desire to become unnecessarily embroiled with her." Alas, Berlin had spoken too soon. What Lippmann called at the time "a diplomatic war in the borderlands of the Soviet Union" commenced in September, bringing with it need-less, peace-shattering embroilment.

To the legions of "world leadership" the U.S.S.R. was not a problem but the solution to a problem, a heaven-sent gift from "providence," in the candid words of the State Department's George Kennan, to *force* the American people into "accepting the responsibilities of moral and politi-cal leadership that history plainly intended them to bear." For the real barrier to an imperial republic was not the Soviet Union but the American people, humbled by Pearl Harbor but not entirely crushed.

The problem facing America's leaders was this: they could not establish an imperial regime without actively dominating the world, but they could offer no honest or persuasive reason for doing so. In the eyes of the nation's leaders, popular resistance to American world leadership led directly to World War II and would lead in turn to World War III. In transforming the old republic, in crushing its spirit beneath an imperial diadem, they were making the world safe *from* the American people. Such was the conviction that fortified America's leaders in 1945, but it made a poor argument in public. Ordinary Americans thought Hitler and the warlords of Japan had started

World War II and they thought America's active membership in the new United Nations organization (which they overwhelmingly supported) would prevent a third global war. Nothing, it seemed, could win them over to the glory and burdens of world leadership.

"A breach of the peace anywhere in the world," claimed their new President, "threatens the peace of the entire world," but Americans did not really believe this because it was patently false. We are "the strongest nation on earth," the new President boasted on Labor Day, 1945. Then why, Americans rightly wondered, was the strongest nation on earth simultaneously so weak and so vulnerable that it had to dominate the world just to be safe? Because "America must behave like the Number One World Power which she is," replied Senator Arthur Vandenberg, foreign policy leader of the Republican Party, begging the question in the safety of his diary. "The position of the United States in world affairs," noted a typical official statement, "is based on the premise that our security and welfare are intrinsically related to the general security and welfare, and upon an acceptance of the responsibility for leadership in world affairs which is called for by that premise." Alas for "world leadership," this kind of high-toned sophistry, reeking with dishonesty in every cant phrase, could neither move a people nor subdue a republic. General George Marshall would speak of "the vast responsibility which history has clearly placed upon our country," but the overwhelming majority of Americans, unenlightened by higher education, did not understand that "history" told their leaders what to do. "No sudden cultural maturation is to be anticipated in the United States," lamented a political scientist named Gabriel Almond as late as 1950, "which would be proportionate to the gravity and power of its newly acquired international status." The only thing Americans want to do, complained Averell Harriman, our ambassador to Moscow, is "go to the movies and drink Coke."

The problem was urgent. "The reluctance of our people to remain on the international scene" was the State Department's greatest fear, said a high-ranking department official. The general solution was obvious. "The United States will not take world leadership effectively," warned Will Clayton, another high-ranking department official, "unless the people of the United States are shocked into doing so." In September 1945 an adviser to Secretary Forrestal warned that unless Americans were persuaded that invasion was perpetually *imminent* they would not support the "complete realignment of government organizations [needed] to serve our national security in the light of our new world power and position."

An ambition pent up for fifty years was not to be thwarted by a nicety of scruple. An imperial republic was not to die stillborn for want of a lie. "Because the masses are notoriously shortsighted," wrote the eminent diplomatic historian Thomas Bailey, summing up the matter in 1948, "and generally cannot see danger until it is at their throats, our statesmen are forced to deceive them into an awareness of their long-run interests." The new imperial republic was to be ruled by official duplicity, provocations, and false alarms. And by a "bipartisan foreign policy" as well, for duplicity cannot long withstand public scrutiny and "world leadership" lacked sufficient merit to bear open discussion and partisan debate.

"Bipartisan foreign policy is the ideal for the executive because you can't run this damned country any other way. . . . Now the way to do that is to say politics stops at the seaboard—and anyone who denies that postulate is a son-of-a-bitch and a crook and not a true patriot. Now if people will swallow that then you're off to the races." Thus Dean Acheson, explaining how to muzzle a free people and stifle their freedom.

So it was (to leap five years ahead) that when a reckless demagogue cried out in February 1950 that Acheson's State Department was a hotbed of pro-communist treason, millions of Americans flocked to that lunatic banner and cheered that manifestly false charge. For in its perverse and twisted way it conveyed the deep forbidden truth of the age, a truth which by then could no longer be spoken, which could scarcely even be thought, which I feel even now my own temerity in uttering: the truth that, while Stalin was a despotic Asiatic brute, the lying pantaloons who sought an imperial diadem, contemptuous of all that Americans had the sacred right to hold dear, who lusted after "the murky radiance of dominion and power," were indeed betrayers of the American republic.

The "diplomatic war in the borderlands of the Soviet Union" had no diplomatic end in view. It was domestic propaganda issued from abroad. Instead of working toward a general European settlement, instead of determining the future of defeated Germany, instead of striving to remove all occupation troops from her territory—the "normal and universally accepted objective at the conclusion and settlement of a war," as Lippmann tartly noted—American leaders at war's end cried out "Bulgaria libre" and "Free Romania," and made it America's first order of postwar business to liberate these two former Nazi allies from Soviet thralldom. No "sphere of influence" is too small, claimed the State Department, to "militate against the establishment and effective functioning of a broader system of peace." We must "further our broad political ideals" in Romania and Bulgaria; it was a "principle interest" of the United States to do so, Harriman urged the fuddled little man in the White House, as did Undersecretary Acheson, as did Admiral William Leahy, the new President's military adviser, as did Secretary Forrestal, who proposed that Truman win over America's skeptical corporations (as late as mid-1947 the National Association of Manufacturers still spoke of the "so-called communist threat") by suspending the anti-trust laws and suppressing domestic radicals as their reward for joining the forthcoming Cold War. Most decisively, Congress pressed hard upon Truman. "Self-determinism" for Romania and Bulgaria or else, warned Senate leaders as soon as the ink dried on the Japanese articles of surrender, thereby rendering the U.S.S.R. dispensable as an ally and accessible as a foe.

From the point of view of "world leadership" the great merit of the borderland campaign lay in this: it was bound to fail and fail badly. This was so not only because we had no force to back up our demands, not only because we had already acquiesced in friendly borderlands for Russia at Yalta, not only because even General Marshall, outgoing army chief of staff, and old Henry Stimson, outgoing secretary of war, thought the Soviets' borderland sphere realistic and tolerable (Truman "was evidently disappointed by my caution and advice," Stimson noted in his diary after telling the new President as much). It was bound to fail because our borderland campaign was so blatantly hypocritical it could only be seen as an act of hostility, provoking hostility in return.

Stalin is "a realist in all of his actions," Harriman warned Truman, "and it is hard for him to appreciate our faith in abstract principles"— especially when applied only to him. The United States was playing "a straight power game" in Latin America—our sphere of influence—"as amoral as Russia's game in Eastern Europe," *Time* had complained in May 1945. On the same score, Stimson, a cabinet member in the Taft Administration, confided to his diary that "some Americans are anxious to hang on to exaggerated views of the Monroe Doctrine and at the same time bite into every question that comes up in Central Europe." Aflame with imperial ambitions, the nation's leaders were leaving the old respectables floundering in their wake. Even Truman's secretary of state, James F. Byrnes, an old-line machine Democrat from South Carolina, worried over the hypocritical diplomacy he was being forced to conduct. In our occupation of Japan "we were going off in a unilateral way as the Russians were going off in the Balkans," he confided in late September to his predecessor, Edward R. Stettinius. American diplomacy was "following a double-standard of morality," complained Lippmann, "nationalist, or if you like, imperialist where we have the power [Japan, Latin America, the Pacific] and universalist where the Russians have it." In other words, the United States in 1945 protected its vital interests—and then some—with unabashed realism and assaulted the Soviets' vital interests with unshakable "faith in abstract principles."

"Was it not certain that here they must fail as in fact they have failed?" Lippmann was to write a year later. Was it not certain, too, that our leaders had gone out of their way to fail, for "contrary to all precedents in settling wars, they chose to begin their peacemaking with the satellites of their principle enemy," Nazi Germany? Was it not obvious, too, that they had gone out of their way to choose precisely "the ground where they [the Russians] were most able to be, and were most certain to be, brutal, stubborn, faithless and aggressive"? Thus did the imperial republic, which so desperately needed a "shock," go about the business of procuring it.

The road to imperium was nonetheless rough. In the autumn of 1945 free elections were held in Czechoslovakia and Hungary; the Hungarian Communist Party was defeated with ease and impunity. The Soviet "shock" was still out of focus. As the State Department's chief of intelligence admitted in December, "the problems of Russian capabilities and intentions are so complex, and the unknowns are so numerous, that it is impossible to grasp the situation fully."

The nation's leaders did what they could to keep trouble brewing. On Navy Day President Truman gave a bellicose speech, crying up the momentous importance of Bulgarian democracy. The day after the Hungarian elections, the Senate Foreign Relations Committee hailed Secretary Byrnes for using the Balkans to prevent any settlements whatever at the first postwar Foreign Ministers' Conference. Yet Byrnes himself was troubled. That failure was true diplomatic success and negotiations a mere sub-branch of government propaganda were ideas too novel, it seems, for the old Bourbon Democrat to grasp.

A revealing little episode ensued. Convinced that deadlock over Romania and Bulgaria had gone far enough, Byrnes flew to Moscow in December to deal directly with Stalin, completely ignoring Truman, whom he held in understandable contempt. After winning from the Soviet despot a faint semblance of liberality in his two Balkan puppet regimes, Byrnes returned home triumphantly and announced in a radio broadcast that the Balkan obstruction had been cleared and the Grand Alliance saved from deadlock and division.

Like a tiger whose prey had been ripped from its jaws, official Washington roared in outrage. Leading senators assailed the secretary for deserting "principle." At the White House, Admiral Leahy spoke ominously of "Munich appeasement." A frightened Truman repudiated his secretary of state and talked instead of using an "iron fist" to crush Soviet ambitions. "There is apparently more anti-Russian spirit than I thought possible," Byrnes's aide in Washington cabled his chief in London on January 14.

Washington's rage was readily understandable. The nation's leaders were determined to subjugate a venerable republic. For so awesome and terrible a task they needed all the self-righteousness they could muster. Byrnes's cheerful pragmatism, the familiar horse-trading of an old-line American politico, exposed their hypocrisy as only an old colleague could. Washington writhed in the agonies of bad faith. Then the U.S. military, ever lacking the visionary gleam, proceeded to make matters worse. In February 1946, the Joint Intelligence Committee of the Joint Chiefs of Staff concluded that the Soviet Union was seeking security from its wartime allies. Where was the "shock" in that? The military blockheads had put the shoe of menace on the wrong foot.

At this painful juncture an obscure State Department intellectual came to the rescue of the imperial enterprise. In an 8,000-word telegram cabled in late February from Moscow, George Kennan brought succor to the imperial hypocrites. Forget Soviet "capabilities and intentions." Forget military blockheads mired in common sense. The Soviet Union was driving for world domination, said Kennan, due to a "psychosis which permeates and determines the behavior of the Soviet ruling caste." Spawned by "internal imperatives," the Soviet drive was unalterable, inexorable, non-negotiable. And what a drive it was! "We have here a political force committed fanatically to the belief that with US there can be no permanent modus vivendi; that it is desirable and necessary that the internal harmony of our society be disrupted; our traditional way of life be destroyed, the international authority of our state be broken if Soviet power is to be secure." Now the right foot had the shoe! Having failed to dislodge Russia from the Balkans, America's leaders joyfully concluded with Kennan that Russia was bent on dominating the world. After pretending with maddening priggishness that a Balkan sphere of influence menaced world peace, the hypocrites of empire now looked forward with utmost eagerness to a world divided into two warring camps.

The author of the "Long Telegram" was at once hailed a savior. Secretary Forrestal, who later jumped from a hospital window in flight from communist bogeys, sent copies of the cable flowing down the corridors of power. Eager to alert its fuglemen and flunkies, the State Department sent Kennan on "a nation-wide tour of off-the-record speaking engagements before groups of foreign policy opinion-makers" to tell them of the mortal danger which "providence" was kind enough to inflict us with, which they in turn would inflict on the Coke-drinking rabble when the nation's leaders deemed the time ripe, some thirteen months later in fact.

"For reasons which I do not understand, Mr. X decided not to consider the men of the Kremlin as the rulers of the Russian State and Empire," Lippmann was to write after the new gospel was publicly set forth in an article by "X"—Kennan—in the July 1947 issue of *Foreign Affairs*. In one of the finest series of political essays ever written for the daily press in America, Lippmann tore the new gospel to shreds from its paltry determinism—first refuge of your modern scoundrel—to its deadly, foreseeable perils. "Mr. X," noted Lippmann, was offering a policy "which does not have as its objective a settlement of the conflict with Russia." He offered instead a dubious theory about the Soviet Union which excluded all possibility of a settlement. What it demanded instead was outright American imperialism, the "recruiting, subsidizing and supporting a heterogenous army of satellites, clients, dependents and puppets" whose internal affairs would require "continued and complicated intervention by the United States." Even worse, the new policy carried the constant threat of borderland war, for one day, warned Lippmann, we would find ourselves compelled to rescue one of our clients "at an incalculable cost on an unintended, unforeseen, and perhaps undesirable issue." Korea and Vietnam were already in utero in 1947, but Lippmann, who was read by everybody who mattered, was ignored by everybody who mattered—except by Acheson, who angrily denounced him at a dinner party for "sabotaging" his country.

To the imperial party the new gospel's radical defects constituted its unsurpassable merit. The Soviets' theoretical drive to dominate the world justified in fullest measure all that the imperialists needed to dominate America. "If it had never existed we would have had to invent it," as one of Kennan's colleagues remarked to him. Here was the grand pretext for imperial dominion, for limitless meddling, for mobilizing the nation as if for war. The imperial republic required an atmosphere of crisis. The new gospel provided a crisis that never ended. "You cannot negotiate with them, their policy cannot change," a State Department official explained in *The New York Times* on February 1, 1947. "Neither Molotov nor Stalin nor the Politburo can change it. It is dogma."

This was a great advantage indeed. From the start "world leadership" was meant to be a permanent regimen, a new "creation," in Acheson's apt term, a permanent tomb for the old republic. The new gospel provided its permanent pretext.

According to its remorseless logic, the very absence of a Soviet threat was a Soviet threat. Since Russia was inalterably bent on our ruin, every Soviet offer of a settlement was merely a trap to lull our suspicions; every feeble Soviet retreat a ruse to bring down our guard. Thus, when General Marshall replaced out-of-step Byrnes as secretary of state in January 1947, his new subordinates, doubtless fearing a military blockhead, greeted their new chief with a warning memorandum. He was advised to treat with public contempt any conciliatory Soviet move. "It is imperative that we not be misled by this tactic— one to which American public opinion had repeatedly shown itself to be vulnerable." The entire body of the American people were potential dupes of the Kremlin! Outright critics were "a sabotage front for Uncle Joe Stalin," as Truman wrote in his diary on September 19, 1946.

Here, in truth, lay the supreme merit of the new Cold War gospel. It allowed America's leaders to wage unceasing war against the American people. As the editors of the *Times* were to put it on December 29, 1949, when Americans were growing unhappy with the Cold War, "It is certainly part of the calculations of the Soviet government that sooner or later the United States will tire of its responsibilities or become divided in its support of the present policy. . . . This would at once provide the signal for a new Soviet advance" on the road to our ruin. Division invited disaster; liberty brought division; therefore liberty must go. Reason of State now ruled the American republic. "The integrity of our system will not be jeopardized by any measures, covert or overt, violent or non-violent," noted a 1950 White House report, "which serve the purpose of frustrating the Kremlin design."

The new imperial regime was formally inaugurated on March 12, 1947, when Truman went before a joint session of Congress to proclaim the leading principles of the new order—soon to be called the "Truman Doctrine"—and to announce its first practical application: U.S. intervention in a civil war in Greece. On the same day, the President signed Executive Order 9835, aimed at making dissent from the new regime a hissing and a byword. For the first time in American history the citizens of the United States were divided into official political categories: the "loyal" and the "disloyal." A "loyal" American acquiesced in the new order without audible complaint. A "disloyal person" voiced doubts about the Cold War gospel; he questioned the Truman Doctrine when asked. Possibly he was "in sympathetic association with" an organization which, in the judgment of the U.S. attorney general, sought to "undermine confidence . . . in the government of the United States." The stigmata of disloyalty was clear and defamatory (as the Supreme Court was to rule in 1951): the "disloyal" were unfit to serve in the general government or to work in a defense plant or a naval shipyard.

Officially restricted to 13.5 million government employees and defense workers, Truman's "loyalty program" was, perforce, applied to the country at large. Those who served the imperial regime fell like wolves upon those who dared question it. With the official encouragement of the first President of the new imperial republic, any American who still thought with John Quincy Adams that America "goes not abroad in search of monsters to destroy" was now open to savage abuse, social ostracism, and the loss of his job. "Liberal internationalists" led the campaign of vilification; "conservative" Republicans followed soon after.

Danger at home and abroad was the initial reason for the campaign against liberty, but it was merely a pretext. It usually is. The 1948 presidential election demonstrated that even the bearer of an illustrious political name—Henry Wallace—could command no popular support if he stood out against the Cold War. The international events of 1948 demonstrated that the U.S.S.R. was utterly outmatched by America's incomparable wealth and power. After Stalin lifted his disastrous blockade of Berlin in May 1949, John Foster Dulles proclaimed "the end of the Cold War in Europe." Returning home from Germany in late 1949, General Lucius D. Clay bluntly advised his countrymen that "we are being frightened by a second-rate people." Yet the abating of danger, such as it was, brought no surcease in the campaign against liberty. Instead, it grew more intense and more systematic. In 1949 alone fifteen states passed anti-subversion laws. In 1949 liberals revived the American Committee for Cultural Freedom to "expose," said its head, "Stalinism and Stalinist liberals wherever you find them." By mid-1949 it was "becoming a state sin," complained a pre-war "isolationist," to oppose the new North Atlantic Treaty. In 1949 university presidents called for campus "loyalty oaths" to protect democracy—meaning the imperial republic—from "the enemies within the walls," while the American Political Science Association solemnly discussed "the problem of setting some limit on freedom of speech as a safeguard against subversive ideas." The political atmosphere grew increasingly poisonous. "It was the popular cant in 1949," Alistair Cooke observed early in 1950, "to say that you could not be too suspicious of your neighbor because the Russians and their agents abroad had adopted a wholly new technique of terrorizing people into conformity." In the year which saw "the end of the Cold War in Europe" those who still dared to defend republican liberties were more savagely denounced than ever. What was the friend of liberty, after all, but the subtlest of national enemies? He was "the fellow traveler of the fellow traveler," Arthur Schlesinger warned in *The Vital Center*, his 1949 credo for liberal Democrats.

The campaign against liberty intensified because the new imperial regime needed something deeper and more durable than mere submission to its current policies. Grave dangers lay ahead. The Soviets' relative weakness could not be concealed from Americans forever, nor could their willingness to throw in the towel—they made their first call for "peaceful coexistence" in December 1949—be denounced as a ruse indefinitely. There were "fair weather internationalists" among us, the *Times* editors warned on January 4, 1950, meaning Americans who supported "world responsibility" only when the international weather looked foul, for fair was foul and foul was fair in the new imperial republic.

Only a people steeped in service bigotry could keep that perverted regime permanently safe from democracy in America. "The fellow traveler of the fellow traveler" upheld the dignity of dissent. The new regime, for its safety, sought to dishonor and defame it. Using every venue of influence available to the modern state, it strove to teach Americans that any questioning of authority in America was sinful, shameful, and, above all, alien. And it succeeded. Long after the end of the "McCarthy era"—that superbly misleading tag—the degraded echoes of the campaign against liberty could still be heard in the country. "America, love it or leave it," cried the well-disposed subject of the imperial regime thirty years after the Cold War began, while millions of less well-disposed Americans skulk to this day in the shadows, speaking to no one, half-ashamed of themselves.

A deeper debasement was wrought in political thought itself. Until the inception of the imperial regime, America had been "a republic if you can keep it," as Benjamin Franklin famously remarked. The American republic was felt to be menaced by a great variety of contradictory causes, conditions, and ambitions: the pride of the rich, the envy of the poor, the pretensions of oligarchs, the ambitions of demagogues, the sheer appetite for power which grows with its exercise. Opinions differed sharply and vehemently, yet, like divergent branches of the soaring American elm, they all sprang from a common set of roots—the principles, the politics, and the history of republics.

The imperial regime tore up those roots. America became a "democracy" endangered only by an enemy without, protected by faithful leaders within. In the public schools of the imperial republic an entire generation of children had this corruption drilled into its soul. In the school history texts of the era, as Frances FitzGerald well observed [see pages 63–78], democracy was no longer subject to political dangers and historical vicissitudes. It had become a "Platonic form abstracted from history," a fixed and immutable attribute of the United States, as a spotted pelt is the fixed attribute of a leopard. "The young were taught to distrust ideas which had been the gospel of the founding fathers," I. F. Stone observed in 1953. What was worse, the precepts of the founders simply ceased to make sense. The founders' fears of irresponsible power and lawless ambition were readily understood in a "republic if you can keep it." So, too, was Jefferson's warning that "eternal vigilance is the price of liberty." Such precepts can find no lodgment in a "democracy" abstracted from history, menaced only by an external enemy and his local agents. Under the new imperial regime the "republic if you can keep it" became a "democracy" kept safe by popular servility and a large standing army, by a vast expansion of official secrecy, by a vast expansion of presidential power, and by a vast system of domestic spying, for in the imperial regime—a new "creation," indeed—"eternal vigilance" was now exercised by the governors over the governed.

Except for McCarthy's mob-revolt against the State Department, which the Korean War effectively sidetracked, the imperial regime went unchallenged for twenty years. To forestall the dreaded abatement of external danger the nation's leaders went to extraordinary, and in due course intolerable, lengths. When the government of the northern half of Korea invaded the southern half—both dictatorships then claiming the whole of it—the American people were grimly advised, in Truman's words, that "communism has passed beyond the use of subversion to conquer independent nations and will now use armed invasion and war." To stop the Soviets' "grand design" for the military conquest of the world, the nation's leaders undertook an enormous military buildup, put the nation on a permanent war footing, established a new system of official secrecy—"classified information," so called—and poured weapons, troops, and a re-armed Germany down the unwilling throats of our allies. As usual, the frenzied alarms were mainly false. "Talk of imminent threat to our national security through the application of external force is pure nonsense," General Douglas MacArthur bluntly told Congress in 1951. The idea of the Soviets invading Western Europe was "silly," said General Eisenhower, opening his presidential campaign in 1952. Our putative defense forces in Europe "were disposed for easy administration and without any regard for their operational role," noted a 1955 report of the North Atlantic Treaty Organization. "It is difficult to imagine dispositions that could be more unsuitable for operations in the event of an aggressor." The invading Red Army only frightened Americans at home.

Thanks to "the misreading by the official Washington establishment of the nature and significance of the Korean War," noted Kennan in 1983, the thirty-third year of his repentance, ". . . the image of the Soviet Union as purely a military challenge was now widely accepted." And thanks to that "misreading"—our leaders never deceive, they only blunder, according to the rules of imperial diction—the old republic seemed snuffed out entirely.

What genuinely frightened America's leaders was the death of Stalin in March 1953 and his successors' open bid for a general European settlement. The redoubtable Winston Churchill, prime minister once more, vainly urged the United States to negotiate in good faith with the Soviets. Even President Eisenhower, still bearing traces of the military blockhead, seemed to lean timidly toward peaceful diplomacy. But the threat of no threat was too menacing to the imperial republic. "The new set of dangers comes from the fact that the wolf has put on a new set of sheep's clothing," Secretary of State Dulles explained to the press. For years every conciliatory Soviet overture was denounced as "communist propaganda" by Dulles, "that slab-faced bastard," as Churchill, who loathed him, called him.

By then the Soviet Union had virtually ceased to be a mere world-conquering military state. It was now regarded, even officially, as the "International Communist movement," to quote Dulles once more. "This failure" to differentiate between the Soviet regime and communism, noted the Cold War historian John Lewis Gaddis, "reflected the belief of many that only the prospect of an undifferentiated threat could shake Americans out of the isolationist tendencies which remained latent among them." Thanks to this "failure"—more imperial prose—a communist rebel in some Asiatic rain forest became a threat to the security of the United States. Even non-communist countries which tried to steer clear of the Cold War became official threats to the security of the United States, for, as a State Department official put it in 1954, "neutralism works only for the enemy." Let some tenth-rate nation escape the American imperium and our "credibility" was said to be weakened. "Once that is done," warned Lyndon Johnson, "the gates are down and the road is open to expansion and endless conquest." By 1961 the only way Americans could demonstrate our "will" to defend what was dear to us was to shed the blood of our youth over trifles. That way lay madness, but that was the way eagerly taken. Corrupted by fifteen years of unchallenged power and determined at all costs to maintain the empire of menace, the imperial republic under President Kennedy was losing every last link to common sense and prudence.

When South Vietnam's president, Ngo Dinh Diem, began seeking a modus vivendi with the communist regime in the north—a policy strongly supported by France's De Gaulle—the imperial regime overthrew him and left him to be murdered by his underlings. Such was the doom meted out to an imperial client who failed to understand that Vietnamese communists were not *his* enemies but *ours.* They were "testing" our credibility and "we dare not weary of the test," as President Kennedy planned to say the day after his scheduled visit to Dallas and three weeks after Diem's murder.

The menace of peace being scotched in Vietnam, Lyndon Johnson decided, soon after entering the presidency, to wage a second major land war in Asia. The military blockheads advised otherwise. The American people were told otherwise. Seeking our votes in the 1964 election, Johnson promised "no wider war" in Asia, then proceeded to launch a vastly wider war at the first opportunity. This time, however, the American people balked and the imperial regime suddenly found itself struggling to survive.

It may be that Johnson had simply over-reached himself, but something else was at work to incite a spirit of popular defiance. This was the civil-rights movement, the unfinished business of the old republic, dating back to Emancipation. It burst in upon the corrupt and imperial republic like a titan's fist smashing through plasterboard. Rebelling against a century of bondage, an oppressed race had won a gallant victory on the eve of that wider Asian war, a glorious republican victory that restored a measure of dignity to dissent and a measure of odium to servility. Americans awoke, as if from a stupor. They began asking awkward questions. Why, precisely, are we in Vietnam? How could a President promise peace and then give us war? What kind of contemptible people did he think we were? The champions of "world leadership" had set out to conquer and degrade the old republic. Now republican virtue and pride, returning as if from the grave, battered the postwar regime.

It fell to President Nixon to restore the imperial republic. The main object of Nixon's diplomacy was to salvage the honor of armed intervention from the debacle in Vietnam. To leave Southeast Asia with some semblance of duty well done and blood not shed in vain, Nixon called on the aid of the Soviet Union, chief supplier of arms to the Hanoi regime. The national enemy was willing to salvage the imperial republic (whose degradation was a Soviet asset), but only at a price— an end, more or less, to the rigors of the Cold War. Specifically, the Soviets wanted recognition as a nuclear "equal," which is to say, a mitigation of the all-too-costly arms race. They wanted formal U.S. recognition of their fragile European empire and they wanted normal trade with the United States to bolster their second-rate economy. The Kremlin had made the same request of Kennedy, but the imperial regime was politically powerful then and saw no reason to temper the Cold War. "Negotiating from strength," in Acheson's phrase, always meant no negotiating at all. Nixon had no such choice. By 1972 an agreement with the Soviets was in place, the first major settlement between the two global rivals after twenty-seven years of wanton, wasteful, and mutually degrading hostility. A popular rebellion against the imperial regime had forced détente upon its leaders.

Yet the imperial republic *sans* Cold War seemed a feeble, foredoomed establishment. Without the Soviet threat, its only real props were the "bipartisan" unity of the governors and the civic degradation of the governed. The unity of the governors was now broken and civic degradation was rapidly abating. For the first time in nearly half a century Americans were actually demanding a greater voice in their own government. Desperately, Nixon sought an antidote to the menace of revived republicanism. Domineering official power was plainly needed, energetically exercised by the White House. Ancient republican trammels stood in the way. Nixon was determined to throw them off. He wanted the White House liberated from a divided Congress by the feigned wall of "executive privilege." He wanted it liberated from the laws by presidential "impoundment" of funds and the claim of a "mandate" supreme over law. He wanted the presidency liberated from its critics by secret harassment of its "enemies." He wanted it liberated from a free press through secrecy, prior censorship, and the expansion of the Espionage Act. And he wanted all that was left of bigotry and servility—and of course there was much—cried up, exalted, and turned against the anti-imperialists. The "Presidential Offensive" this was called at the White House. Degradation was to be lauded; republican virtue, decried and defamed, and, in the person (ostensibly) of one Daniel Ellsberg, tried and convicted of espionage. Since the imperial regime no longer commanded assent, it would rule by presidential fiat. Since it no longer united the people, it would rule them through discord and division.

Looking back over Nixon's failure from the vantage point of the Reagan years, it seems clear that Nixon's measures were premature. When a bungled political break-in led straight to the Oval Office, Nixon discovered that America's need for a "strong" presidency in a dangerous world would not suffice to excuse him. Revived republicanism was still too vigilant for that and congressional leaders were still too weak to dare come to his rescue. And doubtless many a veteran of the imperial regime still thought the Cold War might yet be revived and shed no tear over the departure of the architect of détente.

There is no need to describe in detail the ferocious assault on détente that was launched from the moment Nixon resigned. Under Senator Henry Jackson's driving leadership, Congress in October 1974 destroyed the trade agreement with Russia by demanding free immigration for Soviet Jews in return for normal trade relations. This provided a "liberal" pretext for reviving the Cold War, while "conservatives"—also led by Jackson—concentrated their fire on Nixon's arms-control efforts. Week after week, month after month, year after year the public realm was polluted with new Cold War fears and bogeys: Soviet "adventurism," Soviet "nuclear blackmail," America's dread "window of vulnerability." The United States lay prostrate; Russia was again on the march. Shock and crisis were once more at hand. Under cover of this six-year campaign of fearmongering, the party establishment bound up its wounds and purged party ranks of dissenters, mavericks, and "outsiders." When Ronald Reagan was elected in 1980, the champions of the Cold War were once again in the saddle, booted and spurred and ready to ride.

Yet the imperial regime never regained its lost strength. There was bluster and bragging and petty excursions. The United States, in all its might and majesty, conquered an islet. Then it "punished" for criminal activity an Arab ruler who lived in a tent. It liberated hostages, captured hijackers, arrested terrorists. It hired mercenaries to "contain" communism in the jungles of the world. Under President Reagan, a comical reversal took place in American world leadership. During the heyday of the Cold War, America truly bestrode the world like a titan and modestly called itself a "policeman." Under Reagan America acted like a small-town sheriff and claimed we were bestriding the world. Ephemeral alarums and excursions pleased the electorate, but the moment they bore the faintest resemblance to the old Cold War ambitions, the country rose up to protest in fear and fury. The administration was forced to retreat ignominiously from Lebanon, so deeply offended were the American people by the waste of American lives in yet another out-of-the-way place. The most popular President of modern times could not even secure public support for a war fought by mercenaries against a communist regime in "our own backyard." At the very outset of a huge military buildup, an overwhelming majority of Americans wanted Russia and America to halt at once the development and deployment of all nuclear weapons, despite all that the popular President could do to defame the "freeze" movement.

It was not the strength and menace of the Reagan Administration that brought Mikhail Gorbachev to the negotiating table, that allowed him to admit in public what his Kremlin predecessors never dared admit before—how weak the Soviet Union was, how corrupted it was, how desperately it needed surcease from the Cold War. It was the administration's blustering timidity that emboldened the Soviet ruler. Even with a supremely popular demagogue at its head, the imperial regime could not revive the Cold War, could not conduct a limitless arms race, dared not risk a single American life in a mere anti-communist campaign. What Gorbachev understood with perfect clarity was that the United States had ceased to be a credible threat, even in Soviet eyes, to the security of the Soviet state. The people of the United States saw to that. Flaccid and ductile in so many respects, we were adamantine in this.

The real success of the political leadership lay elsewhere. While alarums and excursions diverted the electorate, the nation's leaders took up where Nixon had been forced to leave off. Quietly, stealthily, and with utter impunity they spent eight years concentrating unprecedented domestic powers in the White House—powers illicit, usurped, and perilous to self-government. Under the new-modeled presidency the very laws of the land can now be altered to conform to the presidential will. The White House is becoming a private legislature, violating the deepest principles of the U.S. Constitution, putting enormous secret influence into its hands. Under the new-modeled presidency the White House now has unprecedented official influence over public opinion. It can keep from the American people virtually any official information which a President's men think it best for people not to know. It can prevent the executive agencies of the government from even investigating a social condition if a President prefers to leave it in darkness. One by one, the new-modeled presidency narrowed or shut down the avenues of public enlightenment. The executive now has the power to censor the writing of tens of thousands of retired government officials, including even letters to the editor. It now has the power to harass, intimidate, and even imprison dissenting officials who dare tell the truth to the American people. It now has the power, equally unprecedented, to review and censor private, unclassified academic research. Under the Espionage Act, judically expanded in 1985, the executive now has a mighty weapon for harassing and subjugating the press, fulfilling one of Nixon's keenest ambitions. If "popular government without popular information, or the means of acquiring it is but the Prologue to a farce," as James Madison long ago warned us, the nation's leaders have spent the past eight years trying to turn popular government into a farce.

"National security" is no longer the main excuse. The President's men spoke of the need for governmental "efficiency," the need to "cut waste," the need for "consistency." They cited the imperious need for "cost-effective" government—harmless-sounding pretexts to supplement the fading pretensions of the imperial regime and the tainted "imperial presidency." Purged of virtually every friend of democracy, the entire political establishment supported the new-modeled presidency. "Conservatives" who once feared concentrated power demanded ever more power for the President and power ever more free of lawful restraint. "Liberals" who had opposed the "imperial presidency" kept their mouths shut for eight squalid years while the new "cost-effective" tyranny exploded. When the Iran-Contra scandal threatened to expose the truly lawless pretensions of the Reagan White House, party leaders in Congress, terrified of that exposure, transformed the scandal into the inconsequent mischief of wayward underlings and renamed it, officially, the Iran-Contra "affair." The power of "bipartisanship" to blind the American people is as strong in our day as it ever was in Acheson's.

While a mendacious White House demagogue pretended to "get the government off the back of the people," the government extended, with utmost rapidity, its sway over the lives and liberties of the people. The central government now has unprecedented authority to spy on the American people, to keep dossiers on the American people, to trace the movements of the American people, to question people without them knowing it, although not the faintest link to a crime attaches to them. The executive now has the power to bar any person from receiving any government or "government-related" loan, grant, or credit, even one given out by a local school board, if the central government declares him a "seriously improper" person. This new, chilling proscription list is kept by the White House budget office.

At every level of government the police power of the state has been rapidly expanded. Stopped and searched at roadblocks, millions of motorists are arrested each year for possession of criminal blood, defined as blood containing .1 percent alcohol—in the name of "safety," which it improves not a whit. Random drug-testing invades our privacy and assaults our dignity in the name of a "productive" work force, which instead it makes sullen and angry. The police invade our households as never before in defense of "family values." Millions of wayward husbands may now be tracked down nationwide and arrested in the service of those "family values." Some 23 million smokers of marijuana, doing harm to nobody, are now subject to federal punishment, threats, and blackmail in the name of a "drug-free" America. Whatever distresses the great electronic audience—missing children and battered wives, AIDS infection, drug-addicted athletes, parolees who commit crimes, arrogant racketeers—has been cried up and exploited with the greatest alacrity to curb personal liberty, to sow fear and discord, to expand the scope of the police spy, the billy club, and the official dossier.

Does anyone suppose that this surging domestic state power bears no relation to the receding imperial tide? The ambition of America's political leaders to subjugate the American republic once and for all had spawned and sustained the Cold War. The Cold War is waning, but the ambition endures. If anything, it has grown more fierce, more reckless, and more radically anti-republican than ever before. Unable to rule us through an external threat, our leaders are prepared to rule us through domestic hatreds, discords, and distempers. Unable to bestride the world, they are ready to bestride a mob; to make us a mob, the better to bestride us. In place of "world leadership" they would give us private virtues enforced with a nightstick; in place of the "International Communist movement," a domineering White House bristling with unprecedented powers, its "bully pulpit" turned into a Ministry of Truth, overwhelming public opinion and popular government along with it.

"Elective despotism," in Jefferson's phrase, tempered by the congressional leadership is the new regime now taking shape in America: the old legislative oligarchy warily united with the new White House autocracy in common defense against a revived, post-imperial republic. That outcome, however, is far from inevitable. We are still "a republic if you can keep it," but perhaps not for long if we do not awaken. Despite the apparent stability of American politics, the bitterest of classical parallels keeps coming to mind: Rome's weakened senate oligarchs calling on Pompey the Great to help them fend off the people of Rome—until the onslaught of Caesar put finish to a republic grown incorrigibly corrupt.

PART II
MEN AND EVENTS

The Political History of Central Park

In the dead center of the long, rectangular island of Manhattan—New York to most people—sits a long rectangle of parkland known appropriately enough as Central Park. On a quiet Saturday morning in springtime, when the automobiles are banned from its drives, it seems wonderfully at odds with the surrounding city. It pits rolling meadows against the city's sharp angles, green life against brick and black asphalt, winding paths against the unbending streets of New York's remorseless grid, into which it has been squeezed as if in a vise. On such a favorable morning Central Park resembles nothing so much as a small, defenseless principality surrounded by a predatory empire, hostile to its spirit, covetous of its green fields, yet miraculously surviving nonetheless—a sort of municipal Liechtenstein.

The Central Park, as it used to be called, has survived now for some 120-odd years and nobody knows quite why. In the least poetical of cities it marks the unexpected triumph of poetry over practicality and of a certain vague yet pervasive sentiment over the hard calculations of interest and profit. As Henry James rightly noted in 1907, Central Park has a "remarkable little history," although it is known to exceedingly few. Most New Yorkers are quite unaware that the park even has any history to speak of. A long time ago, says the native New Yorker, the city fathers set aside a lovely swatch of primeval meadow and forest, laid in some paths and roads, and then more or less washed their hands of it. Such is the prevailing New York view of the matter. In consequence the native New Yorker feels little gratitude toward the city fathers, which only proves that true political understanding can shine through gross historical error. Central Park is most decidedly *not* a piece of primeval Manhattan. It is man-made throughout, every copse, glade, pond, and meadow. On the other hand, the city fathers had precious little to do with its making and would have strangled it at birth had they dared. In this they were being true to the traditions of the city, a city which actually had decreed by law that poetry and sentiment would have to get along on their own and not be a charge on the taxpayers.

The law in question had been enacted in 1811 when the city fathers decided that the future development of Manhattan would proceed along straight lines and right angles and that the future metropolis would become in due course an unbroken succession of rectangular blocks. About the compelling merits of their grid plan the city fathers were forthright and confident. They had dispensed with "circles, ovals and stars," they reported, for the "plain and simple" reason that "right angled houses are the most cheap to build." They had left "few vacant spaces" for posterity, they noted, because New York's posterity would never need them. Those "large arms of the sea which embrace Manhattan" rendered public spaces wholly unnecessary to the health of the citizenry—the felicity of the citizenry counting, of course, for nothing. Besides, the city fathers noted, "the price of land" in Manhattan was "uncommonly great," while salubrious sea breezes were uncommonly cheap. The 1811 grid plan did allow for a large parade ground for New York's militia, but as soon as the expanding city got within a mile of it, the city parceled it off to real estate speculators. That the city fathers ever provided *any* public space for the citizens of New York is the first and fundamental miracle in the little history of Central Park.

It was a poet-turned-newspaper editor who first took public note of the squalid fate in store for a city that was relentlessly marching northward—"uptown" in New York parlance—without a single park to compare with the royal parks of London. This was in 1844, or four years before famine in Ireland and political reaction in Germany were to bring to New York the greatest influx of foreigners it was any city's fate to cope with. The population, nonetheless, was an ample 370,000 and the city already bore most of its characteristic earmarks. It was cramped, noisy, and incorrigibly filthy. In the richest town in America the chief instruments of garbage disposal were unofficial scavengers, human and porcine. On the side streets, wrote a Scottish visitor, "the scene of confused debris was of a kind not to be easily forgotten— ashes, vegetable refuse, old hats without crowns, worn-out shoes, and other household wreck, lay scattered about as a field of agreeable inquiry for a number of long-legged and industrious pigs."

The pace of New York was already so hectic it left foreign visitors nerve-wracked. "Nothing and nobody seem to stand still for half a moment in New York," complained Lady Emmeline Stuart-Wortley in 1849. The huge omnibuses, she reported, "drive like insane vehicles from morning til night [and] appear not to pause to take up their passengers." Private oases in the uproar were few but conspicuous. By 1844 *the* Fifth Avenue (another example of the now-lost "the" in the grammar of old New York) had become the new center of wealth and fashion as far uptown as Fourteenth Street. Beyond lay a lightly populated anyman's land, speckled with "pigtowns" of tin-roofed shanties, a few doomed farmsteads, and here and there little rows of "town" houses waiting for the town to catch up. The undeveloped parts of Manhattan were, in the main, so disagreeable that few wealthy New Yorkers kept pleasure carriages; driving out of town brought no pleasure, a fact that was to have considerable bearing on the future Central Park.

For that future park the poet-turned-editor, William Cullen Bryant, timed his historic first blow for the July 3, 1844, issue of the *Evening Post*, in which he pleaded for the immediate public creation of "an extensive pleasure ground for shade and recreation." The July 3 date was no accident. Bryant hoped to catch the "sachems" of the Tammany Society in a moment of civic weakness. It was on July 4 that the sachems, a semisecret oligarchy that ruled New York in the name of the Democratic Party, made their annual public appearance, wherein they pledged their undying devotion to the precepts of Thomas Jefferson and the well-being of the common man. But Bryant's plea for the common man fell on deaf Tammany ears, which was not surprising even to Bryant. To do as little as possible for the commonality was the abiding principle of Tammany politics. Give the voters an unnecessary inch—clean streets, for example—and they were liable to demand a yard. To the sachems, "an extensive pleasure ground" for the people was not a good idea but a subversive one.

Bryant kept hammering away nonetheless, and by 1850 he had gained the ardent support of a crusading young landscape architect named Andrew Jackson Downing, whose journal, *The Horticulturalist*, enjoyed considerable favor among the liberal spirits in New York's "upper ten thousand" (the days when the city's bon ton would restrict itself to the Four Hundred still lay four decades in the future). Downing's eloquent voice helped considerably, but in 1850, an *annus mirabilis* in the park's history, Tammany helped even more—by blundering. Normally the sachems wanted their mayors to be respectable idlers, but that year they nominated a Quaker businessman named Fernando Wood, blissfully unaware that Wood harbored ambitions of the most dangerous sort. A genuine political desperado, he hoped to become, first and foremost, the boss of all the little Tammany bosses, a second Aaron Burr, and after that, why, the presidency itself seemed not beyond reach. Wood took step one to fulfill this secret ambition in the course of the mayoralty campaign: he came out strongly for a great public park on the lines laid down by Bryant and Downing. With that, the park idea became in a flash a major public issue and a warm public hope, so warm that Wood's successful rival, the Whig candidate Ambrose Kingsland, endorsed the idea with equal vigor and promoted its cause, as mayor, in the Whig-controlled state legislature.

Commercial interests howled in rage. A "People's Park," as Downing called it, would become a den of thieves and ruffians; it would slice a chunk off the tax rolls and wantonly waste the taxpayers' money. Downing could talk all he wanted about providing "a real feeling of the breadth and beauty of green fields." What the mighty

Journal of Commerce saw in Downing's "green fields" was "a perpetual edict of desolation" visited upon acres and acres of building lots. Downing could say of such a park that it is "republican in its very idea and tendency." The park's influential enemies denounced it as a species of monarchical extravagance. The more they raged, however, the more popular the park idea became. The city fathers had lost control of events, thanks to two crusading artists, an ambitious political rascal, and an electorate who knew a good thing when they heard one. And so the primary miracle took place: in 1853 the state legislature authorized the city to purchase a central reservation of land, half a mile wide and nearly two and a half miles long, which carefully respected the still-nonexistent streets of New York's inviolable grid. It was bounded on the south by the future Fifty-ninth Street, on the north by 106th (extended a few years later to its present 110th Street boundary), on the west by Eighth Avenue, on the east by Fifth. It initially comprised some 760 acres, 143 of which came free of charge since the site included two city reservoirs, a bargain regarded as one of the chief merits of the central location.

Socially, however, there was nothing central about "The Central Park," as it was known from the first. The site lay far beyond the inhabited city. Fashionable "uptown" at its uppermost limit still lay two miles to the south; the city's teeming slums lay twice that distance away. As a French visitor remarked, "Nothing is more American than this ambitious name, given at first sight to wild terrain situated beyond the suburbs."

If the park was not yet central, neither did it remotely resemble a park. On the advice of the city fathers the state legislature had allotted New Yorkers an area of peculiarly grim desolation, "a succession of stone quarries interspersed with pestiferous swamps," reported the engineer who surveyed it for the city. Its soil was so thin and poor, a writer was to recall in 1869, that "even mosses and lichen" refused to grow on its high ground. The swamps, created by five muck-filled streams, gave off an unbearable stench and raised a crop of poison ivy so thick it laid a surveyor low for a month. There was scarcely a tree worth saving for a park.

Ill-favored by nature, the future park was equally ill-used by man. It had a population of some five thousand desperate squatters—a few Indians among them—who lived in hovels, caves, and trenches. Most were scavengers who survived by hauling the city's garbage back to the park site in dogcarts, the refuse providing food, bones for boiling, and swill for a number of pig-fattening establishments. The squatters' chief companions in misery were tens of thousands of half-wild dogs as well as an occasional missionary sent up from the city churches in hopes of reclaiming their souls, or at the very least of regularizing their marriages.

Sensing, perhaps, that the public's warm hopes had cooled, Tammany leaders decided that even this disheartening terrain was too generous a gift to the citizenry. Regaining control of the city government, Tammany's minions on the city's council began proposing schemes for chopping down the park. One obstacle was already out of the way: a steamboat explosion on the Hudson River had snuffed out the life of young Downing, the park's most redoubtable champion. In 1854 one committee, bent on truncation, recommended that Seventy-second Street be the future park's lower limit. Equally bent on narrowing, it also recommended that 800 feet be lopped off lengthwise. Strongly supported by all whose "eye," as Bryant angrily wrote, is "accustomed to look upon the dollar as the only attractive object in this world," Tammany decided in 1855 that the future park was ready for the death blow. On March 15 the board of aldermen lumped together both committee recommendations and passed a resolution favoring lengthwise lopping *and* transverse truncation, which would have reduced the park to a bit of public ground bordering two reservoirs; in other words, to a nullity.

But the mayor that year was the ever-untrustworthy Wood, reluctantly nominated by Tammany in 1854 to fend off the Nativist Party, and it was Mayor Wood who saved Central Park with a thunderous veto of the aldermanic attempt to "deprive the teeming millions yet to inhabit and toil upon this island of one place not given up to Mammon." For that act of demagoguery—the last virtuous act in Wood's political career—Tammany never forgave him. Nor did its fuglemen appropriate any funds to create a park out of the exurban wasteland which, as of February 5, 1856, the city officially owned, and which a year later it had done virtually nothing about. Poetry had a foot in the door, but the park seemed doomed to die slowly of inertia and inanition in the hostile environment of the city.

Unbeknownst to anyone, however, the quixotic hero of the park's history—the man who was to create it and whose hovering spirit protects it still—was about to enter the story. He was thirty-five years old in 1857, a sometime farmer, a failed publisher, and an amateur journalist whose description of the slave states, published in *The New York Times*, recently had won him high praise, although not in Tammany circles. His name was Frederick Law Olmsted and, as he often said with bitter irony, he was not a "practical" man.

In the greater history of the American republic, Lincoln's rise to the presidency is rightly accounted a political miracle. In the little history of Central Park, Olmsted's rise was equally remarkable, and the same general force lay behind both. An insurgent political party had been born, a party that embodied, if only for a few glorious years, much that was fresh and vital in the public life of the country. In the 1856 elections the onrushing Republicans won control of the New York State legislature. In April of 1857 they took control of Central Park from the city government and vested it in a nonpartisan "Board of Commissioners of the Central Park." The Republicans appointed the commissioners and by New York City standards—that of the future "Boss" Tweed's Street Commission, for example—they chose remarkably well; which is to say, they chose men who honestly wanted to create a worthy park.

Olmsted gained the first step toward his hero's role in September 1857, when the new board appointed him superintendent of the park's work force, chiefly on the recommendation of the aged Washington Irving. He took the next step several weeks later when an English architect named Calvert Vaux, Downing's former partner, persuaded him to enter the board's public competition for the best park design—first prize, $2,000. For Olmsted the winter of 1857–58 was to epitomize the primary dilemma of the future Central Park. By day, as superintendent, he found himself struggling with New York practicality in one of its most characteristic forms. His workers owed their jobs to Tammany chieftains and, since they were expected to perform political chores for their patrons, they had not the slightest intention of wielding a shovel. "It was as if we were all engaged in playing a practical joke," recalled Olmsted, who was now spending every spare moment with Vaux trying to sketch out a park that would prove the antithesis of New York practicality.

Such was Olmsted's leading idea, his fundamental principle, the key to his design, and the source of twenty years of anguish and frustration. Over the years he was to state the principle again and again—to the Central Park board, to hostile politicians, to cynical editors, to innumerable projectors of schemes for improving his park with museums, cemeteries, and racetracks. The object of the park, Olmsted insisted, was to be all that the metropolis was not. It was to provide New Yorkers with "the most agreeable contrast to the confinement, bustle and monotonous street-division of the city." It was to offer them relief "from the cramped, confused and controlling circumstances of the town." It was to provide, for all who could not afford a country vacation, freedom from "the incessant emphasis of artificial objects."

Such a park was to be no more practical than a poem or a painting. Its "main object and justification," wrote Olmsted, "is simply to produce a certain influence on the minds of people . . . to be produced by means of scenes, through observation of which the mind may be more or less lifted out of moods and habits into which it is, under the ordinary conditions of life in the city, likely to fall." How to produce that "certain influence" was something Olmsted understood with the clarity of genius.

New York was oppressively constricting. Olmsted's park would feature "slightly undulating meadow," pastoral stretches of greensward that would elate hemmed-in New Yorkers with "a sense of enlarged freedom." New York's grid made the city scene depressingly predictable. In Olmsted's park nothing would be predictable. Everywhere the park would offer "uncertainty" and a "sense of mystery," the constant suggestion of surprises to come—the tempting glimpse of soft lawn beyond a rugged rock outcrop, of dense woodland beyond a meadow's vague border. It would have little glades that the visitor would come upon by accident and which he would be hard put to find again. The park's artificial lake would have sharp bays and inlets to lend drama to its shoreline and uncertainty as to its size.

Envisioning the endless rows of buildings that would one day surround Central Park, he wanted the city utterly blotted out of sight. Tall trees bordering the park would do this. He wanted the city blotted out of mind as well. Every building within the park would be made as small and as inconspicuous as possible. Olmsted wanted to banish even New York's grid from the minds of New Yorkers. The one rectilinear element in the park design, a long promenade or mall, Olmsted and Vaux set down at an angle to the future grid, so that promenaders in a half-dozen steps would lose their city bearings altogether and with them, perhaps, their city selves.

The commissioners had stipulated that four commercial roads must traverse the park's width. To nullify that menace, Olmsted and Vaux decided to sink them below the level of the footpaths and carriage drives, which would pass over the roads by bridges blending so gently with the park that visitors scarcely would notice the four commercial incisions. The two designers went further: they envisioned the footpaths crossing under the drives and the bridle path under the footpaths. By keeping every form of locomotion independent and self-contained, Olmsted hoped, he said, to relieve the park's visitors of "anxiety." Such relief was a matter of the utmost urgency to Olmsted. Irritation and fretfulness, the normal state of New Yorkers on the streets, were absolutely fatal to his fundamental principle: "to recreate the mind from urban oppression through the eye."

That last phrase provides the final clue to Olmsted's grand design. To him Central Park was to be, above all else, a noble landscape composition, a work of art to be relished "through the eye." That and that alone, not boating, or skating or riding or ball playing, was what "makes the Park the Park." In a city of business and bustle, of frantic activity and impatient haste, Olmsted offered the alien joys of quiet contemplation. The precarious nature of his conception is readily apparent. His park was to be a gauntlet laid down to the city, a tacit rebuke to its ugliness and misgovernment, a challenge to its habits and to its unquiet spirit. Inevitably the city would turn around and challenge the park. That, however, still lay in the future. In the meantime, the park's history offered up its last major miracle. In April 1858, the "Greensward" plan, as Olmsted and Vaux called their design, was awarded first prize over thirty-two other competitors. Superintendent Olmsted was named the park's architect-in-chief; Vaux was made his principal assistant. They were now to "proceed forthwith" to execute their plan on the wasteland.

Like sculptors working on a vast block of marble, Olmsted and Vaux set about transforming virtually every inch of the site. To turn murky streams into four ornamental lakes they designed an intricate system of underground pipes to collect the streams' water—some sixty-two miles of conduits in all. To turn jagged ground into "undulating meadow" they blasted away at Manhattan bedrock; some 20,800 barrels of dynamite would be consumed in the task. To make the soil fit for green life they brought in half a million cubic yards of topsoil. To make the future park verdant they planted, by the end of 1862, some 166,000 trees and shrubs. The once recalcitrant work force labored with surprising zeal; progress was swift.

On June 11, 1859, that faithful diarist of New York life, George Templeton Strong, noted that the new park, though promising, was still "in most ragged condition: long lines of incomplete macadamization, 'lakes' without water, mounds of compost, piles of blasted stone . . . groves of slender young transplanted maples and locusts, undecided between life and death." Paying a second visit on September 2, Strong was delighted with the summer's progress. "The ragged desert of out-blasted rock, cat briars, and stone heaps begins to blossom like the rose. Many beautiful oases of path and garden culture have sprung up, with neat paths, fine greensward, and hopeful young trees." By the following spring Olmsted's design was beginning to take shape. "The Park below the reservoir begins to look intelligible," Strong noted in his diary on May 28, 1860. "Many points are already beautiful. . . ." It even made him sad to think that the hopeful new park would not achieve its full beauty until "the trees are grown and I'm dead and forgotten."

Eager to gain popular approval, the park board opened up to the public every part of the park as soon as it was completed. In June 1859 the Ramble, a wonderful man-made woodland, received the first strollers on its intricate paths. In November of that year the first three and one-half miles of gravel drives welcomed the carriages of New York's "upper tendom." In the spring of 1861 the great promenade, or Mall, was completed. In April boat service on the lake was installed.

Despite the board's politesse, the park's enemies continued to snarl and plot mischief. The city leaders, recalled Olmsted, used "every device of what in city politics passes for statesmanship" to persuade the voters that the board was up to some "knavish scheme" of graft and corruption. Hostile newspapers reported as fact the accusations of disgruntled ex-employees and disappointed placemen. The "practical hounds," as Olmsted called them, bayed at the board for appointing two "ignorant, incompetent pretenders." It took a state senate investigation to clear the park's directors and designers of all the false charges laid against them. Critics of a more artistic sort dogged Olmsted as well. Missing the whole point of Olmsted's conception, they indignantly complained that Vaux's little bridges lacked dignity and grandeur. Olmsted was hard put to explain that one day when the shrubbery grew thick he hoped they would be nearly invisible. Even during the park's happy first years, the high-strung Olmsted felt frustrated most of the time.

They were halcyon days nonetheless. In a city so starved of outdoor amenities, the park offered heady nourishment even in its raw and unfinished state. In 1862 the gatekeepers clocked in some 2 million visitors entering on foot and more than 700,000 entering by carriage. The broad, tree-lined pedestrian Mall was an instant success.

Free of traffic and noise, it soon was regarded as one of the few public places in New York where unmarried couples could stroll unchaperoned, a sort of semiofficial lovers' lane. With the lake as its terminus and free concerts on Wednesdays and Saturdays, the Mall quickly became the center of the park's busy life. It even brought Herman Melville out of seclusion; he was often seen walking there with his little granddaughter.

Even in winter the young park gave pleasure to the city. Its frozen lakes instantly revived the lost art of ice skating in New York. When the lakes were first opened to skaters, "the variety of skates were few and poor and the varieties of skaters still fewer and poorer," the park board noted in an annual report. But by the end of the Civil War skating had become the winter pastime of scores of thousands of New Yorkers, a spectacular pastime at night when great calcium flares lit up the lake for as many as 20,000 avid skaters. In his *Description of the New York Central Park*, published in 1869, Clarence Cook wryly warned the "countryman" not to venture into the park with his laughable outmoded "double gutters." "Skaters," said Cook, "are now as much exercised over the shape and material of their instrument as horseback riders are over their saddles, and cricket players over their bats and balls." When the lake was safe for skating, the park-bound horsecars would break out flags and New Yorkers would spread the good word to each other. When snow lay on the ground, Central Park seemed to galvanize the entire city, although it still lay a long way uptown. As a British journalist noted in 1862, "On a winter bright day when the whole population seemed to be driving out in sleighs to the great skating carnivals at the Central Park, I have seldom seen a brighter or gayer-looking city."

Every afternoon around four, winter and summer, the young park drew the rich, the famous, the beautiful, and the notorious. The lure was the park's lovely carriage drives, so smoothly graveled, said a contemporary, that "slippered feet might tread them with ease and pleasure." The wealth to buy costly carriages flew into the city on the wings of war, as Strong tartly noted on March 21, 1865. "Fifth Avenue from Forty-ninth Street down was absolutely thronged with costly new equipages on their way to Central Park. . . . It was a broad torrent of vehicular gentility, wherein profits of shoddy and of petroleum were largely represented."

The late-afternoon carriage parade—an immense procession of spanking new landaus, barouches, and Victorias—quickly became one of the famed sights of the city, the flashiest spectacle in New York's postwar "flash age." Of an afternoon on the East Drive, all the city's choice specimens put on their varied displays. Among the 14,000 carriages passing through each day, there were to be seen the enormously wealthy: August Belmont driving an English break and four; the fusty relics of New York's colonial aristocracy—a Livingston or a Schermerhorn secluded in an out-of-date brougham drawn by an equally unfashionable fat horse; the upstart buccaneers of postbellum Wall Street—with Jim Fiske flashing his two French opera stars, Irma and Tosteé, in his red and blue carriage; the notorious and the infamous—elegant Josephine Wood, the "society" brothelkeeper, and Madame Restell, the Fifth Avenue abortionist and blackmailer, the most feared and hated woman in the city. So it was to continue decade after glittering decade until horsepower replaced the horse and altered Central Park's character forever.

Although the strollers thoroughly enjoyed watching the carriage set, few members of the carriage set enjoyed mingling with the foot-sloggers. It was not until years after the park was completed, for example, that Strong determined that it "reveals its full beauty to pedestrians only." Yet public conduct in the early years was exemplary. In 1858 the *Herald* cheerfully admitted its mistake. Those who came to the park by streetcars "always behave well." It was the vehicular gentility that misbehaved. "The more brilliant the display of vehicles and toilettes the more shameful the display of bad manners." The "lowest denizens" actually gave no trouble. "Even men of reckless disposition and unaccustomed to polite restraints upon selfishness," Olmsted recalled, fell under the park's benign influence. In unruly New York this surprising ruliness stemmed from many causes. The most important, quite simply, was that New Yorkers were intensely proud of their raw new park, impressed by its almost daily improvements and by the conscientious zeal of all who worked for it, including Olmsted's gray-uniformed "park keepers," whose task it was to remind the transgressor, as one gentleman to another, just what the park rules were.

Yet there was something ominous about the new park's success, as Clarence Cook shrewdly hinted in 1869. Its visiting throngs were not recreating their minds, they were re-creating the city. They loved the bustle of the Mall and the spectacle of wealth in motion. They loved boating, skating, and driving. In 1868 the park board had to introduce public omnibuses to the carriage drives so that ordinary people, too, could be whisked through the park. Only the seven-mile-per-hour speed limit, strictly enforced, kept the drives from reproducing the tumult of Broadway—deadlocks, collisions, and all.

More ominous still, to Olmsted, was that so many "intelligent citizens" seemed to care so little for his governing principle: that the park was to be a rural landscape as free of the city as possible. They saw no reason why it should not be speckled with edifying buildings and fairground amusements. In 1872 Olmsted listed a few such proposals for the park: a memorial cemetery for the "distinguished dead of the city," a "grand people's cathedral in which all sects might unite in a common litany," an exhibition hall to display the "goods for sale in the city," a street railway running the length of the park, a place for horse racing and steeplechase riding. What made the park so tempting for all the would-be builders in its history—for promoters of swimming pools, circuses, academies, opera houses, radio towers, airfields, and armories—was the irresistible lure of a bargain. The price of New York land was still "uncommonly great," while the price of the park's green fields was uncommonly cheap, as cheap as the salubrious sea breezes that once made green fields so plainly unnecessary. The spirit of New York is amazingly persistent.

As long as the park board loyally beat down all such proposals, time lay on Olmsted's side, time for the landscape to ripen, time for it to exert its "influence" on the moods and habits of the people. Such was Olmsted's faith, and it was by no means entirely misplaced. That

Central Park remains even today something more than what Olmsted called "a desultory collocation of miscellaneous entertainments" is proof of that, for in May 1870, Olmsted's park and Olmsted's principles lost their official defenders with the abolition of the board of commissioners. Under the whip of Boss Tweed, the state legislature returned control of Central Park to the mayor of New York, which meant, for all practical purposes, the Tammany machine. For nearly one hundred years Central Park was to be in the hands of men more or less hostile to the spirit that created it.

The Tweed Ring fell apart too quickly to inflict damage, but it revealed clearly enough the Tammany view of Central Park. There was to be no interference from "landscape architects." Olmsted, studiously ignored and insulted, angrily resigned his post, returning only after the Tweed gang fell. Nothing really changed after that fall. In 1878 Tammany drove Olmsted out of his beloved park forever and reduced Vaux to a distinguished menial. To Tammany the purpose of the park was to fuel the machine. Its work force became petty spoilsmen, the dregs of its ward-heeler brigades. Their salaries consumed what little was spent on maintaining the park, which slowly began to rot from neglect. When horticultural experts warned that the park's trees were doomed unless the soil was enriched, Tammany's parks department paid a small fortune to a well-connected rascal who provided the park with 10,000 cubic yards of cellar dirt more impoverished than the soil he was paid to enrich. To spare equally well-connected builders the trouble of carting their dirt long distances, one park administrator allowed them to dump it in the park, thereby filling up a picturesque ravine.

To the machine Olmsted's park was a political enemy. It inspired hope and idealism, and Tammany battened on cynicism and despair. The "Hall" treated the park accordingly. A succession of park superintendents spitefully hacked away at the shrubs that hid Olmsted's buildings, smashed open his secluded glades, "cleaned up" woodland by lopping off all the lower branches of trees. They invited the city to invade the park. One Tammany superintendent chopped down the tree screen in the northwest border of the park so that visitors could see the Ninth Avenue Elevated line. Above all, Tammany wanted to build—a great zoo on the North Meadow, a mighty World's Fair. But here the machine found itself checked. Too many people protested. They liked Central Park as it was, for in the last years of the nineteenth century it was lovelier than ever before. In March 1892 Tammany met with a particularly stunning defeat. Eager to oblige the sporting set, the party of the common man got the state legislature to authorize construction of a mile-and-a-half-long "speedway" for private trotting races. From every quarter of the city there was an extraordinary outburst of fury. "A dangerous temper developed among workmen," recalled Samuel Parsons, a disciple of Vaux's and the last of the "Greensward dynasty." Tammany beat a hasty retreat. Five weeks after passing the speedway law, the state legislature was forced to repeal it.

Tammany was now determined to teach the meddlesome electorate a lesson. If they persisted in cherishing Central Park they would get a park that nobody could cherish. The city gave up all pretense of maintaining the landscape or of curbing public unruliness. It virtually invited the vandals and the miscreants to come and do their worst. When the wealthy began exchanging their landaus for Daimlers, Tammany paved the carriage drives and turned them into parkways for motorists.

By 1912 Olmsted's rural retreat lay shattered. By 1934, when Robert Moses became the all-powerful commissioner of parks, there was little left of the Olmsted ideal except the commissioner's determination to flout it. He was to do so for twenty-six years. Olmsted had fought desperately to prevent the park from becoming a "collocation of miscellaneous entertainments." To Moses, as *The New Yorker* cheerfully reported in 1941, "the Park is primarily a playground, and he is willing to admit into it any sort of enterprise that will give pleasure to a sufficient number of people." He erected fenced-in baseball diamonds on the expansive North Meadow, which today is no longer a meadow. He blighted the lovely pond with an ugly artificial skating rink, a "prisonlike enclosure" Lewis Mumford called it in 1951.

Olmsted wanted all park buildings to be small, inconspicuous, and rustic. Moses made his buildings of common tenement red brick, little chunks of urban blight. In the cause of cheap maintenance, he turned gravel walks into mean city pavements and rimmed lovely ponds with concrete embankments. Motorists were especially privileged. For their sake Moses bulldozed turf into asphalt parking lots, smashed access roads through Olmsted's glades, straightened the drives so that cars could go faster. Since the park was already a parkway, it might as well be an efficient one.

It was all wonderfully practical and perfectly in tune with the hostile spirit of the city. Under the new policy, the park became so much free land to be shared out among special interests, a perfect reflection of the politics of New York. The habit of favoring a few at the expense of all became so ingrained that in 1955 only a severe public protest prevented the park authorities from turning the priceless Ramble into a fenced-in amusement park for the elderly. Yet it was not to be the last word, for the Olmsted ideal would not die in his park. It would live because Olmsted's poetry proved incomparably more practical than anything the "practical hounds" had visited upon his creation. Far more than any particular amusement, New Yorkers still needed "a sense of enlarged freedom" in an uncluttered pastoral landscape. They still needed relief "from the incessant emphasis of artificial objects" and from the "monotonous street divisions of the city."

In 1966 a reforming mayor stunned New York by banning automobiles from Central Park on the weekends, the park's first triumph over the city since the defeat of the speedway in 1892. That was only a beginning, but a crucial one, for it gave renewed life to the Olmsted ideal. Strolling in a car-free park—it seemed almost miraculous at the time—New Yorkers began to remember what it was that "makes the park the park." Today a vigorous and skillful effort has begun to restore the ravaged landscape of Olmsted's blighted work of art. It will never become what Olmsted envisioned; perhaps that was an impossible dream from the start. Noble and quixotic, Olmsted had assigned to Central Park, in Henry James's words, "a singular and beautiful but almost crushing mission"—to be all that the city was not—and the city proved too powerful for his park. But Olmsted's great creation is a paradox. It is only because its mission is so singular, so beautiful, and so gallant that New Yorkers took it to their hearts, and that is why the little principality still survives in the center of the Empire City.

The America That Was
Free and Is Now Dead

The triumph of Woodrow Wilson and the war party struck the American republic a blow from which it has never recovered. If the mainspring of a republican commonwealth—its "active principle," in Jefferson's words—is the perpetual struggle against oligarchy and privilege, against private monopoly and arbitrary power, then that mainspring was snapped and deliberately snapped by the victors in the civil war over war.

The sheer fact of war was shattering in itself. Deaf to the trumpets and the fanfare, the great mass of Americans entered the war apathetic, submissive, and bitter. Their honest sentiments had been trodden to the ground, their judgment derided, their interests ignored. Representative government had failed them at every turn. A President, newly reelected, had betrayed his promise to keep the peace. Congress, self-emasculated, had neither checked nor balanced nor even seriously questioned the pretexts and pretensions of the nation's chief executive. The free press had shown itself to be manifestly unfree—a tool of the powerful and a voice of the "interests." Every vaunted progressive reform had failed as well. Wall Street bankers, supposedly humbled by the Wilsonian reforms, had impudently clamored for preparedness and war. The Senate, ostensibly made more democratic through the direct election of senators, had proven as impervious as ever to public opinion. The party machines, supposedly weakened by the popular

primary, still held elected officials in their thrall. Never did the powerful in America seem so willful, so wanton, or so remote from popular
control as they did the day war with Germany began. On that day
Americans learned a profoundly embittering lesson: they did not
count. Their very lives hung in the balance and still they did not
count. That bitter lesson was itself profoundly corrupting, for it transformed citizens into cynics, filled free men with self-loathing, and
drove millions into privacy, apathy, and despair.

Deep as it was, the wound of war might have healed in time had
Wilson and the war party rested content with their war. With that war
alone, however, they were by no means content. Well before the war,
the war party had made its aims clear. It looked forward to a new
political order distinguished by "complete internal peace" and by the
people's "consecration to the State." It wanted an electorate that
looked upon "loyalty" to the powerful as the highest political virtue
and the exercise of liberty as proof of "disloyalty." The war party wanted a free people made servile and a free republic made safe for oligarchy and privilege, for the few who ruled and the few who grew
rich; in a word, for itself. The goals had been announced in peacetime. They were to be achieved under cover of war. While American
troops learned to survive in the trenches, Americans at home learned
to live with repression and its odious creatures—with the government
spy and the government burglar, with the neighborhood stool pigeon
and the official vigilante, with the local tyranny of federal prosecutors
and the lawlessness of bigoted judges, with the midnight police raid
and the dragnet arrest.

In this domestic war to make America safe for oligarchy, Woodrow
Wilson forged all the main weapons. Cherisher of the "unified will" in
peacetime, Wilson proved himself implacable in war. Despising in
peacetime all who disturbed the "unity of our national counsel,"
Wilson in wartime wreaked vengeance on them all. Exalted by his
global mission, the ex–Princeton professor, whom one party machine
had groomed for high office and whom another had been protecting
for years, esteemed himself above all men and their puling cavils. He
could no longer tolerate, he was determined to silence, every imperti-

nent voice of criticism, however small and however harmless. Nothing was to be said or read in America that Wilson himself might find disagreeable. Nothing was to be said or read in America that cast doubt on the nobility of Wilson's goals, the sublimity of his motives, or the efficacy of his statecraft. Wilson's self-elating catchphrases were to be on every man's lips or those lips would be sealed by a prison term. "He seemed determined that there should be no questioning of his will," wrote Frederick Howe after personally pleading with Wilson to relent. "I felt that he was eager for the punishment of men who differed from him, that there was something vindictive in his eyes as he spoke."

By the time Wilson reached Paris in December 1918, political liberty had been snuffed out in America. "One by one the right of freedom of speech, the right of assembly, the right to petition, the right to protection against unreasonable searches and seizures, the right against arbitrary arrest, the right to fair trial . . . the principle that guilt is personal, the principle that punishment should bear some proportion to the offense, had been sacrificed and ignored." So an eminent Harvard professor of law, Zechariah Chafee, reported in 1920. The war served merely as pretext. Of that there can be little doubt. In a searing civil conflict that threatened the very survival of the republic, Americans, under Lincoln, enjoyed every liberty that could possibly be spared. In a war safely fought three thousand miles from our shores, Americans, under Wilson, lost every liberty they could possibly be deprived of.

Under the Espionage Act of June 1917, it became a felony punishable by twenty years' imprisonment to say anything that might "postpone for a single moment," as one federal judge put it, an American victory in the struggle for democracy. With biased federal judges openly soliciting convictions from the bench and federal juries brazenly packed to ensure those convictions, Americans rotted in prison for advocating heavier taxation rather than the issuance of war bonds, for stating that conscription was unconstitutional, for saying that sinking armed merchantmen had not been illegal, for criticizing the Red Cross and the YMCA. A woman who wrote to her newspaper that "I am for the people and the government is for the profiteers" was tried, convicted, and sentenced to ten years in prison. The son of the chief justice of the New Hampshire Supreme Court became a convicted felon for sending out a chain letter that said the Sussex Pledge had not been unconditional. Under the Espionage Act American history itself became outlawed. When a Hollywood filmmaker released his movie epic *The Spirit of '76*, federal agents seized it and arrested the producer: his portrayal of the American Revolution had cast British redcoats in an unfavorable light. The film, said the court, was criminally "calculated . . . to make us a little bit slack in our loyalty to Great Britain in this great catastrophe." A story that had nourished love of liberty and hatred of tyranny in the hearts of American schoolchildren had become a crime to retell in Wilson's America. The filmmaker was sentenced to ten years in prison for recalling the inconvenient past.

Fear and repression worked its way into every nook and cranny of ordinary life. Free speech was at hazard everywhere. Americans were arrested for remarks made at a boarding house table, in a hotel lobby, on a train, in a private club, during private conversations overheard by the government's spies. Almost every branch of Wilson's government sprouted its own "intelligence bureau" to snoop and threaten and arrest. By 1920 the Federal Bureau of Investigation, a swaddling fattened on war, had files on two million people and organizations deemed dangerously disloyal. At the Post Office Department, Albert Burleson set up a secret index of "illegal ideas"—such as criticizing Samuel Gompers, the patriotic union leader—and banned from the mails any publication guilty of expressing one. Even if an independent paper avoided an "illegal idea," it could still be banned from the mails for betraying an "audible undertone of disloyalty," as one Post Office censor put it, in otherwise nonfelonious remarks. Under the tyranny of the Post Office, Socialist papers were suppressed outright and country editors sent to jail. Freedom of the press ceased to exist.

Nor did the administration rely on its own bureaucratic resources alone. To cast the net of repression wider and draw the mesh finer, the Justice Department called on the "preparedness" clubs, shock troops of the war party, for help. Authorized by the Justice Department to question anyone and detain them for arrest, the prepareders fell eagerly to their task of teaching "consecration to the State" by hounding free men into jail. Where the "preparedness" clubs were thin on the ground, the Justice Department recruited its own vigilante groups— the Minute Men and the American Protective League—to enforce with the police power "the unity of our national counsel." By August 1917 Attorney General Thomas Gregory boasted that he had "several hundred thousand private citizens" working for him, "most of them as members of patriotic bodies . . . keeping an eye on disloyal individuals and making reports of disloyal utterances, and seeing that the people of the country are not deceived."

Truth and falsity were defined by the courts. According to judicial decisions, public statements were criminally false under the Espionage Act when they contradicted the President's April 2 war message, which became, at gunpoint, the national creed, the touchstone of loyalty, and the measure of "sedition," a crime that Wilson and the war party resuscitated 118 years after it had destroyed forever the old Federalist oligarchy. This time it did not destroy oligarchy. It helped destroy "the old America that was free and is now dead," as one civil libertarian was to put it in 1920. Under the Espionage Act no one was safe except espionage agents, for under the act not a single enemy spy was ever convicted.

The War Enemy Division of the Justice Department had more important war enemies in mind. Every element in the country that had ever disturbed the privileged or challenged the powerful Wilson and the war party were determined to crush. They were the enemy. "Both the old parties are in power," Lincoln Steffens wrote a friend during wartime. "They are the real traitors these days. They are using the emergency to get even with their enemies and fight for their cause." Radicals were ruthlessly persecuted. The International Workers of the World was virtually destroyed in September 1917 when Justice Department agents arrested 166 I.W.W. leaders for heading a strike the previous June. Eugene V. Debs, the Socialist Party's candidate for President, was sentenced to ten years' imprisonment for attributing the world war to economic interests in a speech before a Socialist gathering. Under the cloak of "patriotic bodies" and armed with the federal police power, reactionary local businessmen and machine politicians crushed local radicals and prewar insurgents. The wartime tyranny in Washington spawned and encouraged a thousand municipal tyrannies.

"It was quite apparent," Howe recalled in his memoirs, "that the alleged offenses for which people were being prosecuted were not the real offenses. The prosecution was directed against liberals, radicals, persons who had been identified with municipal ownership fights, with labor movements, with forums, with liberal papers that were under the ban." The entire prewar reform movement was destroyed in the war, said Howe, "and I could not reconcile myself to its destruction, to its voice being stilled, its integrity assailed, its patriotism questioned." The reformers "had stood for variety, for individuality, for freedom. They discovered a political state that seemed to hate these things; it wanted a servile society. . . . I hated the new state that had arisen, hated its brutalities, its ignorance, its unpatriotic patriotism."

Most of all, Wilson and the war party were determined to corrupt the entire body of the American people, to root out the old habits of freedom and to teach it new habits of obedience. Day after day, arrest after arrest, bond rally after bond rally, they drove home with overwhelming force the new logic of "the new state that had arisen": Dissent is disloyalty, disloyalty a crime; loyalty is servility, and servility is true patriotism. The new logic was new only in America; it is the perennial logic of every tyranny that ever was. The new state affected men differently, but it corrupted them all one way or another. The official repression drove millions of independent-minded Americans deep into private life and political solitude. Isolated, they nursed in private their bitterness and contempt—the corrupting consolation of cynicism. Millions more could not withstand the force of the new state that had risen. It was easier, by far, to surrender to the powerful and embrace their new masters, to despise with the powerful the very opinions they themselves had once held and to hound with the powerful their fellow citizens who still held them—the corrupting consolation of submission. Millions more simply bowed to the ways of oppression, to official lies and false arrests, to "slacker raids" and censored newspapers, to saying nothing, feeling nothing, and caring nothing—the corrupting consolation of apathy.

"The war has set back the people for a generation," said Hiram Johnson. "They have become slaves to the government." Yet the tolling of the bells for armistice brought no release to a corrupted and tyrannized people. To rule a free republic through hatred and fear, through censorship and repression, proved a luxury that the victors in the civil war over war refused to relinquish with the outbreak of peace. On Thanksgiving Day 1918, two weeks after the armistice, the war party, as if on signal, began crying up a new danger to replace the Hun, a new internal menace to replace the German spy, a new object of fear and hatred, a new pretext for censorship and repression. "Bolshevism" menaced the country, declared William Howard Taft, although Communist Party members constituted a minuscule .001 percent of the American population. Bolshevik propaganda menaced America, declared a Senate committee in the middle of winding down its investigation of the nonexistent German propaganda menace. Purge the nation of "Reds," declared the National Security League, opening up its campaign against "Bolshevism" a month after completing its hunt for "pro-Germans" and three and a half years after launching its campaign for "preparedness." In Washington the Wilson Administration, too, joined in the new outcry against Bolshevism and continued to wage war unchecked against the liberties of the American people. The Post Office censorship machine continued to tyrannize the independent press. The Justice Department began deporting aliens suspected of belonging to "the anarchistic and similar classes," to cite the federal statute authorizing the mass deportations. For the first time in American history, guilt by association became a formal principle of law.

Everything seemed possible to the powerful and the privileged, so cowed by fear, so broken to repression had the American people become. Wilson even took time out from his messianic labors in Paris to urge passage of a peacetime federal sedition law, "unprecedented legislation," as Harvard's Professor Chafee put it at the time, "whose enforcement will let loose a horde of spies and informers, official and unofficial, swarming into our private life, stirring up suspicion without end." The war was over, but Wilson did not want the American people to regain their freedom of speech and disturb once more "the unity of our national counsel." Although Congress never voted on the bill, the state party machines followed the President's lead. After the armistice almost every state in the Union passed laws abridging free speech. The statutes were sweeping enough in some states to satisfy a dictator's requirements. In Connecticut it became a crime to say anything that, in the words of the statute, "intended to injuriously affect the Government" of Connecticut or of the United States. Striking while the iron was hot, Wilson and the war party were determined, in the immediate aftermath of war, to set up the legal machinery of permanent repression and to reconquer for oligarchy the venerable terrain of liberty in America. Fourteen months after the armistice, the *New York World*, awakening from its Wilsonian raptures, cried out in alarm over the new "despotism of professional politicians." The newspaper wondered why the prewar reform spirit and the prewar insurgents had died away so completely. It wondered, too, why "no other country in the world is suffering so much from professional politics" as America. There was no cause whatever to wonder. The professional politicians had won the only war they cared about, the war against a free republic that Wilson had begun in 1915 in the name of America's "mission."

Defeated in so many ways, Americans in 1919 enjoyed one grim victory of sorts. They witnessed and joined in the personal and political destruction of Woodrow Wilson, whose fall from the heights of glory was swifter and steeper than any other in our history. Ten months after an ecstatic Paris turned out to welcome the savior of the world, ten months after Europe paid him its fulsome homage, Woodrow Wilson was an utterly broken man, crippled in mind and spirit, thoroughly discredited and publicly reviled, his name a stench in his countrymen's nostrils, his deeds publicly denounced as crimes. Popular hatred, party interest, and the unbearable knowledge of what he had done to his country combined to encompass his ruin.

In December 1918 the President had sailed for Europe determined to secure "peace without victory" and to establish a League of Nations to safeguard the just, nonpunitive peace he intended to impose. He appeared to enjoy every prospect of a glorious success. It seemed impossible for Britain and France to withstand the American President's implacable will, to resist his incomparable prestige or the coercive force of their utter dependence on American money and food. So it appeared, but it was all an illusion. The most powerful man at the Paris peace conference was in fact the neediest. Wilson's own deeds had made him so. In the name of "permanent peace" and "an association of nations," he had deceived and betrayed his countrymen, had falsely maneuvered them into war, had robbed them of their peace, their hopes, and the lives of 116,708 of their sons. And because he had done all that, Wilson needed the League of Nations far more desperately than the world did, if indeed the world needed it at all. The League, magical catchphrase, was to justify his life; the League, glimmering panacea, was to set right his betrayals; the League, whose "Covenant" Wilson wrote in Paris, was to hallow Wilson's war. At the peace conference Wilson was fighting neither for the world nor for the good of America. The President whose ambitions transcended his country, whose "idealism" embraced the whole world, was merely fighting to save his own life. Without a League to justify him, Wilson faced truths too crushing to bear. Without a League he was a false messiah who had served himself and called it God's work, an anti-Moses who had led his people from the Promised Land into Egypt. If, as Clemenceau remarked, Wilson "thinks he is another Jesus Christ," it was because megalomania was the condition of Wilson's survival. If he was not mankind's savior, then he was America's scourge. For Wilson there was no middle ground. It was either the League or moral annihilation. At the peace conference he was a weak and desperate man.

The Allies held the one trump card that mattered: they had Wilson's life in their hands. They threatened his League, hinted at postponement, tormented him with doubts, while the demons of guilt crowded in upon their adversary, sapping his strength still further. Driven frantic by Allied demands for territory and pelf, Wilson in early April threatened to leave the conference and sail home. His bluff was pitifully transparent. He, of all men, could least afford to leave

Paris with empty hands. A few days later Wilson caved in to the punitive demands of the Allies in order to save the League and himself. The surrender, however, proved fatal. A catchphrase no longer, Wilson's "association of nations" became in April 1919 a corrupted reality, hardly more than a concert of the victors to safeguard the spoils of victory. So much was obvious even to Wilson's well-wishers. "It was not for this," William Allen White wrote to a member of Wilson's Paris entourage, "that our Americans died."

From that unbearable accusation Wilson fled to the solace of delusion. "The failure here is complete," Steffens reported from Paris, "but that does not matter. What matters is that the President does not see it so." In January Wilson had known quite well that a punitive peace meant an unjust League. What he knew then he denied now, but the demons of guilt could not be eluded so readily. In Paris, after his surrender, Wilson exhibited symptoms of incipient madness, the madness of a man in flight from reality and from himself. He accused his French clerks of spying on him. He accused his once-beloved Colonel House of betraying his secrets to the Allies. He became convinced that visitors were stealing his belongings. Betrayers and Judases lurked everywhere. Four months after coming to Europe as the savior of the world, Wilson began preparing his final sanctuary from the terrors of reality: Wilson the failed savior was to become Wilson the sublime martyr.

Republican Party leaders were now prepared to assist his martyrdom. For years they had vouched for Wilson's deceits, endorsed his flimsy pretexts, and agreed that reality was whatever Wilson said it was. They agreed no longer. The Republican oligarchy was bent on returning to power. Postwar America, degraded and despoiled, was an America made safe for their rule. There would be no trouble with reformers: the prewar reform movement had been destroyed. There would be no perilous popular demands for governmental action: Americans had grown to hate their government so much they merely wanted it lifted off their backs. The Republican Party, however, was not in good odor. Popular hatred of Wilson and the war was its only real asset, and Republican leaders had no choice but to exploit it as best they could. That hatred, as yet unvoiced by a citizenry too cowed to appear "disloyal," was a palpable force in the country nonetheless. It surged powerfully through the Middle West. It burned with white heat among the downtrodden "hyphenates." It waxed strong, too, among America's demobilized soldiers. By June 1919 some 2.6 million of them had returned from Europe, hating the war they had fought and the President who had conscripted them. If the Republicans could somehow identify themselves with that hatred, their triumph was assured and Wilson doomed. The President's power at home was almost as illusory as his power in Paris. For years it had rested on the bipartisan unity of the powerful and the cordon they had thrown up to protect him and his sophistries from the effective judgment of the American electorate. Without that protective cordon Wilson would stand, for the first time, within the electorate's reach, and millions of Americans were ready on signal to reach for his throat. It was not because Wilson had tried to keep America out of war that millions of Americans hated him, just as it was not because war had been forced upon him that he had failed so wretchedly in Paris.

While Wilson was still at the peace conference, Republicans, led by Senator Lodge, launched their attack on the President through a concerted attack on his League. That a large majority of Republican senators favored a League of Nations in principle, that Wall Street supported Wilson almost unanimously, did not deter Republican leaders. For ventilating popular hatred, Wilson's League made the perfect outlet, and the party was not about to pass it up.

To attack Wilson's League was to attack Wilson's war, without incurring the dangers of doing so openly. Republicans assailed the League as a "breeder of war," denounced it as a "supergovernment" concocted by Wilson to snuff out American sovereignty. Unless altered by the Republican-controlled Senate, it would drag America, they said, into corrupt foreign conflicts under the pretense of international "obligation." The implication was clear. Wilson's League would inflict on Americans the kind of war they hated most—the one they had just fought. That Republican leaders had supported that war with the utmost enthusiasm, millions of Americans were past caring.

Unrepresented for so long, they were meanly grateful for whatever crumbs men of power threw them.

To attack Wilson's League was to assault Wilson himself. Of the actual merits and defects of the League of Nations, millions of Americans cared little. They knew only that Wilson wanted it and that was reason enough to oppose it. As the Philadelphia *Public Ledger* complained: "The mere fact that President Wilson wants something is not an argument against it." Wilson was reaping what he sowed. The President had robbed Americans of what they had cherished most. Now, spitefully and vindictively, millions of Americans wanted him deprived of what he cherished most. "Nine out of ten letters I get in protest against this treaty," a pro-League senator complained, "breathe a spirit of intense hatred of Woodrow Wilson. . . . That feeling forms a very large element in the opposition to this treaty." Licensed, as it were, by the Republican oligarchy, pent-up hatred of Wilson poured into the political arena. "No autocracy," shouted Republican foes of the League, and audiences booed "the autocrat's" name to the rafters. "Impeach him! Impeach him!" a Chicago Coliseum audience screamed after Senator William Borah of Idaho finished assailing Wilson's League. It was no edifying spectacle, this picture of free men deliberating grave issues with little thought save personal vengeance. Yet here again Wilson reaped what he sowed. He had been the chief instrument of the republic's degradation. Now hate-ridden millions howled for a degraded revenge.

In July Wilson returned to America, mentally unhinged, morally bankrupt, and politically weak. Unless he acceded to some Republican demands for emendation and interpretive additions, the Treaty of Versailles (which included the League) faced defeat in the Senate, which had once again recovered its voice in foreign affairs. Wilson stood adamant. He would accept no alterations. He would yield not an iota to his Republican betrayers. The League, Wilson claimed, was "ninety-nine percent insurance against war," but compromise with his enemies for the sake of world peace was a price Wilson refused to pay. In the end as in the beginning, Wilson cared only for himself. Compromise would unleash the demons of guilt. It meant admitting that the treaty was flawed, his League corrupted, his war unhallowed. From that admission Wilson had been fleeing in terror since April. Having sacrificed America for the League's sake, Wilson was now prepared to sacrifice the League for his own. Defeat held irresistible attractions. The League, defeated in the Senate, would regain what it had lost at the peace conference: the pristine purity of a noble ideal. The League's defeat would shift from Wilson the burden of guilt that was crushing him. Who could accuse him of vainly inflicting war on his countrymen, after ignoble politicians made his noble war vain? Defeat of the League in the Senate would salvage the one ideal Wilson had ever served—his vainglorious idea of himself.

The defeat, perforce, had to be a noble one, a defeat after heroic efforts to triumph. In the summer of 1919 Wilson drew up his plans for staging a heroic defeat. He decided to undertake a 10,000-mile speaking tour through the Middle West and West—the enemy camp—to arouse popular support for the treaty. Western Republicans who opposed the League root and branch would feel the wrath of constituents spurred to fury by the President's incomparable eloquence. So Wilson claimed. Others knew better. The President's cabinet advised against the tour. Politically it could only do harm. Attacking Republican senators in their home states would not soften Republican opposition to an unamended treaty. It would merely goad partisan Republicans into sterner resistance. The bipartisan days were over. If the President wanted the treaty ratified, his only course was to stay in Washington and quietly work out a compromise. One yielding message to Senate Democrats and ratification was certain. Wilson spurned his cabinet's advice. The message was never to come.

Wilson's personal physician, too, pleaded with him not to go on the tour. A schedule calling for twenty-seven days' confinement in a railway car, ten daily rear-platform speeches, and twenty-six major addresses would exhaust the stamina of a youthful Bryan. Wilson's own health was poor. His appearance was haggard, his hands trembled, his face twitched. At the Paris peace conference the sixty-three-year-old President had become an old man. The tour, Wilson's physician warned him, was sheer suicide. Wilson loftily spurned the warning. "The boys who went overseas," he told his doctor, "did not refuse to go because it was dangerous." Moreover, he added, "You must remember that I, as commander in chief, was responsible for sending our soldiers to Europe." Of course, Americans had not died in France because Wilson was titular head of the American armed forces. His real responsibility was too damning to put into words. Wilson preferred to speak instead of "destiny disclosed" and the "hand of God who had led us into this way," phrases that exalted himself—who was the hand of God?—while relieving him of blame.

As a last resort, Wilson's physician urged the President to ease the tour by adding rest stops. The killing schedule was scarcely a necessity. To Wilson it was. He refused to add rest stops. When Joe Tumulty advised his "chief" that he would be sacrificing his life, Wilson replied grandly, "I will gladly make the sacrifice to save the Treaty." Even Wilson's display of valor was false. It was not dying he feared, but living. And it was not the treaty he was trying to save.

In early September the President set off on his speaking tour—his road to Golgotha—in search of a martyr's death. Fate was to prove cruelly disobliging. The tour, a political disaster, brought Wilson not death but death-in-life.

Even before disaster struck him, Wilson on the stump showed clear signs of onrushing madness. The treaty he stood up to defend was not the Treaty of Versailles, it was the treaty of his dreams. "This incomparable consummation of the hopes of mankind," he called it. Grim reality he brushed aside. How did his vaunted "peace without victory" square with the Allies' annexation of territory and the reparations they were forcing Germany to pay? Wilson's answer was astonishing. The Treaty of Versailles, he assured his listeners, was the first treaty in history ever drawn up by the victors in war "that was not made in their own favor." Addressing the voters, Wilson was consoling himself. As the presidential train hurtled deeper into the West, Wilson fell deeper into fantasy, as if the train's solitary passage were hastening his own flight from reality. On September 17 Wilson described the treaty as an "enterprise of divine mercy," nothing less. The terrible meetings with Lloyd George and Clemenceau, meetings that had broken his will and destroyed his hopes, he now described as "a very simple council of friends . . . men who believed in the same things and sought the same objects." Speeding toward madness, Wilson on September 24 had virtually suppressed all knowledge of the actual treaty. The Allies, he assured a western audience, "did not claim a single piece of territory."

The fantasy was now complete. The Treaty of Versailles had become for Wilson what he so desperately wished it had been—the peace without victory he had failed to achieve. In fantasy so deep and clung to so desperately no man can find safety or peace. The strain on Wilson was beyond enduring. Something had to snap and release him from torment. On September 25, after assuring a Colorado audience that American boys had died in France for the "liberation and salvation of the world," Wilson collapsed on the train, smitten with an excruciating headache. The rest of the tour was canceled. The presidential train rolled home, curtains drawn.

On October 2, at the White House, a blood clot on the brain struck down the President, paralyzing half his body. For three weeks Wilson lay near death, his condition kept secret by the White House entourage. Inevitably rumors sprouted. People promptly concluded that Wilson had gone mad, a testament to the impression his League speeches had made. There was an element of truth in the rumor, for Wilson's stroke had saved his sanity by the narrowest of margins. From October 2 until his death in 1924 Wilson was to be a mere shell of a man. Much of the time his mind wandered fruitlessly, or else it focused obsessively on his customary grievances—the treachery of his friends, the villainy of his opponents. Spasms of self-pity perpetually overwhelmed him; he often wept. His bitterness bordered on lunacy. When he recovered his strength somewhat he fired Secretary of State Lansing for trying to usurp the presidency; Lansing had called a cabinet meeting without him. He continued to console himself with delusions. Too sickly even to perform the routine duties of his office, he planned nonetheless to run for a third term. The people, he believed, would vindicate him. There was a deep irony in that desperate belief, for many years before, Wilson had written that the sovereignty of the American people was a mere legal fiction. Now, in extremis, it was the people's sovereign forgiveness—not God's—that he yearned for and needed. Such is the moral authority that a great republic exerts even on its betrayers. Popular vindication, however, was just another fantasy of Wilson's. By the end of 1919 half the country would have cheered his impeachment. Hatred of Wilson had not abated while the President lay stricken; it had grown more intense. Pitiless toward others, Wilson aroused no pity in others. While the White House fell silent, anti-League orators publicly denounced "the crimes of Wilson."

A madman and a criminal, that was what millions of Americans now thought of their President.

From his wheelchair in the White House Wilson had just power enough to perform one last major act. He could defeat the League of Nations—and he did. In mid-November the Senate, following Lodge, added fourteen interpretive clauses or "reservations" to the Treaty of Versailles. For public consumption Republicans claimed that their reservations had drawn the poison from Wilson's League. The reservations, in fact, were innocuous. Some were superfluous; others asserted the supremacy of the Constitution over the Covenant of the League; none altered anything substantially. For Republicans they served the dual purpose of exploiting hatred of Wilson without openly repudiating the official aims of the war. Republicans were maneuvering for power, not leading an insurrection.

Innocuous though the reservations were, the ailing President rejected them outright. From the shrouded, secretive White House came instructions to Senate Democrats to unite against the treaty with Republican reservations. The Democrats were prepared to follow the President. They had gone too far with Wilson to turn back now; they had nothing to turn back to. On November 19, 1919, Democrats duly voted against the Republican-tinctured treaty. Republicans in turn voted down the unamended treaty. Since there was no third alternative before the Senate, America remained technically at war. For two months thereafter, Democrats and Republicans tried to reach some accord. With ratification threatening, Wilson struck again. On December 14 the White House issued a stern declaration: The President would accept "no compromise or concession of any kind."

On January 8 Wilson repeated the instructions. Let the treaty be defeated now, he advised his party, and let the election of 1920 serve as a "great and solemn referendum" on his noble handiwork. Thanks to Wilson's instructions, no bipartisan accord was reached. On March 19, 1920, the two versions of the Treaty of Versailles once again came to a vote in the Senate. The results were the same as before. Democrats voted against the treaty with reservations; Republicans voted against the treaty without them. The second defeat was final. The United States was never to ratify the Treaty of Versailles or to enter the League of Nations. This was Wilson's final achievement. After wreaking havoc on his country for the sake of the League of Nations, Wilson strangled the League at its birth. It was a noble catch-phrase once more, untarnished, sublime, justifying everything.

Contemporaries saw matters more clearly. The President was now discredited almost everywhere. His selfish, destructive course had disgraced him even in the eyes of admirers. With one year left of his term, he was utterly without power. In May Congress passed a joint resolution terminating the war with Germany. Wilson vetoed it and Congress overrode his veto. A few weeks later, the ailing half-mad President watched in disappointment as his party nominated Governor James Cox, a party hack from Ohio, to run for his office against Senator Warren G. Harding, a party hack from the same state.

Cox never stood a chance of winning. Just as millions of Americans had cared nothing about the merits of the League of Nations, so in 1920 they cared nothing about the merits of the candidates. The chief issue of the 1920 election was Thomas Woodrow Wilson. Wilson's enemies poured their support into Harding's campaign headquarters and it flowed in a torrent. Hatred of the President dominated the campaign. In the denunciations of Wilson the "dictator" and Wilson the "autocrat," Cox himself was virtually forgotten, buried, as the Springfield *Republican* put it, under a "mountain of malice." With nothing to recommend him save the fact that he was not a Democrat, Harding won the election with 16.2 million votes to Cox's 9.1 million. It was the most crushing election victory ever won by a presidential candidate of no distinction whatever. The 1920 election was indeed the "great and solemn referendum" Wilson had called for, and it rendered its judgment on Wilson: guilty as charged. So ended the political career of a President whom Americans for years had been compelled to "stand by," whose lies had been deemed in the courts to be truth itself, whose honest critics had been denounced as "conspirators" and arrested as felons. On his last morning in office this terrible ruin of a man was asked to pardon Eugene Debs, rotting his life away in a federal penitentiary. Unforgiving, Wilson refused. He had pity only for himself. Today American children are taught in our schools that Wilson was one of our greatest Presidents. That is proof in itself that the American republic has never recovered from the blow he inflicted upon it.

In 1920 Americans yearned for the "good old days" before Wilson and war, before everything had gone so wrong. They yearned in vain. The war and the war party had altered America permanently, and since the war party had shaped America to serve its own interests, the change was a change for the worse. In postwar America the "despotism of professional politicians" went unchallenged. Independent citizens ceased to pester the party machines. The "good citizens" whose rise to civic consciousness had spawned the progressive movement now spurned the public arena in disgust. Wilson's hymns to "service" had made public service seem despicable. Wilson's self-serving "idealism" made devotion to the public good seem a sham and a fool's game. "The private life became the all in all," a chronicler of the 1920s has written. "The most diverse Americans of the twenties agreed in detestation of public life." The Babbitt replaced the political insurgent, and what was left of the free public arena was a Kiwanis club lunch. In 1924 three-quarters of the electorate thought it useless to vote.

The nation's Republican rulers governed with impudence and impunity. A major administration scandal scarcely cost them a vote. They not only served the interests of the trusts, they boasted openly of doing so, for the "captains of industry" were now restored to their former glory as if the prewar reform movement had never existed. The

Republican rulers even set about creating multi-corporate cartels to enable the monopolists to govern themselves and the American people as well. This refurbished monopoly economy the rulers and their publicists praised fulsomely as the "American System," although it was a system prewar Americans had fought for thirty years and which the very laws prohibited. Herbert Hoover, the chief architect of the cartels, described the new economy as "rugged individualism," which was very like calling the sunset "dawn" or describing Wilson's neutrality as "America First," for official lies and catchphrases dominated the country after Wilson's demise as much as they had in his heyday. The catchphrases were crass rather than lofty. That was the chief difference.

Magazines that once thrived on exposing the corrupt privileges of the trusts now retailed gushing stories of business "success," supplied recipes for attaining "executive" status, and wrote paeans in praise of big business, although it was even more corruptly privileged in the 1920s than it had been in the days of the muckraker. America basked in unexampled prosperity, the publicists wrote, although half the country was poor and the farmers desperate. In the 1920s the poor became prosperous by fiat. America had entered an endless economic golden age, proclaimed the magnates of Wall Street whose ignorant pronouncements were now treated with reverence and made front-page news. Peace had returned to America, but the braying of bankers, not the voice of the turtle, was heard in the land. There were other diversions, too, for the populace: Babe Ruth, Red Grange, Al Capone, and an endless stream of songs and movies extolling the charms of college life, although most Americans had never graduated from high school. In postwar America the entire country lived on fantasy and breathed propaganda.

Against the fictions and the lies, where were the voices of dissent? There were few to be heard. What had happened to America's deep enmity toward monopoly and private economic power? It had virtually ceased to exist. It was just strong enough to call forth a few euphemisms. Republicans labeled the cartels "trade associations" and that was that. When the indomitable La Follette ran for President in 1924 as a third-party candidate, it was hardly more than the swan song of a cause long lost. Outside of a few of the old insurgent states (now known collectively as the "farm bloc," a mere special interest) the country fell silent. Apathy and cynicism were the universal state. The official propaganda of the 1920s meant little to most Americans, but by now they were inured to a public life that made no sense and to public men who never spoke to their condition. Like any defeated people, they expected their rulers to consider them irrelevant. Even when the Great Depression struck down the postwar economy (it was a house of cards) and toppled the tin gods of the 1920s, Americans remained as if dumbstruck. Foreign visitors to America in the early 1930s were astonished by the American people's docility, for we had never been docile before. In the 1893 depression America had looked like the Rome of the Gracchi; forty years later people whose life savings had been wiped out by the "American System" stood quietly on breadlines as if they had known breadlines all their lives.

Not all of this postwar degradation was destined to last. Some hope, in time, would return to the defeated, and a semblance of civic courage to the servile. What did not return was the struggle for republican reform. That was the lasting achievement of Wilson and the war party. That was the irreparable damage they had done to the American republic. They had destroyed once and for all the republican cause. Never again would the citizenry of this republic enter the political arena determined to overthrow oligarchy (as Lincoln bid his countrymen do), to extirpate private power and eliminate special privilege.

Historians sometimes call this change "the end of American innocence," scarcely realizing (so dead is the republican spirit) what depths of cynicism that airy little phrase betrays. If the republican struggle for liberty and equality was "innocent," what then is "experience"? It means giving up the ancient faith that self-government is worth fighting for; it means growing indifferent to special privilege and private power while forgetting that privilege corrupts and private power enslaves. It means conceding that a few shall monopolize our politics while forgetting that oligarchies serve chiefly themselves. It means comporting ourselves with proper humility, demanding not an end to corrupt privilege, say, but merely a "piece of the pie" or a "piece of the action," a crumb of corruption for ourselves. Such was the new age of "experience" historians say we entered after the First World War, and they are right. Senator William J. Stone of Missouri had foreseen its arrival on that fateful April day when the Senate voted for war against Germany. He was opposed to war, he had told a colleague, not because of the costs or the deaths but "because if we go into it we will never again have this same old Republic."

The new age revealed itself first in the degradation of the discontented. Of the generation that tasted the bitter betrayal of the war, most were too disheartened to speak out. In the early 1920s, there were still Americans angry enough to lash out against their lot, but they had grown too cowardly to fight their real enemies. So they bought white bedsheets from the local Ku Klux Klan and terrorized Negroes, Catholics, and Jews. A few prairie states were all that remained to uphold the old republican cause. The degradation of the discontented proved especially long-lasting. Seventeen years after the war's end, Americans who refused to suffer the shams of the professional politicians turned not to the old reform traditions of the country. They turned instead to the fascistic fulminations of Father Coughlin or to the greedy puerilities of Huey Long's "Share Our Wealth" movement. That, too, was part of our hard-won "experience." Millions of Americans followed a Louisiana dictator and cheered the language of dictatorship, something we had never done in our "innocence." That is how thoroughly the war party had triumphed. It spawned a generation of Americans who mirrored its own corruption, for it no longer cherished the American republic and no longer fought for its principles.

What the war generation ceased to care about, its children were to forget almost entirely. Who was left to remind them? Over the long years since 1917 the "despotism of professional politicians" has suffered its own ups and downs, but it has never been menaced—as it was menaced for so long—by free men struggling to protect their own freedom and regain a voice in their own affairs. From the ruins of the war, the republican cause has never revived to rally free men. It has ceased to make a difference in our politics. What the Spanish-American War deflected and weakened, the First World War obliterated. And who can measure the cost of that loss, both to ourselves and to humanity, in whose name both wars had been fought.

The Fallout-Shelter
Craze of 1961

I t all began on the evening of July 25, 1961, when President John
F. Kennedy went before television cameras to explain to his countrymen the grave meaning and still-graver consequences of the
deepening crisis over Berlin. The Russians were threatening American
access rights to that isolated city, the President told an audience of
fifty million tense and expectant Americans. Those rights might be
terminated on December 31 when Premier Nikita Khrushchev signed,
as he threatened to do, a separate peace treaty with East Germany. If
the Russians used force to override our rights, Kennedy warned, they
would be met with still greater force: "We do not want to fight but we
have fought before." In consequence, he was calling upon Congress to
appropriate $93 million to provide shelter for the population against
radioactive fallout. "In the coming months I hope to let every citizen
know what steps he can take without delay to protect his family in
case of attack." With those few ominous words about civil defense, set
against a looming confrontation with the Kremlin, President Kennedy
triggered what was to become a national craze, a spectacular bubble,
and one of the most revealing moral debates in our history as "one
nation under God." The subject: building fallout shelters for oneself
and one's family in hopes of surviving attack in a thermonuclear war.

On the face of it, that enterprise seemed perfectly practical, prudent,
and straightforward—with or without presidential prompting. For a

half-dozen years Americans had been told the basic facts about radioactive fallout. Should an atomic bomb burst in Times Square with the explosive force of five megatons (equivalent to five million tons of TNT), virtually everything within a two-mile radius would be destroyed by the blast. Several miles from "ground-zero," however, the great peril to human life was the radioactive dust and debris kicked up and sent flying by the explosion. That killing radiation could not penetrate concrete or steel or even earth or brick. Outside the target area a household that built a concrete shelter in its basement or underneath its garden could well survive a thermonuclear war, provided the family stocked its shelter with sufficient provisions to last two weeks. Why not build such a shelter just in case the "unthinkable" burst into reality?

The proposition was not even new on July 25, 1961. New York's Governor Nelson Rockefeller had been an outspoken champion of home fallout shelters for years. Henry Luce and his mighty magazines also had been urging Americans for a long time to build their own private shelters. So had a number of eminent scientists, most notably the Nobel laureate Dr. Willard Libby of the Atomic Energy Commission. So, too, had the Eisenhower Administration. From mid-1958 onward, the administration's Office of Civil Defense and Mobilization not only had promoted home shelters but also had put prototype shelter models on display around the country and had published a small library of manuals teaching Americans how to build one themselves. The results had been virtually nil. When Kennedy took office there were only about 1,500 home shelters in the entire country.

On the morning of July 26, however, the bully pulpit of the White House had once again demonstrated—so it seemed—its awesome power to mold public sentiment. President Kennedy had, quite simply, delivered one of the most frightening speeches in American history, a speech foreshadowing not merely a war but the unthinkable war: a war fought with soaring missiles, a war whose weapons were measured in million-ton units of TNT, a war that would kill not soldiers but the civilian population of the country. And the deadline for the end of peace, the end of the world as men knew it, might be sometime around December 31, just five months away.

On July 27 *The New York Times* reassured its readers that they were "calm" and "confident," that they showed "no shock and no sense of panic." Saying it did not make it so. The President, as James Reston of the self-same *Times* rightly put it, had scared "the daylights out of people," especially, as one Chicago housewife told a reporter, "when he started talking about civil defense and bomb shelters." Nothing had made the prospect of thermonuclear war seem more real than that, and Kennedy was well aware of it. The day after his electrifying speech the President drove home the point again. He was asking Congress for $10 million to build an alarm system for private homes—the National Emergency Alarm Repeater, acronymically known as NEAR. You plugged a little device into your wall socket (price $5 to $10) and the Air Defense Command would activate it when Soviet missiles began flying. That would give you about a half-hour to leap into your home shelter if, as the President had obliquely suggested, you had built one "without delay." On July 29 the administration gave home fallout shelters yet another push forward. Henceforth, announced the Federal Housing Authority, home-shelter builders would be eligible for insured home-improvement loans.

Presidential impulsion—phase one of the shelter craze—sent America flying at once into phase two: a frantic mass search for information, for blueprints, for precise lists of emergency supplies. Once-somnolent civil-defense offices began jangling with the ring of telephones. Mail poured in until, by the end of August, civil-defense officials reported that requests for information had reached "tidal wave proportions." In the aftermath of Kennedy's speech, civil-defense officials distributed no fewer than 22 million copies of the Eisenhower Administration's *Family Fallout Shelter*. And millions of Americans requested another long-neglected government pamphlet: *Family Food Stockpile for Survival*. For the first time in their careers, civil-defense officials found themselves in great demand as public speakers. In school assembly halls, church basements, bowling alleys, and rented movie theaters they lectured to large and avid audiences who wanted to know, first, if they lived outside a targeted area, and, if so, what they could do about it at once. The answers usually made the front page of local newspapers, for civil defense had become news for the first time since the outbreak of World War II.

In the war-darkened summer of 1961, a West Coast woman interviewed after Kennedy's speech seemed to sum up perfectly the national mood: "I don't want a war. I don't want to build a bomb shelter, but I don't see what else we can do about it." The news headlines alone kept the public in a frenzy. On August 13 the world shook with fear and rage when the Communists sealed off East Berlin with barbed wire, preparatory to building the infamous Wall. Several days later the world trembled again when a U.S. military convoy from West Germany made its perilous way along the autobahn to West Berlin. On August 31 fear and tension boiled over into outright hysteria when Khrushchev announced that the Soviet Union, after a three-year hiatus, was going to resume testing atomic weapons at once. That day there was nobody in America who could possibly have predicted that the shelter craze was a bubble that was soon to burst.

The very opposite seemed true. With public interest at fever pitch, fallout-shelter champions, frustrated for years, quickly launched a furious campaign to promote home fallout-shelter construction, "the greatest campaign of persuasion," *The Nation* noted, "in the history of American public relations." Cheerful optimism was the campaign keynote. "We must get the message into every home" that thermonuclear war is survivable, said Kennedy's director of the Office of Civil Defense and Mobilization. Comforting statistics filled the air. On September 2, for example, federal civil-defense spokesmen assured Americans that even if a 100-megaton bomb fell in their vicinity, they stood "an excellent chance" of survival in a home shelter just twelve miles from ground-zero. *Life* magazine estimated that 94 percent of the population could survive a Soviet attack if shelters were available to everyone. Dr. Libby put the figure at 90 to 95 percent in a stirring series of syndicated articles he wrote for the Associated Press.

Shelter advocates even declined to concede that home shelters were merely a grim necessity. They put a halo of heroism around them.

Building shelters, said Stuart Pittman, assistant secretary of defense for civil defense, gave Americans an "opportunity"—an opportunity "to demonstrate their will to face up to a thermonuclear war." The shelter builder was deemed a modern-day pioneer showing the stern stuff that made America great when an American "plowed with a musket in his hand." Linking the thermonuclear present to the comforting pre-atomic past, *The Washington Post* offered plans for a fallout shelter with a "colonial motif," while *Life*, working up the same theme, described a five-family shelter being built on Long Island as a "modern stockade" in a somewhat farfetched comparison between rampaging Iroquois and radioactive isotopes.

In case even the pioneer spirit might sound too grim, shelter advocates cheerfully assured Americans that huddling in an eight-by-eight-foot bunker for two weeks might not be as grueling as it sounded. *Time* magazine suggested decorating one's shelter with a picture of an outdoor scene as a possible cure for cabin fever. The *Library Journal* advised future shelter dwellers to try to learn a new language. "The mental gymnastics would be salutary, if not downright *fun*."

Most of all, insisted shelter advocates, home shelters were cheap and easy to build. Dr. Libby stirred the hopes of millions of modest wage-earners when he announced in his syndicated series that he had built a shelter in the backyard of his Bel-Air, California, home for a mere $30. Even the most complicated shelter recommended by the civil-defense manuals, the double-walled, aboveground concrete shelter, replete with joists, block capping, and toggle joints, could be built "by an enterprising do-it-yourself family," said the editors of *Life*, who appended to their elaborate home-shelter story—"How You Can Survive Fallout"—a letter from President Kennedy urging Americans to "read and consider seriously the contents of this issue of *Life*." The presidentially approved issue bore a cover photograph of a man enveloped in a transparent plastic bag described as a "civilian fallout suit." Its price was $21.95 and its worth as a radioactive shield, when seriously considered, didn't amount to much.

In truth, by the end of the long, weary summer, fallout began to look like a supremely ripe opportunity for profitable commerce. In

September a rash of "survival stores" erupted around the country. There the home-shelter builder could purchase such items as: "a citizen's instrument kit" ($20), which told you how much radiation your body had absorbed while you waited for the all-clear signal; the Surviv-All, Incorporated, food kit ($8.95), which provided two weeks' worth of rations for one; General Mills's MPF, or "multi-purpose food"; Nabisco's seven-pound tins of "survival rations," which reportedly tasted "like animal crackers"; Mead Johnson's Nutrament, originally developed as a quick lunch for assembly-line workers; a variety of blowers ($74) for forcing fresh air into your shelter; air filters ($55) to assure that the fresh air was not radioactive; and a profusion of "lifesaving kits" complete with "anti-radiation" pills and salves which turned out to be the lineal descendants of snake oil and golden elixir.

Despite all the official calls for cheap do-it-yourself construction, shelter manufacturers, too, began appearing in droves. In July 1961, there were only 40 of them in the country. Two months later, reported *The New York Times*, 120 had governmental approval, and there were hundreds more who did not. Most of them were suburban and small-town contractors prepared to make a fast dollar by installing backyard shelters rather than swimming pools. Others, more ambitious, offered completely prefabricated steel or concrete shelters priced, on the average, at around $2,000. The Armco Steel Company of San Francisco combined prefabrication with do-it-yourself by marketing a shelter whose steel modules could be assembled like the parts of an Erector set. Advertising in the press, sending salesmen door-to-door, setting up their sales models in shopping-center parking lots, the "survival merchants," as *Consumer Reports* tartly labeled them, added their own promotional appeals to the national campaign for home fallout shelters. In the autumn virtually every state fair in the country displayed home-shelter models. At the Dallas Fair, the Federal Bomb & Fallout Shelter Company's $1,350 shelter—billed as "the only precast monolithic concrete shelter approved by the Office of Civil Defense!"—reportedly "outdrew the blue ribbon cattle and the midway rides as a popular attraction." People peeked into the concrete igloo, wondered, perhaps, what it would be like to live in a tomb for two weeks, and then went home and argued about shelters with family, friends, and neighbors.

To build or not build a shelter—that, by early October, had become the question of the hour. It was discussed in downtown cafeterias, suburban kitchens, country-club bars, and roadside taverns. To many pro-shelter Americans it was simply a matter of prudence—"insurance," as President Kennedy had put it even before the Berlin crisis. As one New Jersey dentist explained, he carried an umbrella on a cloudy day, and "the world situation looks pretty cloudy today." Others expected war any moment and were determined to survive it. "I want to be one of the quarter of the population to escape and be around to build for the future," a Cambridge, Massachusetts, housewife told a *Times* reporter. There were patriotic arguments, too. Shelter builders insisted, echoing administration spokesmen, that they were helping to strengthen America. A people protected against fallout would discourage a Soviet attack and enable America to get tough with the Russians without fear of "nuclear blackmail." The arguments appeared unassailable, and on October 5 President Kennedy weighed in behind them with all the immense prestige of his office. That day he called on Americans to build private shelters for themselves and their families. Protection from radioactive fallout, said the President, "is within reach of every American willing to face the facts and act."

All the elements of a mass movement seemed firmly in place: millions of shelter manuals now rested in people's hands, a small army of dedicated civil-defense officials were fanned out around the country, an international showdown still loomed, a President was at last openly calling for home shelters, and there were now hundreds of eager contractors ready to supply the expected demand. *The Nation* glumly predicted that the majority of Americans would respond to the call. Amazingly enough they did not. In an age of mass media and mass persuasion, the overwhelming majority of Americans could not be persuaded to do anything. For every American homeowner who decided to build a shelter, there were at least a hundred who still sat on their hands. At the height of the shelter craze the disparity between frantic interest and listless activity was astonishing. According to civil-defense officials, the popular inertia was due to a merely temporary public "confusion." Americans, they said, still did not know exactly how to build an adequate home shelter, nor did they still know for certain whether they lived sufficiently far away from a presumed Russian target to make a fallout shelter worthwhile. According to the *Times*, the inertia was due to a "fatalistic" attitude toward "the possibility of surviving atomic war." The newspaper quoted one Omaha resident who presumably spoke for millions: "Why worry about war? We're all going to be dead in the first five minutes anyway."

There were elements of truth in both explanations. The populace *was* confused about fallout, and millions of Americans *were* fatalistic. Moreover, even Americans who wanted to build shelters found themselves facing a discouraging battery of unexpected difficulties. The experience of Elk Grove Village, Illinois, was typical of many small towns. In August the whole community was determined to dig in for a thermonuclear showdown. The town fathers promised to do all in their power to help residents build shelters in the crawl spaces beneath their homes. Confusion set in at once, however, when civil-defense experts pointed out that Elk Grove crawl spaces were too low to provide two weeks of shelter. The town fathers then urged the citizenry to dig underground. Alas, it turned out, the area's water table was too high to dig a ten-foot hole that stayed dry. "Underground Shelters Would Be Under Water," warned the Elk Grove *Herald*. Despite the enthusiasm of early August, three months went by without a single home shelter being constructed in the village.

Discouraging, too, were reports that fly-by-night operators were stalking the land. One Dallas woman had a steel fallout shelter installed by a contractor for $2,500. In the first heavy autumn rainstorm the roof caved in. When she called the contractor to complain, she found that he already had fled the jurisdiction. By mid-October the Federal Trade Commission was so burdened with complaints about unscrupulous shelter builders that it promised henceforth to monitor "fraudulent advertising campaigns for fallout shelters and survival kits."

Worse than the crooks were the cracks. Despite the cheery do-it-yourself instructions disseminated by civil-defense spokesmen, it took uncommon skill to build the only kind of shelter that could keep out radiation, namely one that was airtight. One hole was fatal, a retired Army officer learned after installing a $1,635 backyard shelter. "Now I have a beehive," he reported from Tennessee. One civil-defense official admitted that of thirty home shelters he had inspected, twenty-seven failed to meet even minimum requirements for fallout protection. The glib advice about easy-to-build shelters began to look suspiciously mendacious, especially when Dr. Libby's nationally famous $30 shelter was partially destroyed in a brush fire.

Yet all these difficulties could have been overcome were it not for a quite unexpected turn of events. Slowly but surely millions of Americans were coming to the conclusion that private fallout shelters were morally indefensible.

Doubts about the morality of home shelters had been bubbling under the surface almost from the moment the frenzy began. What stirred them initially were the widely reported remarks made by an Austin, Texas, hardware dealer when his $90,000 home shelter was completed in early August. He had outfitted his elaborate bunker, he told local reporters, with four rifles in order to shoot any neighbors who tried to invade it when the bombs began to fall. Moreover, in case they jumped into his haven before he did, "I've got a .38 tear-gas gun, and if I fire six or seven tear-gas bullets into the shelter, they'll either come out or the gas will get them." The Texan's views were brutally expressed but they were also undeniably logical. If you built a home shelter you would need a gun to keep out your shelterless neighbors, and in the hysteria of a thermonuclear alert you probably would have to do more than just wave it in the air. Civil-defense officials saw no moral difficulties in that. "There's nothing in the Christian ethic which denies one's right to protect oneself and one's family," said a Riverside County, California, civil-defense official in the course of advising local residents to put pistols in their survival kits to fight off

invading hordes from Los Angeles. In a frank August 18 article entitled "Gun Thy Neighbor?" *Time* came down squarely on the side of
gunning. Why help those who had refused to help themselves?
Against the ruthless moral logic of home shelters there was no public
outcry at first. Because of that very silence an angry teacher of divinity
at Vanderbilt University savagely taunted his fellow clergymen in
print. Writing in the August 23 issue of the *Christian Century,* he sar-
castically called upon "ethicists and theologians" to contrive a new
"nuclear ethics" based on the Gospels but with a few awkward injunc-
tions left out, such as loving one's neighbor. Theologians, he said, now
had a golden opportunity because "thousands of public-spirited
preachers are awaiting some comfortable word which they can proclaim" to their shelter-building, gun-toting parishioners "during the
coming months."

Despite the silence of the nation's clergy, however, those who wanted home shelters often felt qualms of conscience about building one.
According to contractors, their customers would say things like "I feel
sort of ashamed of doing this" or "I know it sounds selfish, or perhaps
immoral, but I have myself and my family to look out for and I don't
want to have to share my shelter with anyone." Other shelter builders
confessed to having "mixed emotions" about their shelters, a *Times*
survey reported. Some contractors, too, felt moral pangs. "What sends
chills up and down my spine," said one shelter manufacturer in
Highland Park, Illinois, "is imagining a child or two out there saying
'Let me in!' when you're full and you just can't let them in."

Such moral qualms remained private until late September, when,
ironically enough, a Jesuit priest made a bold public effort to set them
at rest. Writing in the Jesuit magazine *America,* Father L. C. McHugh,
an associate editor of the magazine and a former teacher of ethics at
Georgetown University, described home shelters as a "grass-roots
movement for survival" being hindered by baseless moral scruples.
The American people, he said, "need a little instruction in the grim
guidelines of essential morality at the shelter hatchway." According to
Father McHugh, the Christian right of self-defense justifies "the use of
violence to defend life and its equivalent goods," such as a lifesaving

shelter. To love one's neighbor as thyself, he argued, was undoubtedly a "heroic" Christian virtue, but it was not a Christian duty. Indeed, it was "misguided charity" not to shoot a neighbor trying to invade one's jam-packed shelter.

Father McHugh's "essential morality" of the hatchway made headlines across the country. Here, stated with force and clarity, was the new "nuclear ethic" predicted by the Vanderbilt divine, but the "thousands of public-spirited preachers" refused to proclaim it. Instead, they assailed it with uncommon fury. On October 13 the Reverend Angus Dun, Episcopal bishop of Washington, D.C., struck the first major blow against "nuclear ethics." To repel with a gun neighbors seeking shelter, thundered Bishop Dun, was "utterly immoral." He professed himself appalled "at this business of preparing people to push their neighbor's children out of a shelter. . . . I do not see how any Christian conscience can condone a policy which puts supreme emphasis on saving your own skin, without regard to the plight of your neighbor." Across the country clergymen echoed Bishop Dun's sense of outrage. A Jesuit priest in Chicago called his fellow Jesuit's arguments the "morality of the cornered rat." The world-famous Protestant theologian Reinhold Niebuhr accused Father McHugh of giving the shelter controversy "a new and horrendous" twist by "justifying murder." Readers of *America,* too, vented their outrage in angry letters to the editor. "Is life so precious," asked one, "that we must turn into savages to protect it?" The Methodist Bishops Council, representing 10 million American Methodists, assailed fallout shelters. The evangelical clergy of the country also took a "dim view" of them, reported the Religious News Service after taking a poll. The leading evangelist of them all, Billy Graham, opposed home fallout shelters. Jewish religious leaders, too, condemned them. Building them meant "abandoning all moral conduct," said one. Shelter builders themselves became the target of moral condemnation. Hailed in August as modern-day pioneers, they found themselves assailed in October as the sort of people America could well do without. As Bishop Dun put it: "The kind of man who would be most needed in a post-attack world is least likely to dig himself a private mole-hole that has no room for his neighbor."

The clergy had drawn the line sharply: a good Christian would not build a home shelter; a shelter builder was not a good Christian. The moral argument, no doubt, was debatable, but who would wish to take the opposing side in a public debate? To the clerical onslaught there was no public reply from home-shelter champions. As for the shelter builders themselves, they presumably disagreed with the clergy but they behaved in remarkably furtive fashion. Shelter contractors reported "an almost universal insistence that their projects be secret." Customers simply could not bear to face the scorn and opprobrium of their neighbors. "We use unmarked trucks," a Milwaukee shelter manufacturer advertised in deference to the passion for secrecy. If, as one shelter advocate had put it, "every man who decides to protect himself and his family adds a stone to the rampart of our total defense," then most rampart builders no longer wished to be caught in the act. The American clergy had voiced the deepest moral sentiments of the country and had strengthened those sentiments immeasurably.

The religious assault on home shelters marked the beginning of the end of the shelter craze, for it encouraged skeptics and critics to speak out strongly for the first time. On the eighteenth of October General Dwight Eisenhower himself informed the press that he would not build a home shelter. "If I were in a very fine shelter and they [his wife and children] were not there," said the former President with simple eloquence, "I would just walk out. I would not want to face that kind of world." Backed by religious leaders and a former President, emboldened, too, by the slow winding down of the Berlin crisis itself, scientists and technical experts, hitherto silent, began giving voice to serious doubts about the efficacy of home fallout shelters. Within a matter of weeks they completely undermined the cheery optimism of the prevailing shelter propaganda. Radioactive fallout, the shelter champions had insisted for years, was the major peril to life in a thermonuclear war. That, it turned out, was not necessarily true, as Rockefeller Institute scientists reported on the first of November. If the Russians chose to explode a bomb high above the ground (as we ourselves did when we bombed Hiroshima), there would be little or no radioactive fallout. Instead, the explosion would produce a mighty firestorm capable of destroying everything miles beyond the blast area. A fifty-megaton bomb, reported Gerard Piel, publisher of *Scientific American*, would generate a firestorm one hundred miles in diameter. Within that vast area every home fallout shelter would become a "fire-trap." If the Russians exploded their big bombs high above America's cities, then suburban and exurban shelters would not be havens but ovens. Fallout shelters, said Piel in a November 10 speech in San Francisco, were "a hoax on public opinion."

Ten days after Piel's speech the famed physicist James Van Allen publicly denounced Dr. Libby's Associated Press articles as "extremely dangerous" and cited facts and figures to prove that they gave Americans "a false sense of security." In December hundreds of Midwestern professors signed an open letter to President Kennedy denouncing fallout shelters as a "quack cure for cancer." As for deter-ring a Soviet attack—an official argument made for shelters—military experts pointed out that shelters could do nothing of the kind. All the Soviet Union had to do in riposte was build more and bigger missiles. A national fallout-shelter program would merely stimulate the arms race. With such considerations in mind, another American elder statesman dealt a blow to the shelter movement. In December the aged Herbert Hoover gave a speech in Nebraska opposing fallout shel-ters of any kind, public as well as private. Instead of digging under-ground, said the former President, "we should keep our heads up looking for honorable solutions." Like the touching words of his fel-low ex-President, this was the voice of an older America, but it proved to be, in this case, the voice of an entire people.

Despite the furious spate of official propaganda, exceedingly few home shelters were ever built, just how many nobody knows to this day. A sampling of figures tells the tale of the boom that never boomed. In Cook County, Illinois, where 260,000 copies of *Family Fallout Shelter* had been distributed, only 19 people out of a popula-tion of 3,500,000 had applied, as of November 19, 1961, for a permit to build a home shelter. A full year after the craze began, the Federal Housing Administration reported that only 3,500 people had asked for a home-shelter loan. The shelter craze died, not with a bang but a whimper, the whimper of shelter merchants going broke. "The market is dead—the manufacturers have had it," reported the president of Chicago's Atomic Shelter Corporation in May 1962. Some 600 shelter manufacturers, he estimated, already had gone out of business. An Oklahoma City contractor reported in May that he had received just one inquiry about shelters in the entire month of April. It was, as one bankrupt Los Angeles manufacturer put it, "a real loused-up deal."

In a symbolic sense, at least, the end came on April 1, 1962. On that day the bankrupt Living Circle Company of Oakland, California, which had sold just one prefabricated shelter in fifteen months, held a public auction of its unwanted wares. Nine shelters were sold for a knock-down price of around $600 each, but the purchasers no longer had fallout in mind. One buyer said he had bought himself a shelter because he thought it would make a "dandy darkroom." Another said he intended to use his as a shed for storing garden tools. Instead of burrowing beneath their gardens, Americans had once more returned to cultivating them.

The Enshrinement of
Bobby Kennedy

I n the last two years of his brief and stormy life, Robert Kennedy
showed a remarkable ability to arouse extravagant political hopes.
California grape-pickers came to look upon him as the savior of
their race. Rebellious ghetto youths, bitter and disaffected, saw in him
a kindred spirit. Young left-wing journalists, who think bankers rule
America, believed that he, and he alone, would prove the glorious
exception to the iron rule of the capitalists.

Such hopes were all the more extraordinary because they rested on
such fragile foundations. Most of what Kennedy had actually done in
his life his most ardent admirers were heartily ashamed of. They hailed
him as the harbinger of peace, yet a few years before he had been a
Cold War bravo of an uncommonly bellicose kind. They saw him as
the one man who could lead America out of its long-standing domestic stalemate, yet a few years before he believed that jailing racketeers
was the most pressing domestic task before the country. Erasing the
inconvenient past, some of Kennedy's admirers spoke of his "conversion": sometime around 1966 he abruptly ceased to be the Kennedy
they detested and became the Kennedy they wished him to be. Others
spoke of his rapid and astonishing "growth" and claimed for him a
unique capacity to learn, to change, and to experience. Just what he
had become none of his admirers could say for certain. To one, he was
"existential man, defining himself by his actions." To another, "there

was something about him—a modern spirit—that reflected the tempo of the times." By 1968 Kennedy had ceased to be, for his admirers, a man of flesh and blood, and had become a sort of pure potentiality, the locus of hope itself.

That was the faith that sustained Kennedy's followers during the last few years of his life. Now, ten years after Kennedy's assassination, Arthur Schlesinger, Jr., one of his closest advisers, has attempted, in a voluminous biography [*Robert Kennedy and His Times,* Houghton Mifflin, 1985], a massive vindication of that faith. The task is worthy of Schlesinger's ingenuity, for there are two formidable barriers to the belief that Robert Kennedy had been the most promising politician of the age, "the most creative man in American public life," according to Schlesinger. The first is common sense, which holds that while people change they still remain recognizably the same. That a man will change drastically between the age of thirty-seven, when Robert Kennedy was manifestly the early, unpromising Bobby (this was 1962), and the age of forty-one the world will accept but grudgingly. The second barrier is our elementary political understanding. That the sharp alteration in Kennedy's public character and opinions took place when it served his presidential ambitions suggests—to put it mildly—that political calculation played a part in that alteration. Protecting Robert Kennedy's reputation from the inroads of common sense and political understanding dictates the strategy of Schlesinger's book. What was truly singular about Kennedy—and he *was* a singular figure—is precisely what his biography is at pains to conceal.

Schlesinger's strategy is fully revealed in his treatment of the first important episode in Kennedy's political career: his decision to join the subcommittee staff of Senator Joe McCarthy, then at the crest of his noxious career. Other admiring Kennedy biographers have treated the episode with candor. They readily admit that Bobby had once been a narrow and surly young man of markedly illiberal views before becoming, many years later, someone different and better. In Schlesinger's account, however, Kennedy's youthful politics do not even enter the matter. We learn in detail *how* Bobby's father got him the job; Joe Kennedy knew McCarthy, liked him, contributed to his campaign, and so forth. Once hired, Schlesinger's youthful job-hunter—for that is all he appears to be in this account—writes a "sober report" on Allied commerce with Red China during the Korean War, a report that McCarthy, in contrast to his sober young aide, turned into blaring, unsober headlines. In July 1953, his report completed, Kennedy resigns. After quoting some critical comments Kennedy published about McCarthy several years later, when his association with the senator had become a political encumbrance, Schlesinger concludes that although Kennedy "had initially shared McCarthy's concern about Communist infiltration"—Schlesinger's sole, glossing reference to the chief point about the episode—he resigned because he owed "a debt to his own inner standards" of probity.

The object of all this obfuscation is plain. Our faith in the metamorphosed Kennedy depends on leaving the political opinions of the unreconstructed Kennedy as vague and as shadowy as Schlesinger can keep them. That is why, in the two hundred pages he devotes to Kennedy's life before becoming attorney general, Schlesinger does not cite, let alone examine, a single one of Kennedy's speeches on the Cold War, remarkable addresses in which Kennedy virtually recommended the global struggle against communism as a means of regenerating an allegedly flabby citizenry and of ridding our politics of "confusion" and "perplexities," as Kennedy himself put it in 1961, the same year in which he privately urged his brother to declare a national emergency, put the government on a war footing, and unleash all his "emergency" powers in order to prosecute more effectively the life-and-death struggle against communism in general and Cuba in particular.

Schlesinger does well to pass over Kennedy's vision of a free people that "toughened" into a clenched fist, a free republic that turned into an armed camp. Such a vision reveals the repugnance for democratic politics and the reckless disdain for the requirements of liberty that Kennedy manifested throughout his career: in his determination as attorney general to use and abuse electronic surveillance (he innocently thought the FBI was using informers, not "bugs," according to Schlesinger); in his efforts to persuade the electorate by every device of cheap publicity that venerable constitutional safeguards crippled government efforts to defeat the nation's chief domestic menace, namely a bunch of Mafia mobsters; in his willingness to harass and bully newsmen, whose stories embarrassed his presidential brother; in his efforts to impede, as far as he could, one of the great grass-roots movements in our history, the Southern civil-rights campaign led by Martin Luther King (the Kennedys' "good intentions" toward the civil-rights movement, notes Schlesinger, "were not solving many problems"). It was manifest, too, in his post-"conversion" effort to liberate black ghetto-dwellers in Brooklyn by putting them in the charge of Wall Street magnates sporting GIVE A DAMN buttons. Kennedy's disdain for democratic politics not only never waned, it eventually became an important part of his later appeal.

The McCarthy episode also reveals the other half of Schlesinger's grand strategy. The same month that Kennedy resigned from McCarthy's subcommittee staff, Democratic committee members began a six-month boycott of the committee, at the conclusion of which they rehired Kennedy as minority counsel. The connection is obvious, but Schlesinger does not make it: Kennedy's "inner standards" prompted him to resign just when Democratic Party leaders decided to pull the rug out from under McCarthy. Schlesinger has attributed to Kennedy's allegedly awakening conscience what he owed to simple political calculation—keeping in step with the leaders of his party. That calculation was entirely characteristic of him. From the outset of his career to the end of his life, the fixed stars of all Robert Kennedy's political calculations were the interests and opinions of Democratic Party leaders. So precarious is Bobby's reputation, however, that Schlesinger dares not concede that he was even ambitious. In his detailed account of Kennedy's career after his brother's assassination, Schlesinger never says outright what was obvious to everyone: that Kennedy wanted to be President of the United States in 1972, when Lyndon Johnson was due to step down. Does Schlesinger think presidential ambition dishonorable? Of course not. In Kennedy's case, however, that otherwise laudable ambition accounts all too fully for his subsequent "growth" and "conversion."

In 1964 the road to the White House lay wide open for Bobby. Democratic leaders were as eager to see the "heir apparent" become President as they had been to elevate his brother. Indeed, the party syndicate's backing was what made Kennedy the "heir apparent" in the first place. Seeking ways to solidify his position, Kennedy had toyed with the idea of forcing himself on the 1964 ticket as Lyndon Johnson's running mate. "Most of the major leaders in the North want me—all of them, really," Kennedy remarked at the time to a *Newsweek* reporter, a quote missing from Schlesinger's biography. When Johnson rudely scotched Kennedy's plans, New York's machine Democrats rallied to support him in his successful bid for a Senate seat.

The only obstacle to Kennedy's ambitions was the deep distrust his political record had aroused among liberals and reformers in the Democratic Party. His obvious task was to win them to his banner without unduly disturbing the Democratic oligarchy, a task that almost every White House–bound Democrat has had to fulfill since 1896. By early 1966, therefore, Kennedy began to manifest in dramatic ways what Schlesinger calls his growing "identification" with the outcasts of American society. The three objects of his compassion no doubt aroused genuine pity in him, but they were also well chosen for his purposes. He became the champion of striking grape-pickers in California by the not very risky feat of championing their champion, a brave trade unionist named Cesar Chavez. He "identified," too, with the Northern black ghettos, principally urging President Johnson to spend more money on his fraudulent "poverty program"; which is to say, the "most creative" politician of the day wanted a program, designed chiefly to keep the poor under control, given larger funds for that purpose. Kennedy also "identified" with American Indians by visiting reservation schools. By the end of 1966, Robert Kennedy, metamorphosed, had become, in Schlesinger's words, "the tribune of the underclass."

Kennedy did his best, too, to make himself the tribune of America's restive and angry underclassmen by delivering on university campuses trite paeans to "youth" and the "revolution of youth." That "revolution," Kennedy liked to tell his campus audiences, had already begun in America with the election of his brother to the presidency at the youthful age of forty-three, surely the most trivial revolution in history. To overcome the distrust aroused by his close ties to machine Democrats, Kennedy, in 1966, sided with party reformers in a local judgeship race, "an impulsive venture," notes Schlesinger, ever on the alert to squelch any suspicion that the "tribune of the underclass" was engaged in the astute management of a political career.

What was *Schlesinger's* Kennedy doing all this while? He was, according to Schlesinger, groping, growing, and undergoing profound learning experiences, for he "possessed to an exceptional degree an experiencing nature." Kennedy's heart was feeling new inner promptings, and these he would boldly express in public with scarcely a thought for the morrow. By 1967, Schlesinger says, Kennedy's "experiencing nature" had turned him into a "radical," had filled him with scorn for "conventional politics," and had led him to dream of building new bases of power outside "established institutions." In fact, by mid-1967 Kennedy had comfortably situated himself at the dead center of "conventional politics." A few painfully cautious criticisms of the Vietnam War had kept him from running too far afoul of the peace movement without forfeiting the trust of the Democratic syndicate. A ringing speech in praise of President Johnson, delivered in June 1967, had signaled to the party establishment that he was perfectly content to wait until 1972 for his appointed turn at the helm. Then fate, in the form of a dynamic party dissident named Allard Lowenstein, stepped in to mangle Kennedy's plans and to expose, inadvertently, the shallowness of his "growth" and "conversion."

Lowenstein was determined to start up a grass-roots party rebellion and wrest the 1968 Democratic nomination from President Johnson. In June, in August, and again in September, he urged Kennedy to run for the nomination as the leader of the "dump Johnson" insurgency. Kennedy refused each time. He would not, he told Lowenstein, take responsibility for "splitting the party." Only if key party leaders invited him to challenge the President would he alter his plans. Otherwise it was out of the question. The foe of "conventional politics" stood aghast at the prospect of defying the magnates of the Democratic Party; the alleged builder of new bases of power flatly refused to lead a rebellion against the old bastions of power; the apostle of the "revolution of youth" had no desire whatever to rid American politics of the grizzled party despots in whose bosom his family had flourished so mightily; the man deeply moved by the degradation and oppression of black people in Northern cities had no wish to weaken the one established institution, his party, chiefly responsible for that degradation and oppression. He just wanted the party bosses to nominate him for the presidency in 1972.

On October 17, however, Kennedy received a stunning blow: Eugene McCarthy, an eccentric, gifted, and frustrated senator, had accepted Lowenstein's invitation to challenge Lyndon Johnson and the Democratic organization. "I cannot recall in the conversations I had with Bob," said Senator George McGovern, bearer of the ill tidings, "anything that so much disturbed him as McCarthy's announcement." McCarthy was not only going to split the party; he wanted to split the party. He would "become the hero of countless Democrats across the country," Schlesinger himself warned Kennedy. What was even worse, McCarthy's candidacy threatened to puncture the inflated claims and pretensions of the timorous "tribune of the underclass."

Recovering his composure, Kennedy detected a silver lining in the McCarthy cloud. At a council of war held on November 3, 1967, Kennedy informed his assembled courtiers and advisers that he was canvassing the party bosses to find out whether, in the event McCarthy's insurgency proved menacing, "state leaders might ask him to run in the interests of party unity. . . . 'Joe Dolan has been working almost full time on this for the past ten days,' " Schlesinger noted in his personal minutes of the meeting. That the "state leaders" would abandon Johnson for Kennedy in order to "rescue the party" from its own rank and file, Schlesinger himself was hopeful. Kennedy's canvass, however, brought only discouragement. In January 1968 Kennedy explained to Lowenstein that he could not run because (I quote from *An American Melodrama*, an account of the 1968 campaign written by a trio of Englishmen) "his aides had consulted the various power-brokers in the party, Mayor Daley among them. But the advice they received had been virtually unanimous; it was not

Kennedy's year, his chance would come in 1972." What else could "the most creative" politician of the day do but wait upon the pleasure of the Democratic syndicate? To support McCarthy himself was, of course, "out of the question," Schlesinger notes; it would have "put him in an odd position with Dick Daley and other professionals."

Unfortunately for Kennedy, in 1968 the "professionals" had ceased to be what Kennedy had always regarded them as being: the only serious factor in the calculations of ambition. While he sat on his hands, countless rank-and-file Democrats were beginning to regard him with open scorn and contempt. They were not likely to forget four years hence that in the crisis of 1968 the erstwhile leader of the "new politics"—another claim Kennedy's followers made for him—had proved himself the craven myrmidon of the old pols. By March 1968 Kennedy saw his long-sought objective—the presidency in 1972—slipping out of his grasp. Cruel circumstance left him no choice but to enter the race without the formal approval of the "state leaders," but not without hope that they might turn to him, in Schlesinger's words, as "the rescuer of the party" from its followers. At the very least they would reward him in 1972 for splitting their enemy's camp in two in the supreme crisis of their political careers.

Kennedy himself understood this quite well, which explains the remarkable conclusion he appended to the announcement of his candidacy: "At stake is not simply the leadership of our party or even our country—it is our right to moral leadership on this planet." Chagrined when they saw the draft, some of Kennedy's more youthful advisers vainly begged him to delete the passage. It was just the kind of thinking, they complained, that had gotten America into the Vietnam War. Exactly so, and that was why Kennedy included it. It was his message to the party leaders that, if they nominated him for the presidency, he would never neglect those vast global duties and burdens that for thirty years had done so much to keep "the underclass" under; that despite the exigencies of ambition he had not, in fact, changed at all. As Hubert Humphrey said shortly before Kennedy's assassination, "He's a party regular in spite of everything."

That is what was truly singular about Robert Kennedy: he aroused extravagant political hopes while standing opposed to all that was best and most promising in his day. The years from 1964 to 1968 were preeminently democratic years. For the first time in many decades Americans had begun to exercise their liberties, to act for themselves in political affairs, and to demand their rightful voice in their own government. Millions had become fed up with faithless leaders, with capricious government and inexplicable wars. They were growing intolerant of the party "professionals" and the self-serving power of the few. On the other side stood Robert Kennedy, who thought it a crime to "split" a party oligarchy whose power itself is a crime, and a virtue to protect it from a rebellious citizenry. He was a man who regarded grass-roots movements as something for the "professionals" to bring under control, who spent most of his adult life envisioning this republic turned into a hideous Sparta. In Robert Kennedy, Democratic politics had produced the first important national figure in our history who completely embodied the spirit of its old municipal machines—despotism, disguised as party loyalty, and a deep contempt for the larger republic in which they flourished like cancer cells. He was a man so thoroughly estranged from the principles of a democratic republic that the foolish left-wing journalists, who think the Constitution a bankers' plot, saw in Kennedy another Julius Caesar come to rescue the peasantry from republican trammels. That estrangement revealed itself even in Kennedy's best moments, for while he calculated how to serve a corrupt party oligarchy he offered his compassion to its more conspicuous victims, the benevolence of a prince toward his impotent subjects. Had he lived, there is no doubt that he would have restored public confidence in the Democratic syndicate, which for decades has blighted and betrayed every hope it aroused. Such is the man Arthur Schlesinger wants us to revere as the most promising public figure of his time. That millions of Americans do, in fact, cherish Kennedy's memory is one of the more unpromising aspects of our present political condition.

The Hour
of the Founders

Exactly ten years ago this August, the thirty-seventh President of the United States, facing imminent impeachment, resigned his high office and passed out of our lives. "The system worked," the nation exclaimed, heaving a sigh of relief. What had brought that relief was the happy extinction of the prolonged fear that the "system" might not work at all. But what was it that had inspired such fears? When I asked myself that question recently, I found I could scarcely remember. Although I had followed the Watergate crisis with minute attention, it had grown vague and formless in my mind, like a nightmare recollected in sunshine. It was not until I began working my way through back copies of *The New York Times* that I was able to remember clearly why I used to read my morning paper with forebodings for the country's future.

The Watergate crisis had begun in June 1972 as a "third-rate burglary" of the Democratic National Committee headquarters in Washington's Watergate building complex. By late March 1973 the burglary and subsequent efforts to obstruct its investigation had been laid at the door of the White House. By late June Americans were asking themselves whether their President had or had not ordered the payment of "hush money" to silence a Watergate burglar. Investigated by a special Senate committee headed by Sam Ervin of North Carolina, the scandal continued to deepen and ramify during the summer of 1973. By March 1974 the third-rate burglary of 1972 had grown into an unprecedented constitutional crisis.

By then it was clear beyond doubt that President Richard M. Nixon stood at the center of a junto of henchmen without parallel in our history. One of Nixon's attorneys general, John Mitchell, was indicted for obstructing justice in Washington and for impeding a Securities and Exchange Commission investigation in New York. Another, Richard Kleindienst, had criminally misled the Senate Judiciary Committee in the President's interest. The acting director of the Federal Bureau of Investigation, L. Patrick Gray, had burned incriminating White House documents at the behest of a presidential aide. Bob Haldeman, the President's chief of staff, John Ehrlichman, the President's chief domestic adviser, and Charles Colson, the President's special counsel, all had been indicted for obstructing justice in the investigation of the Watergate burglary. John Dean, the President's legal counsel and chief accuser, had already pleaded guilty to the same charge. Dwight Chapin, the President's appointments secretary, faced trial for lying to a grand jury about political sabotage carried out during the 1972 elections. Ehrlichman and two other White House aides were under indictment for conspiring to break into a psychiatrist's office and steal confidential information about one of his former patients, Daniel Ellsberg. By March 1974 some twenty-eight presidential aides or election officials had been indicted for crimes carried out in the President's interest. Never before in American history had a President so signally failed to fulfill his constitutional duty to "take care that the laws be faithfully executed."

It also had been clear for many months that the thirty-seventh President of the United States did not feel bound by his constitutional duties. He insisted that the requirements of national security, as he and he alone saw fit to define it, released him from the most fundamental legal and constitutional constraints. In the name of "national security," the President had created a secret band of private detectives, paid with private funds, to carry out political espionage at the urging of the White House. In the name of "national security," the President had approved the warrantless wiretapping of news reporters. In the name of "national security," he had approved a secret plan for massive, illegal surveillance of American citizens. He had encouraged his aides' efforts to use the Internal Revenue Service to harass political "enemies"—prominent Americans who endangered "national security" by publicly criticizing the President's Vietnam War policies.

The framers of the Constitution had provided one and only one remedy for such lawless abuse of power: impeachment in the House of Representatives and trial in the Senate for "high Crimes and Misdemeanors." There was absolutely no alternative. If Congress had not held President Nixon accountable for lawless conduct of his office, then Congress would have condoned a lawless presidency. If Congress had not struck from the President's hands the despot's cudgel of "national security," then Congress would have condoned a despotic presidency.

Looking through the back issues of *The New York Times*, I recollected in a flood of ten-year-old memories what it was that had filled me with such foreboding. It was the reluctance of Congress to act. I felt anew my fury when members of Congress pretended that nobody really cared about Watergate except the "media" and the "Nixon-haters." The real folks "back home," they said, cared only about inflation and the gasoline shortage. I remembered the exasperating actions of leading Democrats, such as a certain Senate leader who went around telling the country that President Nixon could not be impeached because in America a person was presumed innocent until proven guilty. Surely the senator knew that impeachment was not a verdict of guilt but a formal accusation made in the House leading to trial in the Senate. Why was he muddying the waters, I wondered, if not to protect the President?

It had taken one of the most outrageous episodes in the history of the presidency to compel Congress to make even a pretense of action.

Back on July 16, 1973, a former White House aide named Alexander Butterfield had told the Ervin committee that President Nixon secretly tape-recorded his most intimate political conversations. On two solemn occasions that spring the President had sworn to the American people that he knew nothing of the Watergate cover-up until his counsel John Dean had told him about it on March 21, 1973. From that day forward, Nixon had said, "I began intensive new inquiries into this whole matter." Now we learned that the President had kept evidence secret that would exonerate him completely—if he were telling the truth. Worse yet, he wanted it kept secret. Before Butterfield had revealed the existence of the tapes, the President had grandly announced that "executive privilege will not be invoked as to any testimony [by my aides] concerning possible criminal conduct, in the matters under investigation. I want the public to learn the truth about Watergate. . . ." After the existence of the tapes was revealed, however, the President showed the most ferocious resistance to disclosing the "truth about Watergate." He now claimed that executive privilege—hitherto a somewhat shadowy presidential prerogative—gave a President "absolute power" to withhold any taped conversation he chose, even those urgently needed in the ongoing criminal investigation then being conducted by a special Watergate prosecutor. Nixon even claimed, through his lawyers, that the judicial branch of the federal government was "absolutely without power to reweigh that choice or to make a different resolution of it."

In the U.S. Court of Appeals the special prosecutor, a Harvard Law School professor named Archibald Cox, called the President's claim "intolerable." Millions of Americans found it infuriating. The court found it groundless. On October 12, 1973, it ordered the President to surrender nine taped conversations that Cox had been fighting to obtain for nearly three months.

Determined to evade the court order, the President on October 19 announced that he had devised a "compromise." Instead of handing over the recorded conversations to the court, he would submit only edited summaries. To verify their truthfulness, the President would allow Senator John Stennis of Mississippi to listen to the tapes. As an independent verifier, the elderly senator was distinguished by his devotion to the President's own overblown conception of a "strong" presidency. When Nixon had ordered the secret bombing of Cambodia, he had vouchsafed the fact to Senator Stennis, who thought that concealing the President's secret war from his fellow senators was a higher duty than preserving the Senate's constitutional role in the formation of United States foreign policy.

On Saturday afternoon, October 20, I and millions of other Americans sat by our television sets while the special prosecutor explained why he could not accept "what seems to me to be non-compliance with the court's order." Then the President flashed the dagger sheathed within his "compromise." At 8:31 P.M. television viewers across the country learned that he had fired the special prose-cutor; that Attorney General Elliot Richardson had resigned rather than issue that order to Cox; that the deputy attorney general, William Ruckelshaus, also had refused to do so and had been fired for refusing; that it was a third acting attorney general who had finally issued the order. With trembling voices, television newscasters report-ed that the President had abolished the office of special prosecutor and that the FBI was standing guard over its files. Never before in our his-tory had a President, setting law at defiance, made our government seem so tawdry and gimcrack. "It's like living in a banana republic," a friend of mine remarked.

Now the question before the country was clear. "Whether ours shall continue to be a government of laws and not of men," the ex–special prosecutor said that evening, "is now for the Congress and ultimately the American people to decide."

Within ten days of the "Saturday night massacre," one million let-ters and telegrams rained down on Congress, almost every one of them demanding the President's impeachment. But congressional leaders dragged their feet. The House Judiciary Committee would begin an inquiry into *whether* to begin an inquiry into possible grounds for recommending impeachment to the House. With the obvious intent, it seemed to me, of waiting until the impeachment fervor had abated, the Democratic-controlled committee would con-sider whether to consider making a recommendation about making an accusation.

Republicans hoped to avoid upholding the rule of law by persuad-ing the President to resign. This attempt to supply a lawless remedy for lawless power earned Republicans a memorable rebuke from one of the most venerated members of their party: eighty-one-year-old Senator George Aiken of Vermont. The demand for Nixon's resignation, he said, "suggests that many prominent Americans, who ought to know better, find the task of holding a President accountable as just too difficult. . . . To ask the President now to resign and thus relieve Congress of its clear congressional duty amounts to a declaration of incompetence on the part of Congress."

The system was manifestly not working. But neither was the President's defense. On national television Nixon bitterly assailed the press for its "outrageous, vicious, distorted" reporting, but the popular outrage convinced him, nonetheless, to surrender the nine tapes to the court. Almost at once the White House tapes began their singular career of encompassing the President's ruin. On October 31 the White House disclosed that two of the taped conversations were missing, including one between the President and his campaign manager, John Mitchell, which had taken place the day after Nixon returned from a Florida vacation and three days after the Watergate break-in. Three weeks later the tapes dealt Nixon a more potent blow. There was an eighteen-and-a-half-minute gap, the White House announced, in a taped conversation between the President and Haldeman, which had also taken place the day after he returned from Florida. The White House suggested first that the President's secretary, Rose Mary Woods, had accidentally erased part of the tape while transcribing it. When the loyal Miss Woods could not demonstrate in court how she could have pressed the "erase" button unwittingly for eighteen straight minutes, the White House attributed the gap to "some sinister force." On January 15, 1974, court-appointed experts provided a more humdrum explanation. The gap had been produced by at least five manual erasures. Someone in the White House had deliberately destroyed evidence that might have proved that President Nixon knew of the Watergate cover-up from the start.

At this point the Judiciary Committee was in its third month of considering whether to consider. But by now there was scarcely an American who did not think the President guilty, and on February 6,

1974, the House voted 410 to 4 to authorize the Judiciary Committee to begin investigating possible grounds for impeaching the President of the United States. It had taken ten consecutive months of the most damning revelations of criminal misconduct, a titanic outburst of public indignation, and an unbroken record of presidential deceit, defiance, and evasion in order to compel Congress to take its first real step. That long record of immobility and feigned indifference boded ill for the future.

The White House knew how to exploit congressional reluctance. One tactic involved a highly technical but momentous question: What constituted an impeachable offense? On February 21 the staff of the Judiciary Committee had issued a report. Led by two distinguished attorneys, John Doar, a fifty-two-year-old Wisconsin Independent, and Albert Jenner, a sixty-seven-year-old Chicago Republican, the staff had taken the broad view of impeachment for which Hamilton and Madison had contended in the *Federalist* papers. Despite the constitutional phrase "high Crimes and Misdemeanors," the staff report had argued that an impeachable offense did not have to be a crime. "Some of the most grievous offenses against our Constitutional form of government may not entail violations of the criminal law."

The White House launched a powerful counterattack. At a news conference on February 25, the President contended that only proven criminal misconduct supplied grounds for impeachment. On February 28 the White House drove home his point with a tightly argued legal paper: if a President could be impeached for anything other than a crime of "a very serious nature," it would expose the presidency to "political impeachments."

The argument was plausible. But if Congress accepted it, the Watergate crisis could only end in disaster. Men of great power do not commit crimes. They procure crimes without having to issue incriminating orders. A word to the servile suffices. "Who will free me from this turbulent priest," asked Henry II, and four of his barons bashed in the skull of Thomas á Becket. The ease with which the powerful can arrange "deniability," to use the Watergate catchword, was one reason the criminal standard was so dangerous to liberty. Instead of having to take care that the laws be faithfully executed, a President, under that standard, would only have to take care to insulate himself from the criminal activities of his agents. Moreover, the standard could not reach the most dangerous offenses. There is no crime in the statute books called "attempted tyranny."

Yet the White House campaign to narrow the definition of impeachment met with immediate success. In March one of the members of the House of Representatives said that before voting to impeach Nixon, he would "want to know beyond a reasonable doubt that he was directly involved in the commission of a crime." To impeach the President for the grave abuse of his powers, lawmakers said, would be politically impossible. On the Judiciary Committee itself the senior Republican, Edward Hutchinson of Michigan, disavowed the staff's view of impeachment and adopted the President's. Until the final days of the crisis, the criminal definition of impeachment was to hang over the country's fate like the sword of Damocles.

The criminal standard buttressed the President's larger thesis: In defending himself he was fighting to protect the "presidency" from sinister forces trying to "weaken" it. On March 12 the President's lawyer, James D. St. Clair, sounded this theme when he declared that he did not represent the President "individually" but rather the "office of the Presidency." There was even a National Citizens Committee for Fairness to the Presidency. It was America's global leadership, Nixon insisted, that made a "strong" presidency so essential. Regardless of the opinion of some members of the Judiciary Committee, Nixon told a joint session of Congress, he would do nothing that "impairs the ability of the Presidents of the future to make the great decisions that are so essential to this nation and the world."

I used to listen to statements such as these with deep exasperation. Here was a President daring to tell Congress, in effect, that a lawless presidency was necessary to America's safety, while a congressional attempt to reassert the rule of law undermined the nation's security.

Fortunately for constitutional government, however, Nixon's conception of a strong presidency included one prerogative whose exercise was in itself an impeachable offense. Throughout the month of March the President insisted that the need for "confidentiality" allowed him to withhold forty-two tapes that the Judiciary Committee had asked of him. Nixon was claiming the right to limit the constitutional power of Congress to inquire into his impeachment. This was more than Republicans on the committee could afford to tolerate.

"Ambition must be made to counteract ambition," Madison had written in *The Federalist*. On April 11 the Judiciary Committee voted 33 to 3 to subpoena the forty-two tapes, the first subpoena ever issued to a President by a committee of the House. Ambition, at last, was counteracting ambition. This set the stage for one of the most lurid moments in the entire Watergate crisis.

As the deadline for compliance drew near, tension began mounting in the country. Comply or defy? Which would the President do? Open defiance was plainly impeachable. Frank compliance was presumably ruinous. On Monday, April 29, the President went on television to give the American people his answer. Seated in the Oval Office with the American flag behind him, President Nixon calmly announced that he was going to make over to the Judiciary Committee—and the public—"edited transcripts" of the subpoenaed tapes. These transcripts "will tell it all," said the President; there was nothing more that would need to be known for an impeachment inquiry about his conduct. To sharpen the public impression of presidential candor, the transcripts had been distributed among forty-two thick, loose-leaf binders, which were stacked in two-foot-high piles by the President's desk. As if to warn the public not to trust what the newspapers would say about the transcripts, Nixon accused the media of concocting the Watergate crisis out of "rumor, gossip, innuendo," of creating a "vague, general impression of massive wrongdoing, implicating everybody, gaining credibility by its endless repetition."

The next day's *New York Times* pronounced the President's speech "his most powerful Watergate defense since the scandal broke." By May 1 James Reston, the newspaper's most eminent columnist, thought the President had "probably gained considerable support in the country." For a few days it seemed as though the President had pulled off a coup. Republicans on the Judiciary Committee acted accordingly. On the first of May, sixteen of the seventeen committee Republicans voted against sending the President a note advising him that self-edited transcripts punctured by hundreds upon hundreds of suspicious "inaudibles" and "unintelligibles" were not in compliance with the committee's subpoena. The President, it was said, had succeeded in making impeachment look "partisan" and consequently discreditable.

Not even bowdlerized transcripts, however, could nullify the destructive power of those tapes. They revealed a White House steeped in more sordid conniving than Nixon's worst enemies had imagined. They showed a President advising his aides on how to "stonewall" a grand jury without committing perjury: "You can say, 'I don't remember.' You can say, 'I can't recall. I can't give any answer to that, that I can recall.'" They showed a President urging his counsel to make a "complete report" about Watergate but to "make it very incomplete." They showed a President eager for vengeance against ordinary election opponents. "I want the most comprehensive notes on all those who tried to do us in. . . . They are asking for it and they are going to get it." It showed a President discussing how "national security grounds" might be invoked to justify the Ellsberg burglary should the secret ever come out. "I think we could get by on that," replies Nixon's counsel.

On May 7 Pennsylvania's Hugh Scott, Senate Republican minority leader, pronounced the revelations in the transcript "disgusting, shabby, immoral performances." Joseph Alsop, who had long been friendly toward the President in his column, compared the atmosphere in the Oval Office to the "back room of a second-rate advertising agency in a suburb of hell." A week after Nixon's seeming coup Republicans were once again vainly urging him to resign. On May 9 the House Judiciary Committee staff began presenting to the members its massive accumulation of Watergate material. Since the presentation was made behind closed doors, a suspenseful lull fell over the Watergate battleground.

Over the next two months it was obvious that the Judiciary Committee was growing increasingly impatient with the President, who continued to insist that, even in an impeachment proceeding, the "executive must remain the final arbiter of demands on its confidentiality." When Nixon refused to comply in any way with a second committee subpoena, the members voted 28 to 10 to warn him that "your refusals in and of themselves might constitute a ground for impeachment." The "partisanship" of May 1 had faded by May 30.

Undermining these signs of decisiveness was the continued insistence that only direct presidential involvement in a crime would be regarded as an impeachable offense in the House. Congressmen demanded to see the "smoking gun." They wanted to be shown the "hand in the cookie jar." Alexander Hamilton had called impeachment a "National Inquest." Congress seemed bent on restricting it to the purview of a local courthouse. Nobody spoke of the larger issues. As James Reston noted on May 26, one of the most disturbing aspects of Watergate was the silence of the prominent. Where, Reston asked, were the educators, the business leaders, and the elder statesmen to delineate and define the great constitutional issues at stake? When the White House began denouncing the Judiciary Committee as a "lynch mob," virtually nobody rose to the committee's defense.

On July 7 the Sunday edition of *The New York Times* made doleful reading. "The official investigations seem beset by semitropical torpor," the newspaper reported in its weekly news summary. White House attacks on the committee, said the *Times*, were proving effective in the country. In March 60 percent of those polled by Gallup wanted the President tried in the Senate for his misdeeds. By June the figure had fallen to 50 percent. The movement for impeachment, said the *Times*, was losing its momentum. Nixon, it seemed, had worn out the public capacity for righteous indignation.

Then, on July 19, John Doar, the Democrats' counsel, did what nobody had done before with the enormous, confusing mass of interconnected misdeeds that we labeled "Watergate" for sheer convenience. At a meeting of the Judiciary Committee he compressed the endlessly ramified scandal into a grave and compelling case for impeaching the thirty-seventh President of the United States. He spoke of the President's "enormous crimes." He warned the committee that it dare not look indifferently upon the "terrible deed of subverting the Constitution." He urged the members to consider with favor five broad articles of impeachment, "charges with a grave historic ring," as the *Times* said of them.

In a brief statement Albert Jenner, the Republicans' counsel, strongly endorsed Doar's recommendations. The Founding Fathers, he reminded committee members, had established a free country and a free Constitution. It was now the committee's momentous duty to determine "whether that country and that Constitution are to be preserved."

How I had yearned for those words during the long, arid months of the "smoking gun" and the "hand in the cookie jar." Members of the committee must have felt the same way, too, for Jenner's words were to leave a profound mark on their final deliberations. That I did not know yet, but what I did know was heartening. The grave maxims of liberty, once invoked, instantly took the measure of meanness and effrontery. When the President's press spokesman, Ron Ziegler, denounced the committee's proceedings as a "kangaroo court," a wave of disgust coursed through Congress. The hour of the founders had arrived.

The final deliberations of the House Judiciary Committee began on the evening of July 24, when Chairman Peter Rodino gaveled the committee to order before some 45 million television viewers. The committee made a curious spectacle: thirty-eight strangers strung out on a two-tiered dais, a huge piece of furniture as unfamiliar as the faces of its occupants.

Chairman Rodino made the first opening remarks. His public career had been long, unblemished, and thoroughly undistinguished. Now the representative from Newark, New Jersey, linked hands with the Founding Fathers of our government. "For more than two years, there have been serious allegations, by people of good faith and sound intelligence, that the President, Richard M. Nixon, has committed grave and systematic violations of the Constitution." The framers of our Constitution, said Rodino, had provided an exact measure of a

President's responsibilities. It was by the terms of the President's oath of office, prescribed in the Constitution, that the framers intended to hold Presidents "accountable and lawful."

That was to prove the keynote. That evening and over the following days, as each committee member delivered a statement, it became increasingly clear that the broad maxims of constitutional supremacy had taken command of the impeachment inquiry. "We will by this impeachment proceeding be establishing a standard of conduct for the President of the United States which will for all time be a matter of public record," Caldwell Butler, a conservative Virginia Republican, reminded his conservative constituents. "If we fail to impeach . . . we will have left condoned and unpunished an abuse of power totally without justification."

There were still White House loyalists, of course; men who kept demanding to see a presidential directive ordering a crime and a documented "tie-in" between Nixon and his henchmen. Set against the great principle of constitutional supremacy, however, this common view was now exposed for what it was: reckless trifling with our ancient liberties. Can the United States permit a President "to escape accountability because he may choose to deal behind closed doors," asked James Mann, a South Carolina conservative. "Can anyone argue," asked George Danielson, a California liberal, "that if a President breaches his oath of office, he should not be removed?" In a voice of unforgettable power and richness, Barbara Jordan, a black legislator from Texas, sounded the grand theme of the committee with particular depth of feeling. Once, she said, the Constitution had excluded people of her race, but that evil had been remedied. "My faith in the Constitution is whole, it is complete, it is total and I am not going to sit here and be an idle spectator to the diminution, the subversion, the destruction of the Constitution."

On July 27 the Judiciary Committee voted 27 to 11 (six Republicans joining all twenty-one Democrats) to impeach Richard Nixon on the grounds that he and his agents had "prevented, obstructed, and impeded the administration of justice" in "violation of his constitutional oath faithfully to execute the office of President of the United States and, to the best of his ability, preserve, protect, and defend the Constitution of the United States, and in violation of his constitutional duty to take care that the laws be faithfully executed."

On July 29 the Judiciary Committee voted 28 to 10 to impeach Richard Nixon for "violating the constitutional rights of citizens, impairing the due and proper administration of justice and the conduct of lawful inquiries, or contravening the laws governing agencies of the executive branch. . . ." Thus, the illegal wiretaps, the sinister White House spies, the attempted use of the IRS to punish political opponents, the abuse of the CIA, and the break-in at Ellsberg's psychiatrist's office—misconduct hitherto deemed too "vague" for impeachment—now became part of a President's impeachable failure to abide by his constitutional oath to carry out his constitutional duty.

Lastly, on July 30 the Judiciary Committee, hoping to protect some future impeachment inquiry from a repetition of Nixon's defiance, voted 21 to 17 to impeach him for refusing to comply with the committee's subpoenas. "This concludes the work of the committee," Rodino announced at eleven o'clock that night. Armed with the wisdom of the founders and the authority of America's republican principles, the committee had cut through the smoke screens, the lies, and the pettifogging that had muddled the Watergate crisis for so many months. It had subjected an imperious presidency to the rule of fundamental law. It had demonstrated by resounding majorities that holding a President accountable is neither "liberal" nor "conservative," neither "Democratic" nor "Republican," but something far more basic to the American republic.

For months the forces of evasion had claimed that impeachment would "tear the country apart." But now the country was more united than it had been in years. The impeachment inquiry had sounded the chords of deepest patriotism, and Americans responded, it seemed to me, with quiet pride in their country and themselves. On Capitol Hill congressional leaders reported that Nixon's impeachment would command three hundred votes at a minimum. The Senate began preparing for the President's trial. Then, as countless wits remarked, a funny thing happened on the way to the forum.

Back on July 24, the day the Judiciary Committee began its televised deliberations, the Supreme Court had ordered the President to surrender sixty-four taped conversations subpoenaed by the Watergate prosecutor. At the time, I had regarded the decision chiefly as an auspicious omen for the evening's proceedings. Only Richard Nixon knew that the Court had signed his death warrant. On August 5 the President announced that he was making public three tapes that "may further damage my case." In fact, they destroyed what little was left of it. Recorded six days after the Watergate break-in, they showed the President discussing detailed preparations for the cover-up with his chief of staff, Bob Haldeman. They showed the President and his henchmen discussing how to use the CIA to block the FBI, which was coming dangerously close to the White House. "You call them in," says the President. "Good deal," says his aide. In short, the three tapes proved that the President had told nothing but lies about Watergate for twenty-six months. Every one of Nixon's ten Judiciary Committee defenders now announced that he favored Nixon's impeachment.

The President still had one last evasion: on the evening of August 8 he appeared on television to make his last important announcement. "I no longer have a strong enough political base in Congress," said Nixon, doing his best to imply that the resolution of a great constitutional crisis was mere maneuvering for political advantage. "Therefore, I shall resign the Presidency effective at noon tomorrow." He admitted to no wrongdoing. If he had made mistakes of judgment, "they were made in what I believed at the time to be in the best interests of the nation."

On the morning of August 9 the first President ever to resign from office boarded Air Force One and left town. The "system" had worked. But in the watches of the night, who has not asked himself now and then: "How would it all have turned out had there been no White House tapes?"

The Reagan Revolution
and Its Democratic
Friends

Someday an inquisitive historian will try to explain a very odd and disturbing phenomenon: how it was that from 1981 to 1984 an American President who undermined liberty and laid siege to equality managed to be held in esteem by a normally democratic people. What strange immunity shielded a President who promised to get "government off the backs of the people" while making government more intrusive than ever; who showered favors on the favored while hounding, with unexampled severity, the poor, the disabled, and the powerless; who promised to control government spending while generating the most enormous deficits in American history; who promised steady economic growth sustained by savings while giving us a false recovery fed by a spending spree; who promised to make America "proud again" while vaunting his military triumph over a country a good deal smaller than Long Island?

If that future historian pursues his inquiry free of glib misanthropy, he will discover, I believe, that the chief agency sustaining that President was his putative political opposition, the Democratic Party. He will be able to show, with a richness of detail that I can only suggest, how the Democratic leadership in Congress served as the witting confederate of that President and of the counterrevolt of the privileged that he headed. He will show, too, for the history cuts deep, how this policy of collusion marked the culmination of a twelve-year drive by Democratic leaders to root out democracy from the Democratic Party and regain control of the presidential nomination, with Walter Mondale as their chosen instrument.

When Ronald Reagan announced his "program for economic recovery" on February 18, 1981, he made public for the first time the depth and the extent of the counterrebellion of the favored. It might have been expected that the Democrats in Congress would have felt a surge of hope for the revival of their party. For the President's program and the extravagant military buildup so oddly conjoined to it lay open to the most damaging doubts and the most alarming suspicions, the kinds of doubts and suspicions that a bold opposition can use to mobilize, in the words of historian James MacGregor Burns, "the support of tens of millions of Americans presently antagonized or bored with both parties."

In 1980 surveys had consistently shown that most Americans opposed deep cuts in spending for health, education, and other social programs. Yet the principal element in the President's plan was a call for immense cuts in social spending that would reduce the income of the poorest Americans by up to 25 percent. Reagan assured Americans that he was mainly eliminating "waste and fraud," but they had heard that from conservatives before. The program seemed destined not to withstand congressional scrutiny.

The second important element in the President's program was a proposal to reduce federal revenues by $750 billion in the space of five years by means of the most massive—and the most inequitable—tax cut in American history. The economic justification of this "rich people's tax bonanza," as *The New Republic* called it, convinced almost nobody. Even *Fortune* tore most of the tax plan to shreds.

In the name of "recovery"—Franklin Roosevelt's old gambit—a President and his supporters were calling for the most brutal class legislation ever proposed in America: "gross economic favors for the privileged, the powerful, and the well-to-do, and blatant deprivations for the distressed and the needy," in the somber judgment of the

Southern historian C. Vann Woodward. (After its enactment by Congress, the Reagan program would *take* nearly $400 away from households with incomes of $10,000 a year or less and *give* $8,000 to households with incomes of $80,000 a year or more.)

There was a third element in Reagan's legislative program, and it shed sinister light on his plan to enrich the rich with the pittance of the poor. The President's ambitious proposals to increase defense spending made a mockery of "Reaganomics." An administration that blamed so many of the nation's ills on excessive government spending and inflationary government deficits might have been expected to exercise the keenest thrift in examining the Pentagon's requests. Instead, the White House discovered countless pretexts for the largest peacetime military buildup in America's history. It exaggerated the Soviet military buildup by confounding rubles and dollars. It lied about Soviet nuclear "superiority" by counting weapons instead of warheads. It subjected the country, in the words of Theodore Draper, to "a rolling barrage of unprecedented panic-mongering along with the most grandiose plans for actually fighting a nuclear war," plans that General David C. Jones, former chairman of the Joint Chiefs of Staff, characterized as throwing money down "a bottomless pit."

Did a President who proposed to create a giant global war machine in order to make America "proud" and "impressive" really care a fig about excessive government spending, excessive government deficits, or excessive government interference in our lives? The question, once raised, answered itself. Concerted Democratic opposition to the President's military extravagance would lay bare something dark and menacing at the core of the Reagan White House: a President seemingly bent on fighting "proud" little wars abroad to distract popular attention from gross privilege at home.

In the spring of 1981, Arthur Schlesinger, Jr,. warned in *The Wall Street Journal* of the "explosive possibilities when an economic establishment wages a class war against the poor." The political possibilities were indeed explosive. To awaken the electorate no rabble-rousing demagoguery would be needed. Calm and thorough examination by

Congress would be sufficient to expose a "program" for America that entitled the rich to devour the fisc and the military to devour the needy. Steven Weisman of *The New York Times* had just such a Democratic challenge in mind when he wrote in April 1981 that "the political risks Mr. Reagan faces are probably even more severe than the economic risks."

For Democratic leaders, however, the Reagan Revolution was seen as no opportunity at all. To awaken the vast plurality of apathetic and alienated citizens was the very last thing they wished to accomplish as they prepared the ground for Walter Mondale's nomination in 1984. After all, it was the angered and the disregarded who had risen up in the wake of 1968 and wrested control of the party from the bosses. The problem Reagan's program posed for the erstwhile party of the people was not how to oppose its folly and favoritism but how to shepherd it through Congress without awakening anybody.

The spring of 1981 was to prove a magical season in American history, for it was a time of strange transformations. The Speaker of the House, Massachusetts Democrat Thomas P. O'Neill, Jr., had been known during the 1970s as the "crafty Old Pro"; overnight he would become a sniveling, sentimental "liberal" of unsurpassed ineptitude. Reagan's brutal class legislation would be turned by glozing Democrats into a benign question of fairness, then into "fairness," and finally into the "fairness issue." Reagan, too, would be transformed—from a President who had won an election over a weak opponent with a mere 50.7 percent of the vote into the political equivalent of the great god Juggernaut. Such is the wizardry of collusive politics.

The February 28, 1981, *Congressional Quarterly* reported that House Democrats harbored "profound doubts that the Reagan plan would work." Six weeks later all their doubts were resolved in Reagan's favor. On April 9 the House Budget Committee proposed to cut domestic spending by $18 billion and taxes by $38 billion in a striking demonstration of "the new fiscal conservatism of the party," as *Congressional Quarterly* put it. That estimable journal could scarcely conceal its surprise. Democratic leaders had "accepted to the letter a majority of [Reagan's] proposals. . . . They had acceded to his request for an overall cutback in government spending." Nothing attested more vividly to the Democrats' collapse than the Budget Committee's call for a $219.6 billion defense authorization for fiscal 1982. This was only $6.7 billion less than the President's request, and it was $73 billion more than Congress had given the Pentagon in 1980. With no questions asked, the Democratic leadership had given a ringing endorsement to Reagan's most questionable proposal.

That same day, the new chairman of the House Ways and Means Committee, an Illinois Democrat and Cook County ward boss named Dan Rostenkowski, reduced still further "the political risks Mr. Reagan faces." The chairman, like the President, called for a sharp reduction in the taxes paid by wealthy individuals and large corporations. This Democratic "counterproposal," in the words of *Congressional Quarterly,* was "carefully designed to embrace the basic principles of the Reagan plan."

After embracing Reagan's "basic principles," Democratic leaders took prompt measures to justify their party's newfound belief that the rich were not rich enough and the poor were not poor enough. It was the irresistible power of a uniquely popular President that had brought about their transformation. To demonstrate the irresistible power of a President whose approval rating was actually *lower* than that of any other new President in recent times, the Democrats employed crude but effective methods.

As soon as the party leaders had announced their budget, every major administration figure began telephoning House Democrats to urge them to vote for the President's budget. The House Democratic leadership was too busy to lobby for its proposal. On April 10, Speaker O'Neill, Chairman Rostenkowski, and assorted other members of the loyal opposition embarked for the Antipodes. While Reagan invaded the ranks of House Democrats, and while liberal congressmen privately fumed, the Speaker and the chairman idled away the Easter season in Australia and New Zealand, celebrating the glories of the ANZUS pact.

The President was scheduled to make a speech to Congress on

April 28—he actually believed his program might be in trouble. O'Neill returned to Washington on April 27 and instantly ensured the success of the President's upcoming speech. He told reporters that the Democrats had no chance to defeat Reagan's budget. The Speaker's prophecy fulfilled itself. "We were behind maybe twenty votes when [O'Neill] started his press conference, and then he announced we were behind by fifty votes," a liberal Democratic congressman said at the time. "At that moment, we fell behind by fifty votes."

On May 3 Martin Tolchin of *The New York Times* noted that "the leadership failed to initiate the kind of lobbying campaign for which the Democrats are famous. No effort was made to exploit redistricting, for example, through enlisting the aid of 27 Democratic governors and 28 Democratic legislatures"—powers that can redistrict unruly members of Congress into oblivion. "We have no game plan," a legislative whip complained. "We're just going to get killed. It's pathetic." O'Neill went out of his way to assure pro-Reagan Democrats that they could vote for the President's budget with impunity. "He made it easy for everyone to get off the hook," said Representative Benjamin Rosenthal of New York. "He gave them a free ride. He should have called them in and said, 'If you're not with us on this, don't come into my office and ask for anything.' " Close votes, however, do not a juggernaut make.

On May 7 the Democratic leadership's campaign to achieve its own crushing defeat was crowned with a brilliant success. In the Democratic House, Reagan and his budget swept all before them by a vote of 253 to 176. The victory was a "milestone" for Reagan, as *Congressional Quarterly* observed. The Democrats were said to be in complete "disarray," but the conservative columnist William Safire came much closer to the truth: " 'Tip' O'Neill," he wrote in *The New York Times* on May 11, "has become Ronald Reagan's secret weapon." Democrats, noted Safire, were "profoundly embarrassed at the amateurish leadership of the man who used to be called the Old Pro." This once guileful and effective leader had become "a boon to Republicans seeking to portray the Democratic party as a listless hulk." Did anyone wonder at this sea change?

The "milestone" victory of May 7 gave Reagan only preliminary approval for his overall budget. Ahead lay the task of specifying the $36.6 billion worth of domestic spending cuts called for in the May 7 resolution. For this the most delicate management was required. The chairman of the House Education and Labor Committee, Carl Perkins of Kentucky, pleaded with the Democratic leadership to give House committees a chance to show the voters what Reagan's budget really entailed. His plea fell on deaf ears. Awakening the electorate's spirit of fairness was the last thing the party of fairness wanted. Instead, O'Neill and his lieutenants proposed and promoted a novel parliamentary device designed to conceal from the American people what their amiable President was up to.

Known as "budget reconciliation," its aim, as explained by *Congressional Quarterly*, "is to deter challenges to individual spending cuts by packaging them in omnibus legislation." Each House committee was instructed to authorize a portion of the total spending figure contained in the May 7 budget. Because these instructions involved huge spending cuts, the committees could fulfill them only by making changes in existing laws. Since the reconciliation deadline was June 12, the committees had to make these changes with minimum publicity and maximum haste, thus effectively shielding the President, gagging his critics, and making it difficult for the public to realize, as *Congressional Quarterly* pointed out, "precisely what the spending cuts [Reagan] is seeking mean in terms of slashing social programs."

Democratic "disarray" miraculously vanished as committees scrambled to meet the June 12 deadline, slashing appropriations and altering laws with little or no debate. Carl Perkins cried out in anguish over the Democrats' self-gagging. "In all my years in Congress," he said, "I have never witnessed an action more ill advised, more insensitive, or more threatening to the rightful operation of the legislative process than these so-called reconciliation instructions."

Reagan's tax proposals posed the most formidable problem for the Democratic policy of nonopposition. Had the House leaders wished it, the Ways and Means Committee could have subpoenaed business leaders, bankers, brokers, and economists to testify against some portion or other of what former Secretary of Defense James Schlesinger has called "the most irresponsible fiscal action of modern times." Rostenkowski, however, hit upon a wonderful device for quashing opposition. Proclaiming himself a tough, practical politician, he decided that the Democrats should pursue a tough, practical "win" policy. Instead of subjecting "the most irresponsible fiscal action of modern times" to the scrutiny it surely merited, Rostenkowski resolved to match it dollar for dollar, bonanza for bonanza, inequity for inequity, until he had produced its Democratic replica. "The Democrats had their chance for glory by exposing the economic fallacies and risks in the President's plan," a *New York Times* editorial lamented. "Instead, they pursued him over the same cliff." The Reagan Revolution was moving safely into place, but not because of any Reagan juggernaut.

"If it's a normal year we win," Walter Mondale's campaign manager predicted in 1981. By "win" he meant not the presidency in 1984 but the party's presidential nomination. The difference is crucial. In the end, the Democrats' policy of connivance and collusion with the Reagan Administration came down to this: making sure that in 1984 all would be conveniently "normal," that the populace would be politically as lukewarm and complacent as the former vice president himself. Only then would Democrats cast their primary votes for the Democratic leader's chosen instrument for regaining what they had so stunningly lost after 1968—control of the party's presidential nomination.

That loss was a momentous event in America's history, a "quiet revolution," as a Russell Sage Foundation study put it. Swept by fierce demands for a more "open" party, Democratic leaders, disgraced and discredited, were forced to scuttle long-established arrangements that gave a few score party magnates the authority to name a majority of delegates to the Democratic National Convention. That authority was essential to the security of party leaders, for it ensured that no enemy of the party oligarchy, however popular, would ever carry the banner of the party of the people. Preventing such enemies from gaining the presidency had long been the first principle of American party politics. Given a choice between winning the White House with a foe of the party organization or losing in a landslide with a trusted confederate, party leaders invariably chose the latter. It was only after 1968, the year Democratic magnates abused this privilege by ramming Hubert Humphrey, Mondale's patron, down the throats of the rank and file, that demands for a more democratic nominating procedure were made. As a result of the disastrous Chicago convention and Humphrey's Election Day defeat, rank-and-file voters in Democratic primaries and participants in open caucuses were, in 1972, given a decisive voice in choosing the party's presidential candidate.

This was revolutionary indeed. For the first time in 140 years, the Democratic gateway to the White House was not guarded by a few party potentates. For the first time since the days of Andrew Jackson, a man favored by the plain people stood a fair chance of becoming President of the United States. For the first time in American history, the banner of the party of the people was in the people's hands. This was considerably more than a loss of the party potentates' power. It was a dire menace to the entire political establishment. Suppose the voters swept into the mighty office of the President a genuine tribune of the people, a Jacksonian enemy of privilege and private power? Whether he triumphed or failed in office, American politics would never again be the same.

At the 1972 national convention Democratic spokesmen proclaimed the party "purged" and "purified" of its former corruption. They cited the nomination of Senator George McGovern, chairman of the party's reform commission, as proof of that democratic rebirth. The party oligarchs, however, had not become giddy converts to popular rule. They were resolved to wrest from the people the power that had been placed in their hands.

Actually, the discredited Democratic leaders had already begun gingerly altering party rules to favor their own candidates and hobble outsiders. Democrats in Congress amended the federal election laws toward the same end, first by legalizing (in 1971) and then by enhancing (in 1979) the political role of trade unions, whose manpower, wealth, and organization were essential to recapturing the presidential nomination. This legislation also legalized political action committees and encouraged the influx of corporate money into politics. The new financial flood is a direct result of the efforts of the Democratic bosses to restore the party hierarchy and curtail party democracy: money flowing into politics in quest of special privilege invariably aids the few with the power to dispense it. The drive to strengthen the party at the expense of the people involved not only political machinations but seemingly ideological matters as well. Thinly disguised as "the (Henry) Jackson wing of the Democratic Party," the party barons waged, in the words of William Safire, "a guerrilla campaign to discredit dovish policies" and so drive from the party's ranks precisely those younger, more liberal members most prone to challenge the leaders' efforts to regain their power.

Most important, the discredited party leaders set about to discredit democracy. By crushing the hopes of the voters, by sabotaging their chosen candidates, they hoped to teach the American people that the democratic reform of the Democratic Party had all been a terrible mistake. "Politics is not the nursery," Hannah Arendt reminded us, and the ambitions of oligarchs are as pitiless as the passions of princes.

As soon as McGovern was nominated, party leaders began systematically slurring and belittling him, while the trade union chieftains refused to endorse him on the pretense that this mild Mr. Pliant was a being wild and dangerous. A congressional investigation of the Watergate scandal was put off for several months to deprive McGovern's candidacy of its benefits. As an indiscreet Chicago ward heeler predicted in the fall of 1972, McGovern "is gonna lose because we're gonna make sure he's gonna lose." The party jettisoned McGovern and concentrated on keeping its grip on Congress. So deftly did party leaders "cut the top of the ticket" that while Richard Nixon won in a "landslide," the Democrats gained two Senate seats.

Having wrecked McGovern's candidacy, Democratic leaders promptly drew a lesson from the wreckage. Here was proof, they said, that the popular nomination of Presidents could not "pick a winner." (That the party barons had not picked a winner in 1968 was not discussed.) Here was evidence that primaries and caucuses produce losing "factional" candidates appealing chiefly to cause-oriented activists and upper-middle-class suburbanites who are cut off from the party's "broad constituency" of blue-collar toilers. This brazen nonsense was not only hawked by a credulous press, which always depends on politicians to explain politics; it was endlessly elaborated by a special branch of political science devoted to proving that the rule of party barons is democratic and the rule of the people "elitist."

Party leaders could not prevent the nomination of Jimmy Carter, but they trashed him—and the ideas he represented—on a grand scale after his election. By the time Democratic congressional leaders had finished demolishing virtually every major proposal submitted to Congress by that weak, unwanted outsider—"During the Carter years congressional opposition to Presidential proposals was almost routine," noted *Congressional Quarterly*—the electorate had been given another political lesson. According to Democratic leaders, the press, and the Democratic Party branch of political science, the demolition of President Carter proved that the popular nomination of Presidents made America "ungovernable." As David Broder of *The Washington Post* put it, popular nomination deprives a President of "the alliances that [make] it possible for him to organize the coalitions and support necessary to govern." As James Reston of *The New York Times* put it: "The people have acquired the power to nominate presidents and even to determine foreign policy they know very little about. The Governments they elect have in the process lost the authority needed to govern." As James Sundquist of the Brookings Institution put it: "Jimmy Carter, the outsider, would not have been the nominee in 1976 of an organized political party; he is what can happen when the choice of party leader is taken entirely out of the hands of the party elite and turned over to the people." As Beth Fallon of the New York *Daily News* put it: "We overdosed on democracy."

Popular rule had become an orphan. The Democrats' destruction of a Democratic President had regained for the party oligarchy the "right" to control presidential nominations. Party leaders could now openly alter party rules to further strengthen the party organization, to further favor the party's candidate, and to reduce still further the chances of an outsider gaining the nomination. Trade union chiefs would be free to place their vast resources behind the oligarchy's chosen aspirant. These were great assets indeed (as Senator Gary Hart has learned), but they would not suffice if 1984 were not "normal," if aroused citizens stormed back into party caucuses and angry primary voters looked to new men and women for leadership. Ronald Reagan, in short, could not be opposed; the more extreme his program, the more dangerous it would be to oppose him. Such a collusive policy would make the 1984 Democratic nomination something considerably less than the high road to the White House, but Democratic leaders had no choice. They could not nominate their tame creature and also offer opposition to the counterrevolt of the privileged. What electorate that cared deeply about anything could possibly care about Walter Mondale? For the Democrats, power and popularity had parted company.

Seated in his office in the Rayburn Building one afternoon in February, Representative Richard Ottinger, the New York Democrat from Westchester County, took in all of Capitol Hill with a sweep of his hand. "This enormous institution has just been sitting here for three years," he said. "On key votes in the House you hardly see the leadership." Ottinger said that O'Neill didn't count votes or know how people voted. He ruled "by abdication." The congressman, who is fifty-five, smiled wearily. "You can't lead by rewarding your enemies and punishing your friends. The guys who get rewarded are the real troublemakers—the conservative element."

Since the enactment of Reagan's program, Ottinger said, the Democratic leadership had done little to convince Americans of the severe impact of the President's budget cuts. "We have a real potential for bringing these issues before the country, but Congress does not bring them before the country dramatically. Two million kids are not getting measles and polio shots due to budget cuts. That's something you can dramatize." If the leadership supported bills that remedied the damage, "they would fly" through Congress, Ottinger said. "You put through a bill restoring student loans and grants and it would sail through the House. We could be sending up a barrage like that." Instead, he said, "the leadership has not done anything to help Democrats embarrass Republicans. When five hundred people froze to death in the winter cold snap, Congress provided weatherization funds for low-income people. The only thing the leadership did was water down the bill." O'Neill, Ottinger believes, "has given the ball game to Reagan." After eight terms in Congress, Ottinger is retiring.

Virtually everything congressional Democrats have done since the Reagan Revolution of the spring of 1981 reflects their policy of non-opposition. In July 1982 the House Ways and Means Committee was considering its own version of a Republican bill to raise $98 billion in taxes. Senate Republicans had proposed the tax increase to reduce the deficits, but, said *The New Republic,* "they are also scared that the Democrats will make fairness the main issue of the 1982 congressional campaign." What particularly frightened Republicans was a scandalous provision of the 1981 Economic Recovery Tax Act that enabled some of the largest and most profitable companies to pay virtually no taxes in the first quarter of 1982. The Republican bill had considerable merit, but House Democrats were expected to better it. What more, it seemed, could the party of "fairness" want than this golden opportunity to close more corporate loopholes than the Republicans had proposed to do? *The New Republic* looked forward to "a bidding war in the name of fairness." At the last minute, however, the Democratic leadership snuffed out the chance. At the urging of O'Neill's lieutenants, the Ways and Means Committee decided to offer *no* tax bill at all. In a "surprise move" committee members resolved to go into a House–Senate conference with empty hands. Having stifled opposition the previous year with a show of trying to "win," House leaders now stifled it by refusing to compete. By that brazen refusal, as *The Washington Post* noted, the Democrats had abandoned "any attempt to exploit what ought to be their best issue of 1982, the apparent 'unfairness' of the Reagan economic program." Moreover, said the *Post,* "the Democrats' posture of inaction accelerates their departure from the center of debate over national issues." Both results served the

Democratic leadership's interests. With the recession deepening and Reagan's approval rating below 50 percent, "debate" was more dangerous than ever and fairness yet more explosive.

To make sure the President's popularity slipped no lower, the Democrats turned a blind eye to malfeasance and official corruption. The Reagan Administration consigned statutes to limbo, debauched public agencies, and arbitrarily suspended federal regulations; Democratic "oversight" committees contented themselves with *pro forma* complaints and one-day hearings. "Even critics supportive of deregulation," wrote Martin Tolchin in his book *Dismantling America*, "warned that the Reagan Administration's efforts may backfire politically if the public eventually sees the program for what it is: totally geared to business." Such fears proved groundless; the Democrats were making every effort to prevent the public from seeing anything Reagan did "for what it is." In the September/October 1981 issue of *Regulation,* an ardent supporter of the President voiced fears that his "efforts to reform regulation" would provoke "a new wave of anti-business populist sentiment." Those fears, too, were groundless, for "populist sentiment" was precisely what the Democrats were laboring to quash.

The corrupting of the Environmental Protection Agency was the exception that proved the rule. The Democrats dropped their promising investigation of a scandal that reached into the White House almost as soon as the President gave them a sacrificial lamb named Rita Lavelle, whom Congress cited for contempt, 413 to 0, and, coward-like, destroyed. At the suggestion of the White House, Congress left further inquiry to the attorney general, although the attorney general's office was itself suspected of complicity in the scandal, having allowed subpoenaed EPA documents to be shredded while in the agency's care and having gone to outrageous legalistic lengths to block *any* congressional investigation of the EPA. When the Justice Department issued a report absolving the White House of any blame in the scandal, House Democrats let it pass, although the department had reached this conclusion by the simple expedient of not asking anyone in the White House about contacts with the EPA.

Time and again, Democratic leaders rescued Reagan from his own follies. The moment the President's "peacekeeping" force in Lebanon became perilously entangled in a civil war, O'Neill rushed to the White House with an offer of "bipartisan" support for a policy that had become insupportable, thereby transforming an unpopular presidential policy into a great national commitment. After the death of 241 Marines cried out against the President's wanton folly, the Democrats rushed once more to Reagan's rescue. The Democratic majority on the House Armed Services Committee issued a scathing denunciation, not of Reagan but of the Marine Corps, which it condemned for trying "to be more diplomatic than the diplomats." Coming from a committee supposedly dominated by supporters of the Pentagon, this was a perfect two-step of collusive politics. First the churlish Democrats made a scapegoat of the Marines. Then Reagan graciously stepped forward to forgive them in their hour of grief. This is what is meant by the President's "uncanny" ability to walk away unscathed from disaster, to quote a recent *New York Times Magazine* article that asked: "Will the magic prevail?"

Perhaps it has been in the rescue of the MX missile that the Democrats have revealed most starkly the strength of their determination to protect Reagan from the judgment of the people. The President's MX problem began on October 2, 1981, when he announced that the missile, which was supposed to be an invulnerable replacement for the Minuteman missile, would be placed in the Minuteman's vulnerable silos. Friends of the arms buildup could scarcely conceal their chagrin. "Opponents of the decision will have a field day pointing to the contradictions and inconsistencies" in the President's plan, wrote Leslie Gelb of *The New York Times*. "Mr. Reagan is now in a box. He continues to assert that there is a real and present danger to the ICBM's, yet his new programs do nothing to alleviate that danger."

The President seemed entangled in his own deceits beyond all hope of extrication. If a "window of vulnerability" to a Soviet attack really existed, then there was no earthly reason to deploy a new missile in old silos. If the "window of vulnerability" did not exist, then the President was an arrant liar and all the cries about Soviet nuclear "superiority" were merely another shabby pretext for another American quest for nuclear ascendancy.

Putting an MX missile in a vulnerable silo did more than cast doubt on the missile itself. It cast the gravest doubt on the administration's panic-mongering, and so cast doubt, too, on the military buildup and on the domestic budget cuts that were paying for the buildup. Reagan's vulnerable missile was the loose thread that might unravel a whole fabric. The party in opposition acted accordingly. Democratic leaders in the House were conspicuously numbered among the 112 Democrats who voted "development" funds for the MX on November 18, 1981.

By March 1982 the great body of the American people, arisen as if from the dead, made thunderously clear their opposition to Reagan's renewal of the arms race. Millions of Americans from all walks of life were marching, preaching, and organizing in favor of a "nuclear freeze." Opponents of the arms buildup were elated. "This movement is too powerful," wrote George Kennan in *The New York Review of Books*, "too elementary, too deeply embedded in the natural human instinct for self-preservation, to be brushed aside" by the government. But Kennan had seriously underestimated the power of the Democratic Party. Under intense public pressure to voice the common sense of the American people, and with no apparent reason to do otherwise, Democratic leaders stood firmly beside the President. They managed to keep the MX alive with further development funds while waiting for Reagan to persuade the voters that the MX was an arms-control bargaining chip.

But here was one message the Great Communicator could not get across. As *Congressional Quarterly* put it, the President labored "under the political burden of an apparently widespread suspicion that he may be unwilling to seek a diplomatically feasible arms control agreement with the Soviet Union." What too many Americans suspected was that Reagan used arms negotiations "as a mask to cover new deployments," in the words of Averell Harriman. The only way to res-

cue the MX and secure that loose thread was to take the missile out of
Reagan's tainted hands. The White House and Democratic leaders,
therefore, agreed to place the fate of the MX at the disposal of a
"bipartisan commission" of "defense experts"—former secretaries of
defense and the like. "Appointed to solve a political problem disguised
as a technical one," in Senator Daniel Patrick Moynihan's apt description, the experts were expected to urge the deployment of the MX and
so enable Congress to bow to the expertise of the few while mocking
the wisdom of the many. Congressional emissaries dispatched by
O'Neill kept the expert advisers closely advised on just what pretexts
and shams "moderate" Democrats thought they could get away with
when it came time to vote.

Thus emboldened, the experts neatly uprooted the main obstacle to
the MX, namely its pretext. To the argument that the MX failed to
close the "window of vulnerability," the commission replied that no
such window existed after all. To the argument that the nonexistence
of the threat made the MX unnecessary, the commission replied that
the MX possessed "political symbolism." Abandoning a weapon on
which $5 billion had already been spent, said the experts, "does not
communicate to the Soviets that we have the will to deterrence. Quite
the contrary."

President Reagan humbly vowed to heed the experts' advice to
deploy 100 MX missiles in vulnerable silos. A more palpable confidence trick could scarcely be imagined. On July 20, 1983, the House
of Representatives voted at long last to produce the MX. O'Neill's
emissaries to the commission had procured the necessary margin of
victory. In order to save the arms buildup and the credibility of the
Reagan Revolution, Congress had made what Senator Moynihan calls
"probably the most fatal mistake in our history." Ten months later, the
calamitous weapon still hung by a thread devised by Democrats.

Such is the "magic" of Ronald Reagan: pull back the curtain and
you find the Democrats moving all the levers. With the nomination of
Walter Mondale all but safely secured, that conniving will probably
end, at least in its present extreme form. The real question is how long

the self-serving of the powerful few will prevail over the just sentiments of the American people.

The citizenry, for the moment, is quiet; the listless chatter of a "normal year" clogs the political realm. Democratic leaders have not only regained control of the presidential nomination; they have done so with impunity. In state after state, the raw exercise of party and trade union power—still regarded as scandalous as recently as 1976—incited no furious backlash. To a great extent Gary Hart's vote measures what is left of the insurgent spirit after the Democrats' trashing of democracy.

But the signs of a "normal year" are deceiving. Democratic leaders recaptured the presidential nomination only by betraying the popular cause more thoroughly and more outrageously than ever before. A great deal of power, in consequence, lies loose and explosive in the streets. Some of it has gravitated toward Jesse Jackson; others will come forward, too, to seek their share of it. The millions of Americans whom the Democrats sacrificed to the Moloch of the Democratic machine will call one day for a reckoning, and they will either be heard or be crushed. In their hour of triumph to be savored this month in San Francisco, the Democratic oligarchs may gain the most disastrous victory in their long, checkered history.

Liberty Under Siege

T he Reagan Administration came to power firm in its resolve to liberate corporate enterprise from government regulation, to free the economy from the incubus of the welfare system, and to reduce the government's role in the life of the country. It never said that these far-reaching goals could not be achieved by the ordinary methods of democratic persuasion and the established procedures of congressional lawmaking. The administration never contended in public, and perhaps not even in private, that the exercise of liberty gave its enemies an unfair advantage, or that the traditional sources of public information kept the electorate too well informed, or that popular government in general was a hindrance to its aims. Only once did any ranking member of the administration publicly admit that the "Reagan Revolution" included—indeed necessitated—a program of drastic political change. This occurred in late 1981, when David Stockman, the White House budget director, said that the new administration's success "boils down to a political question, not of budget policy, or economic policy, but whether we can change the habits of the political system." After Stockman's outburst of perilous candor, the curtain came abruptly down. It has not risen again on the political intentions of the Reagan Administration, for the habits the administration has striven to change have been, by and large, the habits of freedom.

"What we are witnessing," said the American Civil Liberties Union in November 1981, "is a systematic assault on the concept of government accountability and deterrence of illegal government conduct."

Alas, "we," the people, were not witnessing a thing, and have not been witnessing a thing for almost five years. In politics, what is seen is what is talked about, and the "systematic assault" has not been talked about—not by the administration, not by Congress, not by the opposition party, not by the press.

Nothing is more important, however, than what public men prefer *not* to discuss. For nearly five years now the Reagan Administration has been engaged in an unflagging campaign to exalt the power of the presidency and to undermine the power of the law, the courts, the Congress, and the people. That is what our politicians have not discussed with us, and what lies hidden behind the screen of political rhetoric and the smile of a popular President.

What follows is a chronicle of that campaign, told simply by the means of recounting the deeds that comprise it. This chronicle is not the secret history of an alleged secret plot. Most of the events have been duly reported in the daily newspapers. The chronicle is simply a matter of paying attention to public deeds that have been largely ignored or made light of outside the confines of congressional hearings. The chronicle is remorseless because the campaign is remorseless, and it is shocking because the campaign is shocking. When a concerted assault on the habits of freedom ceases to shock us, there will be no further need to assault them, for they will have been uprooted once and for all.

I. 1 9 8 1

The newly elected Reagan Administration promised to "hit the ground running" and it does—like a company of commandos fanning out in a hostile country that just happens to be its own.

What it besieges at once is the old, unsung bulwark against overweening presidential power: the open, garrulous, decentralized executive branch itself. Bureaucrats practiced in rudeness and evasion are put in place of helpful press officers. Telephone requests for information are suddenly given short shrift. Press briefings become so grudging, notes one veteran reporter, that a State Department spokesman says "no comment" and "I can't say" more than thirty times in the course of one forty-five-minute session. Pentagon officials are warned that the polygraph test—which accuses the guilty and the innocent alike—will be used to identify those who "leak" classified information to the press.

In late April the President declares a moratorium on the preparation and dissemination of government publications, and the huge, habitual outflow of official reports, bulletins, and pamphlets is quickly brought under control. The administration's stated goal is the "elimination of wasteful spending on government periodicals." Dropped in the moratorium is a government booklet on bedbugs, which Edwin Meese III, counselor to the President, brandishes for reporters with a hearty chuckle, as well as Central Intelligence Agency reports on "U.S.–Soviet Military Dollar-Cost Comparisons," which disappear unbrandished. Meanwhile, the White House musters every specious argument it can find to justify the biggest arms buildup in history. Something considerably more important than thrift lies behind this moratorium.

Whatever can be hidden the administration hides. "The White House is structuring key advisory panels," reports *The New York Times* in July, "so that they do not fall under the public meeting rules of the Advisory Committee Act." Under the direction of the White House the agencies of the executive branch evade the public accountability provisions of the Administrative Procedure Act. New regulations are issued as "guidelines" so that the public need not be notified. Existing regulations are altered by internal memorandums.

On June 6 *The Washington Post* runs a story under the headline "Administration Attempting to Stem Information Flow to Trickle." This is only the beginning, however, for the President is determined to redress the balance between, in his words, "the media's right to know and the government's right to confidentiality."

This latter "right" is a figment of the official imagination: in America the governed have rights, not the government. But one reason the administration is determined to uphold it becomes clear on

July 8, when a legal analysis of the gravest importance begins circulating in the House Committee on Energy and Commerce. Prepared for the committee by the American Law Division of the Library of Congress, it describes a far-reaching seizure of power carried out by the President on February 17, when he signed Executive Order 12291. That order, says the report, "sets up a framework for [presidential] management of the rule-making process that is undeniably unprecedented in scope and substance," one that "does not appear to draw its authority from any specific congressional enactment." It "provides no explicit safeguards to protect the integrity of the process or the interest of the public against secret, undisclosed, and unreviewable contacts . . . the Order, on its face, deprives participants of essential elements of fair treatment required by due process." Most important, the order threatens to make "cost-benefit principles," imposed and manipulated by the White House, supreme over the statutory mission given by Congress to the executive agencies of the government—in violation of the doctrine of separation of powers. The warning falls into the public arena as noiselessly as a feather.

The administration's most ambitious efforts to censor and suppress lie in the future, but even in mid-1981 it begins to choke off various sources of objectionable opinions.

Cuba is one such source. On July 10 the secretary of the treasury notifies thirty thousand subscribers of the Communist Party weekly *Granma*, which was impounded by Treasury agents in May, that "it will be necessary for you to obtain a specific import license from this office" in order to "import" Cuban periodicals in the future. The maximum penalty for subscribing without a license is ten years in prison and a $10,000 fine under the Trading With the Enemy Act of 1917; this act has never before been applied to periodicals, owing to the long-standing national "habit" of distinguishing printed matter from merchandise. By treating Cuban periodicals like Cuban cigars the administration claims control over a hitherto free activity—until it is stopped by a First Amendment lawsuit brought by the ACLU. This is not the last time, however, that the administration will try to use commercial regulations to suppress non-commercial activity.

Political refugees from friendly tyrannies are another source of objectionable opinions: they know too much about the regimes they fled. After seeing its February white paper on El Salvador, which presented "evidence" that the Salvadoran guerrillas were being heavily armed by Cuba and the Soviet Union, exposed as a pack of lies, the administration begins to deport Salvadorans en masse. In August the tortured corpse of one deportee turns up by a Salvadoran roadside.

To the administration, however, the most dangerous source of objectionable opinions is its own documents. On October 15 the White House submits legislation to Congress that would keep these documents out of the public's hands by "reforming" the Freedom of Information Act into oblivion. Politically, this is the administration's first truly perilous moment, for the act is no ordinary piece of legislation. It has behind it the entire weight and authority of the democratic tradition in America: the sovereignty of the people, the accountability of government, the old republican distrust of official secrecy and bureaucratic caprice. "The Freedom of Information Act is a blessing for those who value a check on Government snooping," William Safire, the conservative columnist for the *Times*, wrote in May when the White House, testing the waters, first indicated its hostility to the law. "Individuals can now find out what the FBI file says about them. Even better, individuals can force the Federal bureaucracy to disgorge rulings made without public scrutiny, and documents more politically embarrassing than secret."

Yet one "improvement" in the administration's Freedom of Information Improvement Act of 1981 would put out of the public's reach precisely those documents that give the governed their "check on government snooping." Another "improvement" would make it difficult to discover how the agencies of the executive branch are enforcing the health, safety, and environmental laws that the White House is bent on subjecting to cost-benefit analysis. A third improvement would make it dauntingly expensive for the act to be used by those who inform the public—scholars, writers, newspaper reporters, public-interest organizations—the very users that, under the unimproved act, pay little or nothing.

"Freedom of information is not cost-free. It is not an absolute good," Jonathan C. Rose, an assistant attorney general in charge of abridging the freedom of information, would say a year later. But the administration's cant about thrift rings false. "If the Freedom of Information Act is rescinded or crippled," says Kurt Vonnegut at a symposium on the FOIA, "the American people will have been treated as spies for a foreign enemy." An administration which prates about getting the government off the backs of the people has revealed its real ambition: to get the people off the back of the government.

On October 14 that ambition could scarcely be plainer, as the President invokes "executive privilege" to withhold from Congress thirty-one documents, many of them unsigned memorandums, prepared by junior officials in the Department of Interior. In the most sweeping assertion of executive secrecy in our history, the President declares that all information that is "part of the executive branch deliberative process" lies beyond the oversight of Congress. President Reagan, who invents his own constitution as he goes along, has expanded the confidentiality of the Oval Office to cloak the entire executive branch. In the space of twenty-four hours he has proposed to cut off the government not only from the people but from their elected representatives as well.

By October 15 Congress has every reason to ask—and loudly—on what meat doth this our Caesar feed. But Congress asks nothing. The opposition leaders are silent; "liberals" are as mute as "conservatives." The elected representatives of the people apparently prefer to deal privately with the White House rather than awaken the sleeping electorate. Quietly, Congress will preserve the Freedom of Information Act, and quietly it will challenge "executive privilege"; but the administration's assault on accountability it will not make known to the people.*

---

*The administration's FOIA bill never came to a vote. Other legislation incorporating many of the administration's proposals passed in the Senate but stalled in the House. In late 1981 the House Committee on Energy and Commerce cited Interior Secretary James Watt for contempt; the documents at issue were subsequently turned over.

On December 4 the President signs an executive order authorizing the CIA for the first time to collect "foreign intelligence" in the United States by surreptitiously questioning the citizenry. It also authorizes the CIA to employ the entire local police force of the country in this undercover questioning, which can take place in a barroom, a barbershop, or the aisle of a K-Mart—as if the U.S. government needed to monitor the unguarded conversations of private citizens to keep itself informed about foreign countries. Getting the government off the backs of the people is the very last thing this administration wants.

II. 1982

On January 7, at the annual meeting of the American Association for the Advancement of Science, in Washington, the administration opens an assault on the old, slack habits of scientific freedom. The "hemorrhage of the country's technology" overseas is so severe, says Admiral Bobby Inman, deputy director of central intelligence, that the government must step in to "control" the public dissemination of private research. If the nation's scientists do not submit voluntarily to such censorship, Admiral Inman warns the assembled audience, a "tidal wave" of public outrage "could well cause the federal government to overreact" against the liberties of science. Anger and indignation sweep the meeting. What the government wants "is clearly more compatible with a dictatorship than a democracy," says Peter Denning, a computer scientist from Purdue University, in a sharp rebuttal to Inman. The administration mistakes the very source of the "hemorrhage," reports the March issue of the *Bulletin of the Atomic Scientists. Commerce* is what transfers technology abroad, according to a 1979 study made by the Pentagon itself, and commerce is what the 1979 Export Administration Act was designed to control.

To all arguments against censorship, however, the administration is deaf. As Lawrence J. Brady, an assistant secretary of commerce, tells the press in March, the government is determined to combat "a strong belief in the academic community that they have an inherent right . . . to conduct research . . . free of government review and oversight." Accordingly, the Commerce Department informs universities across the country that any faculty member who lectures on advanced technology to even a single foreign student may be considered a "U.S. exporter" under the 1979 law and fined $100,000 for exporting technical data without a government license. At a scientific conference in August, one hundred optical engineers are forced to withdraw their research papers at the last minute when government agents warn them that they may violate export control regulations. Once again, an administration which regards the lawful regulation of commerce as unwarranted oppression uses commercial regulations to suppress noncommercial activity. Yet about the transfer of technology overseas the administration evidently cares little. Due to its slack enforcement of the *real* export control laws, California's Silicon Valley, in the words of an FBI official, is "as leaky as a sieve."

The pretexts are shifted around like the three shells in the shell game—efficiency, thrift, and national security—but the aim is always the same: to give the White House the power to withhold from the American people whatever the President thinks it best for the people not to know.

On February 4 the President shows Congress the final draft of an executive order on "classified information." The order betrays an appetite for secrecy so wanton that the White House declines to send a representative to defend it at a congressional hearing. Under the order a bureaucracy which already withholds from the public about 16 million documents each year is instructed to resolve all doubts about secrecy in favor of public ignorance. The order creates a new category of technical data ("vulnerabilities or capabilities of systems, installations, projects, or plans relating to the national security") so vast and so vague that it enables the government for the first time to classify private technical research—thereby giving the White House another way to clamp down on the campus and the laboratory and the Freedom of Information Act. The new category has the additional advantage of greatly thickening the wall of secrecy surrounding the administration's wasteful, fraud-ridden military buildup.

The new secrecy order treats history itself as a menace to national security. The systematic declassification of documents, begun by President Eisenhower in 1953, is brought to a virtual halt, and its unprecedented antithesis—reclassification—is introduced in its place. Under the new order government officials can reach into the public domain and re-conceal what is already public. After high-ranking officials use classified information to present their version of events, the government can now deny that information to others. "We are encouraging the distortion of history," says Anna K. Nelson, representing the American Historical Association at the March 10 hearings. "The knowledge that documents and records are equally available to all has kept many a participant an honest observer. This provision has no place in a representative democracy."

The one-day hearing makes no public stir. But the White House is still anxious to preserve its "conservative" reputation. At a meeting of the National Newspaper Association on March 14, Ed Meese blames the draft order on "overzealous bureaucrats"; but the President signs it just the same. On April 1, armed with their new authority to suppress private research, Pentagon officials telephone the technical journal *Spectrum* and order an editor to start shredding a manuscript about high-tech Army weapons systems "immediately."

The White House in 1982 is steadily consolidating its new legislative powers. Under Executive Order 12291, which elevates cost-benefit principles over acts of Congress, a new mode of lawmaking is being set up before our unseeing eyes. Under this new system Congress continues to enact legislation after years of study and deliberation. And it continues to delegate to the appropriate agency the authority to issue regulations carrying out the aims of each law. But after that a few dozen clerks in the White House budget office virtually dictate the promulgation of any new regulations, thereby nullifying acts of Congress that the President considers too costly. "The result is a return, to some extent, to autocratic government," says

Kenneth Culp Davis, one of the country's leading experts on administrative law, writing in the April issue of the *Tulane Law Review*.

And what is the purpose of inserting autocracy into the American republic? To "reduce the burdens of existing and future regulations," says the White House, but that is all it dares say in public. Like the arms buildup, like domestic snooping, this "good," too, thrives best out of sight of the electorate. Under the direction of the budget office the Nuclear Regulatory Commission in June suspends some of its most important safety regulations without the knowledge of the millions of people who live near nuclear power plants. Under the control of the White House the Environmental Protection Agency turns into a massive conspiracy against the environmental protection laws. The *Times*, reporting on the 1983 congressional testimony of John E. Daniel, the second-ranking official at the EPA, notes that the budget office "tried to dictate regulations to the agency, threatened reprisals, urged that cost factors be built into health rules when the law prohibited them and showed proposed rules changes to officials of the industries being regulated before the changes were available to the public." With the White House acting as influence-peddler—exactly what the American Law Division's report on Executive Order 12291 had warned of a year earlier—a field report on dioxin contamination is altered to delete a sentence reading: "Dow's discharge represents the major source, if not the only source, of TCDD contamination" in Saginaw Bay, Michigan. EPA field officials are ordered not to submit a new report until Dow "endorsed" it.

These are public benefactions so desperately in need of public inattention that when a congressional subcommittee subpoenas EPA documents on October 21, the President is compelled once again to invoke his personal constitution. On November 30 he declares that "the Constitutional doctrine of separation of powers" obliges him to withhold from Congress the documentary evidence of the agency's efforts to give America "cost-effective" toxic waste dumps. The "dissemination of such documents outside the Executive Branch," says the President, "would impair my solemn responsibility to enforce the law."

Under White House control the Department of Labor nullifies the occupational safety laws by cutting down on inspections, reducing fines, weakening the old rules, and delaying the enactment of needed new ones. The department also quietly undermines a law ensuring fair employment opportunities for Vietnam veterans by suspending key regulations without public notice or comment. According to the department, it is "unnecessary and contrary to the public interest" to let the American people know how their President treats the veterans of a war he is trying to glorify.

In June the Department of Health and Human Services proposes that all changes in rules affecting the aged, the poor, the young, and the disabled henceforth be promulgated without public notice or comment. A cost-benefit analysis has persuaded the department that the "delay" caused by public participation in the rule-making process "outweigh[s] the benefits of receiving public comment." Alas for democracy, it cannot make the poor run on time.

A few weeks before making its secrecy proposal the department had direct experience of the utter incompatibility of democracy and cost-benefit analysis. In May it tried unsuccessfully to save nearly $1 billion by gutting a program that provides preventive medical checkups to 2 million poor children. When this came to public notice, the shysters of "cost-effectiveness" had a hard time explaining why an ounce of prevention was no longer worth a pound of cure, this being the well-known result of a cost-benefit analysis made by humanity at large and not readily rescinded except in the dark. What an enemy of the "good" is common humanity!

As long as a free people can bring the executive to court, however, presidential power is under constraint, for the courts do not yet recognize the new legislative system. In July Federal District Judge Harold Greene stops the Department of Labor from nullifying two laws it considers too costly to enforce. "It is not for the Secretary of Labor or his subordinates to make that judgment," wrote Judge Greene. "Under our constitutional system, policy decisions are not made by Government administrators; they are made by the Congress." What an enemy of the "good" is the old Constitution!

To free arbitrary power from the constraints of the courts, the administration tries to cut off the courts from the people. To prevent the citizenry from enforcing the civil-rights laws themselves, the administration will try in 1983 (in vain) to amend those provisions that allow people to sue the government in order to compel it to enforce those laws. To make it financially difficult for the public-spirited to uphold the law against lawless bureaucracy the administration will also try in 1983, again in vain, to curtail government payment of fees to lawyers who vindicate the law. To weaken the "habit" of judicial review the administration rails at the federal courts for what Attorney General William French Smith calls "constitutionally dubious and unwise intrusions into the legislative domain"—the domain which the White House itself has lawlessly invaded. To put the old, the young, the poor, and the disabled beyond the protection of the courts the Department of Health and Human Services announces in June that in the future the internal rules it issues to administer its programs will not create any rights or benefits that are "enforceable" in court.*

To deprive the poor of their legal rights, the White House asks Congress in November to abolish the Legal Services Corporation, which provides the poor with counsel to help them protect their rights in court. When Congress refuses the White House installs its own agents at the corporation. In late November they unfurl their handiwork: pettifogging rules (later dropped) that make it almost impossible for Legal Services lawyers to sue on behalf of large groups of people, the single most efficient weapon in vindicating the legal rights of the poor. And what is the "cost-effectiveness" of compelling the victims of official justice to sue for their rights one at a time? The inestimable "benefit" of liberating lawless power from the constraints of the law.

*Although a final regulation was never published, this proposal, as well as the one stipulating that the department's rules be promulgated in secret, remains on the agenda.

I I I . 1 9 8 3

On January 24 the budget office proposes a change in its Circular
A-122—"Cost Principles for Nonprofit Organizations." What is proposed are new accounting rules for the thousands of private organizations that receive federal grants to carry out government functions in
lieu of an extended bureaucracy. The new rules say, in effect, that all
such organizations—from the Girl Scouts and the Izaak Walton
League to the Association for Retarded Citizens—must forfeit federal
funds if they speak out on public affairs.

The new rules "would inhibit the free flow of information between
these parties and all levels of government," says an angry Chamber of
Commerce. "Operated in tandem, the scope and inherent vagueness
of the terms 'political advocacy' and 'unallowable costs' can easily
become a giant pincers for the stifling of the free and unfettered exercise of First Amendment rights," says the National Association of
Manufacturers, which finds itself puzzled at the spectacle of the White
House discouraging "citizen involvement in the political process."
Representatives of both organizations testify on March 1 before the
one forum left in Washington for a republican opposition to arbitrary
power: the House Government Operations Committee, under the
chairmanship of Jack Brooks of Texas.

Frank Horton of New York, the senior Republican on the committee, cannot hide his anger or his shame. "We are talking about what a
citizen can do with his own money on time not paid for by the
Government. . . . [The revision] says that if he receives any money
through an award based on cost, he cannot express an opinion on
public matters and still be compensated. Mr. Chairman, this is posi-
tively outrageous. I cannot believe that this could possibly be the
intent of the Administration, and yet the language is painfully clear."

Two weeks after issuing its proposed revision of A-122 (which will
be only slightly modified before being adopted in April 1984), the
President signs an executive order banning "any organization that seeks
to influence . . . the determination of public policy" from participating

in the federal government's lucrative on-the-job charity drives. A month later the White House calls for the elimination of postal subsidies for the blind, libraries, schools, and other nonprofit organizations.

Why does the White House wish to silence so many thousands of public-spirited people who have firsthand knowledge of the effects of its policies? The question answers itself: so that the American people cannot judge for themselves the costs and benefits of those policies, and so cannot hold the administration accountable. That is why the administration stops funding the publication of the *Survey of Income and Program Participation,* which assesses the effects of its welfare policies; stops publishing the *Annual Survey of Child Nutrition* and the *Annual Housing Survey;* stops publishing several bulletins on occupational health hazards; stops issuing warnings about newly discovered toxics; withholds health care data from local officials; and eliminates or reduces "at least 50 major statistical programs," the Government Operations Committee reports, on such matters as nursing homes, medical care expenditures, monthly department store sales, and labor turnover.

According to administration spokesmen, the "free market" will attend to these things, so the government need not inform the electorate about them. But how can the American people judge the merits of the "free market" if they are kept in ignorance of its effects? This question, too, answers itself. The market is not for the American people to judge. Although it is the highest good of all, the market, too, apparently thrives best in darkness.

On a radio program devoted to "Defunding Anti-Family Organizations," Michael Horowitz, general counsel of the budget office and mastermind of the A-122 revision, describes the kind of Americans the White House favors: "Americans who live in real-world communities, have real-world jobs, real-world concerns, who are not political in character."

Under Justice Department guidelines issued on March 7, Americans who are "political in character" are put within easy reach of police surveillance. In addition to permitting FBI agents to infiltrate political organizations in the cause of "domestic security," the new guidelines allow the bureau to collect "publicly available information" on any

American it chooses to monitor for any reason whatever. Thanks to an administration which pretends to oppose official oppression, any citizen who emerges from "real-world" obscurity now falls within the purview of, and possibly into the files of, the federal police power.

On March 11 the White House attempts to do for national security affairs what A-122 was meant to do for domestic affairs: stop up the mouths of those who know too much. Under the President's National Security Decision Directive 84, all government employees with access to "sensitive compartmentalized information" must sign contracts which subject them to an extraordinary system of official censorship. If they wish to publish a book, an article, or even submit a letter to the editor containing "any information" related to "intelligence"—a category vast enough to take in most of the domain of national security—they must first show it to the government for review, and, if need be, alteration, not only while in office but for the rest of their lives.*

The White House does not give a clear-cut justification for this system of lifetime censorship, possibly because there is none. The administration's statement accompanying the directive describes it as both a harmless effort to give government policy "a greater consistency" and an urgent effort to prevent the unauthorized disclosure of important state secrets. The press briefing at the Justice Department borders on the theater of the absurd.

"How many employees are you talking about here?" a reporter asks an official.

"SCI access is given out only to a handful of employees."

"Hundreds, thousands?"

"It would probably be classified."

"Can you provide one or two examples of concrete damage to national security" from unauthorized disclosures?

No, he cannot: "When we officially confirm information that has been disclosed in this manner, it compounds the damage."

The truth comes out later and the truth is devastating. The "hand-

---

*On February 17, 1984, the President orders the censorship provisions of NSDD-84 "held in abeyance," but does not revoke them.

ful" is 128,000 officials. And, according to the State Department, the total number of damaging "leaks" conveyed through the writings of government officials during the preceding five years is *none*, not one.

"Well, I just can't believe it," says Lucas A. Powe, Jr., a professor of law at the University of Texas, in testimony before a Government Operations subcommittee. "It is as if in coming up with the proposal the Administration weighed censorship in the balance as a positive good instead of a presumptively unconstitutional evil."

That their highest officials might be the enemies of their freedom Americans find hard to believe, but such is the case. On a pretext so false its falsity cries out to heaven, the White House is determined to censor the writings of the only class of citizens who can effectively challenge a President in affairs of state—all those retired State and Defense Department officials whose character and patriotism cannot be impugned and whose judgments command attention even when they run counter to a President's. The administration is apparently bent on turning the White House into the unopposable voice of Authority.

On February 24 a prizewinning Canadian film about the horrors of nuclear war is labeled "political propaganda" by the Justice Department and placed under the restrictions of the Foreign Agents Registration Act of 1938. The name of every organization and individual to whom the film is distributed must be filed with the government. On March 3 the State Department denies a visa to Salvador Allende's widow, who had been invited to address church groups in San Francisco. It is "prejudicial to United States interests," says the department, to let a few Americans hear, perhaps, that the present Chilean regime is a tyranny.

On April 1 the Department of Energy introduces a new kind of official secret. According to the department's proposed regulations, which were later modified, a vast mass of published books, articles, and reports must henceforth be concealed from the public if they could possibly contribute to "nuclear terrorism." Any library that lets such "unclassified controlled nuclear information" fall into unauthorized hands could be fined up to $100,000 for failing to help the government achieve what Stanford University, in a stinging rejoinder, calls "the futile and repugnant object of making known and unclassified information secret."*

On May 25 the President fires three members of the six-person Civil Rights Commission—something no other President has ever done—for daring to monitor the administration's non-enforcement of the civil-rights laws. At a single stroke the commission's statutory independence is destroyed, but the White House has little patience for contrary voices. Americans have a right to speak out about their "concerns," says the President at a press conference in mid-June, "but let us always remember, with that privilege goes a responsibility to be right."

On September 12 the White House takes another step toward centralizing control of government information. The budget office proposes that all government agencies must consider that "information is not a free good but a resource of substantial economic value and should be treated as such." In light of this they must submit to the White House clear proof that any information they make public passes the supreme test of "cost-benefit analysis."** Half in shock, half in anguish, the American Library Association asks how such an analysis can properly be made. "What is the dollar benefit of an informed citizenry?"

"You can't let your people know" what the government is doing, the President explains at an October 19 press conference, "without letting the wrong people know—those who are in opposition to what you're doing." (On October 20 the Senate votes 56 to 34 against lifetime censorship for government officials.) Reporters are so inured to the President's artless press conference remarks that nobody asks him why the people's right to know chiefly benefits "the wrong people."

---

*The final regulations, passed in April 1985, allow the DOE to restrict access to such information only if it is contained in material acquired by a library after that date.

**Although formal guidelines were never issued, this has become the administration's de facto policy.

The meaning of the President's remarks becomes clear on October 25, when U.S. forces invade the island of Grenada and the American press is barred from the scene at gunpoint, forced to huddle on a nearby island, and compelled to transmit to the public only official lies and evasions. This wanton act of government censorship reveals "a certain mind-set" among the nation's leaders, *Time* angrily observes: "the notion that events can be shaped by their presentation, that truth should be a controlled substance." Indeed so, but this flaunting of censorship reveals something more than a "mind-set": it reveals a determination to habituate a free people to official news and to regarding a free press as the national enemy. "It seems as though the reporters are always against us. They're always seeking to report something that's going to screw things up," says Secretary of State George Shultz, "pandering," writes Safire on December 18, "to the most dangerous I-Am-the-State instincts of his boss."

And who is "us," Secretary Shultz is asked. "Our side militarily—in other words, all of America."

IV. January – October 1984

In early January the administration makes its first crude attempt to revive seditious libel—the ancient crime of speaking ill of the government. On January 3 Justice Department officials obtain a court order barring a publisher from printing a legal opinion of a Colorado judge because the department thinks it is "slanderous" to three of its lawyers. Three weeks later the sear of notoriety forces the U.S. Court of Appeals in Denver to recollect what country it is in, but America has had its first inkling of a future in which the executive may punish with prior restraint the sin of slandering the state.

In January, too, the administration experiments with new ways to deter government officials from disclosing classified information to the public. "Leaks are consensual crimes," says Acting Assistant Attorney General Richard Willard. Willard shows Senate aides the draft of unprecedented legislation that would authorize the federal government to punish with crushing financial penalties any person with access to classified information—more than 4 million people— who divulges the most trivial fact concealed within the bloated empire of national security."*

The administration takes a parallel step against leaks in late January, when two Air Force investigators approach Professor Jeffrey Richelson of American University an hour before he is to deliver a technical paper on arms control verification to an academic audience in Los Angeles. They warn Richelson that if he delivers his paper he could be prosecuted under the 1917 Espionage Act.** On February 3 *The Washington Post* reports that FBI agents have warned two former National Security Agency officials that their research into the downing of the Korean Air Lines jet "technically violated" the Espionage Act.

The word "technically" betrays the administration's intention. It seeks to turn a law aimed at the transfer of vital secrets to a foreign power with the intent to harm the country into an instrument for prosecuting those who transfer information to the public with the intent to help the country. The great advantage of this law over other methods of stopping leaks, notes a confidential White House memorandum circulated in 1982, is that it "could also be used to prosecute a journalist who knowingly receives and publishes classified documents or information."

Behind the President's "leakomania," as Safire calls it, lies the force of a very practical necessity. Ordinary means of concealment can no longer hide the scandalous truth about the administration's trillion-dollar military buildup; it is a colossal squandering of the public wealth. The established secrecy rules are good enough to silence time-

---

*The White House never formally proposed this legislation, in large part because the details of Willard's draft were reported in the press, generating widespread public opposition.

**Richelson delivered his paper anyway. He later provided the Justice Department with evidence that it was based on published information, and a decision was made not to prosecute.

servers, but they cannot prevent men of honor from supplying Congress, the press, and the public with the sordid evidence of wanton waste—the evidence that "the vast majority of money we put into major weapons systems is pure waste and inefficiency," according to Senator Charles E. Grassley, a conservative Iowa Republican; the evidence that "we are not buying airplanes, we are buying the contractors' costs," according to A. Ernest Fitzgerald, the Air Force official who gave "whistle-blowing" a good name; the evidence that the entire weapons buildup "had nothing to do with a strategy, nothing to do with a program of what we needed for defense," according to Richard A. Stubbing, who served in the budget office as deputy chief of national security during the first years of the buildup.

To help it conceal this hideous engine of waste from the American people, Congress has quietly handed the Department of Defense extensive new secrecy powers. Slipped into the voluminous folds of the Omnibus Defense Authorization Act of 1984 is a provision that gives the Pentagon statutory authority "to withhold from public disclosure any technical data with military or space application" that could not be released to a foreigner without obtaining an export license. After all, why should Americans have a right to know any more than foreigners? We are a thousand times more dangerous than foreigners. This *congressional* assault on accountable government gives the executive the authority to conceal the entire domain of national defense from the American people. But the Pentagon waits until after the election to exercise its new powers.

Secrecy rules are one thing; enforcing them is another. Hence the importance the administration places on expanding the Espionage Act.

On October 1 the administration takes the next step toward the act's expansion when it arrests a civilian Navy official for selling three classified satellite photographs of a Soviet aircraft carrier under construction to a venerable British military magazine. There is no question of disclosing information damaging to our national security. The Defense Department releases satellite photographs whenever it suits the administration's purposes. Nor is there anything surreptitious about the sale: the arrested official, Samuel Loring Morison, is an editor of *Jane's Fighting Ships*, and the photographs were duly published in August. The only question is whether the administration can find a judge willing to rule that the Espionage Act is in fact an official secrets act under which no one has been convicted in sixty-seven years.

V. November 1984 – November 1985

The President's great popular victory in November does not reconcile the administration to the habits of freedom and popular government. It merely gives the President and his faction greater power to besiege and subvert them.

On November 20 the Defense Department exercises its new statutory power to conceal itself from the country. It issues a directive stating that every Pentagon official must henceforth withhold from the public all "technical data," including any pertaining to "contractor performance evaluation"—fraud—and "results of test and evaluation of . . . military hardware"—waste—if such data "are likely to be disseminated outside the Department of Defense." In other words, if the American people want to know about something, then, for that very reason, it must be kept from their knowledge. That is the plain English of the regulations. The maximum penalty for enlightening the country is ten years' imprisonment and a $100,000 fine for violating the export control laws, now distorted beyond recognition.

The great administration engine for squandering the public wealth, the machine which generates crushing budget deficits, which in turn serve as a permanent force for reducing "social spending," has at last become what it so desperately needs to be: a single, all-embracing secret of state. Wanton waste, under heavy concealment, will enforce needless sacrifice, and the sovereignty of a free people will be crushed under a fabricated necessity. Social programs will be abolished, public benefits reduced, social services left to decay; and a blinded electorate will no more understand why their country has grown so impoverished than a savage can understand why the sun rolls around in the heavens.

Also in the aftermath of the election the administration reveals what the President means by "the responsibility to be right." It will try to make falsehood a federal crime. A writer named Antoni Gronowicz has published a book about Pope John Paul II, *God's Broker,* containing extensive interviews with the pontiff which the Vatican says are fictitious. This is gross falsehood—the pope says so—and this the White House is determined to punish. An administration which thinks it is oppressive to prevent corporations from poisoning the air thinks it is the government's duty to prevent an author from misleading a few readers. The Justice Department seeks a grand jury investigation in Philadelphia, hoping to have Gronowicz indicted, not precisely for publishing a book containing falsehoods but for violating the mail fraud statutes.*

In late November the administration finds a still more potent way to curtail the freedom of the press in America. The CIA files a complaint with the Federal Communications Commission against the American Broadcasting Company that could result in the loss of its broadcast licenses for airing a false charge, later retracted, against the agency. Since the CIA's unprecedented suit has the backing of the White House, the FCC proves obliging. Even though it eventually rules against the CIA, the FCC declares that any agency of the government henceforth has the right to file such a complaint against a broadcaster (under the Fairness Doctrine) if it feels it has been unfairly abused on the airwaves. Thus has the FCC reinvented seditious libel. By bureaucratic fiat, it is now an offense punishable by the threat of extinction for any broadcaster to treat the executive branch unfairly— in the judgment of the executive branch.

As long as Americans still cherish a free press, however, the administration cannot successfully subjugate the news media. Accordingly,

---

A grand jury was convened, and ordered Gronowicz to turn over his notes. He refused, and has asked the Supreme Court to overturn lower court rulings ordering that he do so.

the administration renews its efforts to turn the people against their own newspapers. Another flaunted drama of censorship provides the instrument. On December 17 the Defense Department calls in the press to announce that the scheduled January 23 flight of the space shuttle *Discovery* will be treated as a military secret of the gravest kind. The public learns that Secretary of Defense Caspar Weinberger has personally asked the Associated Press, NBC News, and *Aviation Week & Space Technology* to suppress their stories about the shuttle mission in the interests of "national security"—and that the three organizations have dutifully complied. The public learns, too, that even "speculation" about the purpose of the flight is forbidden and will be punished by a full-out investigation of the offender—a truly extraordinary threat.

This sudden, officious announcement stuns the Washington press corps. There is simply no warrant for such elaborate secrecy. The military purpose of the shuttle flight has been publicly available information for months. To kill a news story merely because the government orders it would set a "dangerous precedent," warns John Chancellor on the *NBC Nightly News*. True enough, but the administration evidently wants something more than that servile precedent. Its insolent warning against "speculation" is a goad to defiance, "an enticement for people to go after what the mission was about and then to publish what they found out," as former Defense Secretary James R. Schlesinger tells the press.

Taking up the gauntlet, *The Washington Post* refuses to keep secret what is not a secret and publishes a story about the shuttle flight based on information from available sources. Secretary Weinberger denounces the paper for daring to "violate requests" from the Pentagon. Disobedience to a government decree, he says, "can only give aid and comfort to the enemy." This is more than mere calumny; it is the precise wording of the constitutional definition of treason, and it suggests a motive for the shuttle affair. What the administration has done is stage a little morality play before the eyes of the country, a corrupting drama in which the servility of the press appears in the bright garb of patriotism and the freedom of the press in the black hues of treason.

Some weeks later the administration stages a second act of the vicious play when the *Times* publishes a secondhand story by Leslie Gelb against the wishes of the State Department. The department's Bureau of Politico-Military Affairs orders Gelb ostracized and ostentatiously denounces him for "willingly, willfully, and knowingly" publishing information "harmful and damaging to the country." That the information has been previously published is irrelevant, the department explains. "The Secretary of Defense and Secretary of State and National Security Adviser were against printing it," and this alone makes it treasonable conduct in the new tyrannized republic. As Floyd Abrams, the famed constitutional lawyer, observes, the administration is "attacking the legitimacy of the press, not its performance."

Under the administration's powerful assault the press grows timid. The Morison case passes through various preliminary stages but the public hears almost nothing about it. Tyranny is not "news." That is the new rule of American journalism. The truth is, the press is too frightened to write about what frightens it. It cowers in dread of being called "too powerful." For the myth of media power, which the media never contested in their salad days, is now being used by the enemies of liberty to incite the people against a free press.

On January 4, without the slightest public notice, the White House issues an executive order that concentrates still greater legislative power in the hands of its budget office. Under Executive Order 12498 the White House gives itself the formal power not only to impose cost-benefit analysis but to review, control, approve, or suppress any agency activity "that may influence, anticipate, or could lead to the commencement of rule-making proceedings at a later date." Regardless of the laws they are supposed to implement, the executive agencies of government can now do virtually nothing the White House disapproves of. For the first time in American history a President has the formal power to turn acts of Congress into mere husks for secret White House legislation. Under the new executive order the President also has the unprecedented power to bar any executive agency from even studying anything the White House prefers to leave unstudied. No official information that might allow the

American people to question the wisdom of a President may be collected without that President's permission—which will be given or withheld in secret. Under this new dispensation the old, decentralized executive branch stands on the verge of extinction. The traditional bulwark against presidential despotism has been reduced to silence and servility.

On March 12 a federal judge in Baltimore, deciding a motion in the Morison case, rules that the Espionage Act applies to unauthorized disclosures of classified information to the press. According to Judge Joseph H. Young, "the danger to the United States is just as great when this information is released to the press as when it is released to an agent of a foreign government." For decades it was plain to Congress and the courts that the vital secrets of 1917 bear little resemblance to the half-billion "classified" documents concealed by the modern security establishment. For decades it was evident to everybody that informing the American people is different from informing a foreign government, that the wish to enlighten the country is different from the intent to harm it. But this administration believes that an enlightened citizenry is a menace to the state. Thanks to Judge Young's ruling, patriotic officials may no longer menace the great engine of Pentagon waste. Morison himself faces up to forty years in prison for putting three harmless photographs into a well-known magazine.

Imagine a faction that would throw honorable men into prison so that it could impoverish the public treasury with impunity and bend a sovereign people to its will, not just this year and the next, but long after it has fallen from power. Imagine a venerable republic, the hope of the world, where the habits of freedom are besieged, where self-government is assailed, where the vigilant are blinded, the well-informed gagged, the press hounded, the courts weakened, the government exalted, the electorate degraded, the Constitution mocked, and laws reduced to a sham so that, in the fullness of time, corporate enterprise may regain the paltry commercial freedom to endanger the well-being of the populace. Imagine a base-hearted political establishment, "liberal" as well as "conservative," Democratic as well as Republican, watching with silent, protective approval this lunatic assault on popular government. Imagine a soft-spoken demagogue, faithful to nothing except his own faction, being given a free hand to turn Americans into the enemies of their own ancient liberties. Imagine this and it becomes apparent at last how a once-great republic can be despoiled in broad daylight before the unseeing eyes of its friends.

All the
Congressmen's Men

On November 9, 1984, Arthur Ochs Sulzberger, publisher of *The New York Times*, inadvertently shed fresh light on one of the all-too-settled questions of American life: Who decides what is news in America—that is, who tells us what we know about our country's ongoing political life? The enlightening occasion was a speech that Sulzberger delivered at Yale University, warning of new dangers to liberty in America. Silently and relentlessly, the Reagan Administration was expanding official secrecy, intimidating the press, and constricting public access to public information. "The disdain toward the press displayed in the Grenada action was part of a frightening information policy by the administration," said Sulzberger. What made that policy even more insidious, he added, was that it had "gone largely overlooked by the general public"—including the readers of *The New York Times*, which had covered the near-weekly installments of the "frightening" policy without giving any inkling that the installments added up to a policy and that it was frightening indeed.

Now the eminent publisher had spoken; surely his newspaper would speak out, too. What could possibly stand in the way? Is the American press not powerful and autonomous, famously accountable to no one? Is it not, as we so often hear, a "shadow government," a "second adversarial government," a "newsocracy" that exercises, in the words of former publisher Walter H. Annenberg, "at least as much

power in determining the course of the republic as the executive, legislative, and judicial branches set forth in the Constitution? Virtually
every media study says so; the entire political spectrum says so. Our
press is "imperial," says William Rusher, publisher of the *National
Review*, a voice of the right. It exercises "perhaps the greatest power
there [is] in politics: the power to define reality," says Mark
Hertsgaard, a voice of the left. The leading media moguls are
America's "powers that be," says David Halberstam, a voice of the center. And one of his five ruling "powers" is none other than Arthur
Ochs Sulzberger. Who can possibly doubt his power over the news?
He is a leading member of Hertsgaard's "class of super-rich and powerful businessmen who ultimately controlled the U.S. news media," a
class whose members "have virtually unlimited power and can suggest,
select, and veto stories whenever they choose," says Herbert Gans, a
sociologist of the news. Nor is Sulzberger a mere absentee capitalist.
On the contrary, notes Rusher, he is one of the relatively few media
chieftains who "still exercise a major editorial influence" as "an owner
in the 'hands-on' tradition." Since "subordinates learn by habit to conform to owners' ideas," says Ben Bagdikian, former ombudsman of
The Washington Post, and even "overreact" to them, according to
Gans—what diversity of opinion in America!—was it not certain that
the menace to liberty "largely overlooked" for nearly four years must
soon itself become nationwide news?

Moreover, on the issue of the government's "frightening information policy," Sulzberger had right as well as might on his side. As a
matter of principle the press has a "constitutional obligation to act as a
check on the government," claims Tom Wicker, a *New York Times*
columnist. It is "the vehicle through which we learn about government," notes Stephen Hess of the Brookings Institution. A free press
enables "a free citizenry . . . to play an intelligent part in the political
process," says Rusher. Yet here was an American President trying to
prevent us from playing that part. What could be more newsworthy
than that? "The journalist's role is to serve as an advocate or celebrant
of consensual values," says Daniel Hallin, a professor of communications quoted by Hertsgaard. And what consensual value could be

more authoritative in America than democracy, which Sulzberger, armed cap-a-pie with right and might, stood up to defend from danger on November 9, 1984.

What happened? Nothing at all. The "frightening information policy" remained almost as "overlooked by the general public" four years after Sulzberger's speech as it had been the day he delivered it, although the policy remained unaltered and even grew bolder for a time. Just three days before Sulzberger spoke, the administration had proposed new regulations that made it a felony under the export control laws for a Defense Department official to "export" to his fellow Americans any *non-classified* technical information—for example, by talking to a newspaper reporter. Heavy fines and long prison terms would await the public servant who gave his countrymen documentary evidence of waste and fraud in the administration's waste- and fraud-ridden military buildup.

To this latest installment of the frightening information policy Sulzberger's editors replied on November 10: "Casting a penumbra over all non-secret scientific and technical information will deny the Pentagon the benefit of valuable public criticism." What frightening policy? What policy at all? The Reagan Administration was not trying to stifle public criticism. It was guilty, at most, of underestimating its benefits. So said the editors of *The New York Times*, tacitly rebuking citizen Sulzberger. The mighty publisher of the mighty *Times* had dared champion liberty, and his own editors sided with its powerful foes by casting a penumbra of servile blather over their plans and ambitions.

So let us start afresh and ask again: Who decides what is news in America?

The answer lies right on the surface, as obvious as Poe's purloined letter. Reporters themselves know the answer, and talk of it candidly enough in their memoirs. Newspapers carry the answer in almost every news story they publish. What keeps us looking in the wrong direction, as I recently discovered while wading through an ample supply of media studies and books by working journalists, is a deep-seated linguistic habit. Instead of speaking of news, we speak of "the press" and "the media"—corporate entities with wealthy owners, paid employees, profits, holdings, forests in Canada. And, thinking of these, it is almost impossible not to speak of "the press" doing this or that—which is exactly what hides the purloined letter. For to say that the press *does* things conceals the fundamental truth that the press, strictly speaking, can scarcely be said to do anything. It does not act, it is acted upon.

This immediately becomes clear when one considers how and where reporters find the news. Very few newspaper stories are the result of reporters digging in files; poring over documents; or interviewing experts, dissenters, or ordinary people. The overwhelming majority of stories are based on official sources—on information provided by members of Congress, presidential aides, and politicians. A media critic named Leon V. Sigal discovered as much after analyzing 2,850 news stories that appeared in *The New York Times* and *The Washington Post* between 1949 and 1969. Nearly four out of five of these stories, he found, involved official sources. Had Professor Sigal limited his study to national political news, and had he been able to count all the stories that had been instigated by official sources who went unmentioned, nearly five out of five would probably be closer to the truth. The first fact of American journalism is its overwhelming dependence on sources, mostly official, usually powerful. "Sources supply the sense and substance of the day's news. Sources provide the arguments, the rebuttals, the explanations, the criticism," as Theodore L. Glasser, a professor of journalism, wrote in a 1984 issue of the *Quill*, a journalist's journal. To facts derived from sources, reporters add "a paragraph of official-source interpretation," according to Wicker, for powerful people not only make news by their deeds but also tell reporters what to think of those deeds, and the reporters tell us.

David Broder, in his recent memoirs, recalls that while covering the Democratic Party for *The Washington Post* in the late 1960s he learned that the grass-roots rebellion against President Johnson and the Democratic Party establishment, as he then put it, "degrades the Democratic Party"—having been told so by his sources, that is, by members of the Democratic National Committee, Democratic leaders in Congress, and local party officials. Covering Congress means talking to the most powerful legislators and their legislative aides. For years, recalls Broder, the Associated Press covered the House of Representatives for scores of millions of Americans through daily chats with Representative Howard W. Smith, a conservative Virginia Democrat who chaired the powerful Rules Committee. Covering the White House means dancing daily attendance on the President's aides and spokesmen. "We're in small quarters with access to only a small number of official people, getting the same information. So we write similar stories and move on the same issues," says a White House correspondent interviewed in *The Washington Reporters*. A dozen great venues of power and policy—Defense, State, Justice, Central Intelligence, FBI, and so on—form the daily beats of small claques of Washington reporters "whose primary exercise is collecting handouts from those informational soup kitchens," as Alan Abelson once put it in *Barron's*.

Sources are nearly everything; journalists are nearly nothing. "Reporters are puppets. They simply respond to the pull of the most powerful strings," Lyndon Johnson once said. Reagan's secretary of state, Alexander Haig, explained to an interviewer in March 1982 that "even if they write something that I think is terribly untrue, I don't consider that it was a writer who did it. It's always someone who gave that writer that information." So pervasive is the passivity of the press that when a reporter actually looks for news on his or her own it is given a special name, "investigative journalism," to distinguish it from routine, passive "source journalism." It is investigative journalism that wins the professional honors, that makes what little history the American press ever makes, and that provides the misleading exception that proves the rule: the American press, unbidden by powerful sources, seldom investigates anything.

Under the rule of passivity a "leak" is a gift from the powerful. Only rarely is it "an example of a reporter's persistence and skill," as William S. White noted in *Harper's Magazine* more than thirty years ago. "Exclusives" are less a sign of enterprise than of passive service to the powerful. When Reagan's State Department wanted to turn its latest policy line into news, department officials would make it an "exclusive" for Bernard Gwertzman of *The New York Times*, former State Department spokesman John Hughes recently recalled in the pages of *TV Guide*. Hughes could then count on "television's follow-up during the day," since TV news reporters commonly used the *Times* reporter as *their* source, knowing that he was the trusted vessel of the highest officials. It is a bitter irony of source journalism that the most esteemed journalists are precisely the most servile. For it is by making themselves useful to the powerful that they gain access to the "best" sources.

So passive is the press that even seemingly bold "adversarial" stories often have the sanction of the highest officials. In December 1982 *Time* questioned President Reagan's queer mental equipment in a cover story entitled "How Reagan Decides." This was the first such story given prominence in a major news outlet. Yet the story's source, it turned out, was none other than the President's own White House aides, who thought it would help them club Reagan awake. Without White House approval the story would never have run, as the *Time* editor involved, Steve Smith, told the inquisitive Hertsgaard. Five months later, with an economic summit conference scheduled for Colonial Williamsburg, the same White House aides set about repairing any damage to Reagan's image they might have inflicted in December. To make sure that the President's fictive competence would be the media's line at the conference, Reagan aide Michael Deaver invited Hedrick Smith, a star reporter at the *Times*, to lunch at the White House in order to press home the point. This kind of source journalism is almost irresistible to a reporter. As Wicker tells us with admirable candor, "I regret . . . to say I have on too many occasions responded like one of Pavlov's dogs when summoned to the august presence of a White House official; whatever information he had for me, I usually grabbed and ran," knowing full well that it was almost certain to be "a self-serving bill of goods." Hedrick Smith, author of *The Power Game*, did likewise. "A few days later the *Times* ran a page-one story on President Reagan's vigorous preparations for the summit," *The Wall Street Journal* reported. "But the real payoff was how

Mr. Smith's piece set the tone for the television networks' coverage of the summit. All of the TV broadcasts conveyed the image of a President firmly in charge." As Lyndon Johnson once remarked, "There is no such thing as an objective news story. There is always a private story behind the public story."

While serving as Reagan's treasury secretary, James Baker promoted Third World debt policies that were profitable to himself. Yet that gross impropriety, though part of the public record, went completely unnoticed by the press for nearly two years, and continued unnoticed while the Senate was ostensibly examining Baker's appointment as secretary of state. The new secretary had no sooner entered upon his duties, however, when "someone in the administration"—White House counsel C. Boyden Gray, as it turned out—peached on Baker to the press, thereby turning the newsworthy into news. For some reason one of President Bush's White House henchmen had used the press to humiliate the President's most powerful adviser. That was the private story, now becoming public, seen darkly through the looking glass of news.

The private story behind our national news is usually found in Congress. The powerful sources seen darkly through the glass of news are congressional leaders telling the press what to think and say about anything that happens in the capital and anyone who matters in the capital—excluding themselves. "This is a well-known 'secret' in the press corps: *Washington news is funneled through Capitol Hill*," notes Hess, rightly italicizing a secret well worth knowing: that congressional leaders make and unmake the nation's news.

As long as Congress made aid to El Salvador contingent on improvement in human rights, Salvadoran death squads and political crimes were news in America. To keep well supplied, the *Times* put a local investigative reporter on its staff. As soon as Congress lost interest in El Salvador, in 1982, the murderous regime virtually ceased to be news; the *Times* investigative reporter—Raymond Bonner—was promptly replaced by a reporter more amenable to the new congressional line.

For some years evidence of Pentagon waste and corruption had been available to the press in the uncommonly graphic form of $660 ashtrays and $7,622 coffeepots. Yet this well-documented information lay in a sort of journalistic limbo until mid-September 1984, when certain political leaders held a well-orchestrated Senate hearing on Pentagon waste. Thus licensed as news, outrageous ashtrays became common knowledge and struck home with extraordinary force. The entire country was so enthralled and appalled that the wanton arms buildup stood in political peril. Something had to be done to stanch the flow of enlightening news. At the urgent request of congressional leaders (frightened perhaps of their own temerity), President Reagan established in mid-1985 a bipartisan commission to take charge of investigating Pentagon procurement. In typical mock deference to lofty presidential commissions—those black holes in political space—Congress fell silent about defense corruption. No official source remained but the Pentagon soup kitchen, which ladles out no news of Pentagon malfeasance. Once again minus its congressional news license, Pentagon waste and corruption disappeared into journalistic limbo. On matters of public consequence, it is not news editors but the powerful leaders of Congress who decide what is news and how it will be played.

Do we harbor a clear and distinct impression about national affairs? Quite likely it comes from congressional leaders. "To a large extent, the reputations of Presidents and their top political appointees—cabinet members, agency heads, etc.—are made or broken on Capitol Hill," Broder notes in his memoirs. The "news" that President Carter failed to "consult with congressional leaders" came to us from congressional leaders. (The truth of the matter was quite another story.) Similarly, the preposterous "news" that President Bush was haplessly "adrift" six weeks after his inauguration was whispered to reporters by congressional Democrats and "Republican insiders"—leading politicians of both parties. That is surely Hertsgaard's "power to define reality," and just as surely, that power is not in the hands of a passive press and its source-bound reporters. The myth of media power is nothing more than a political orthodoxy that conveniently masks the purloined truth: the professional politicians of Washington quietly shape our national news to suit their interests. It should not come as a surprise that an orthodoxy so useful to the powerful (not to mention flattering to the press) has achieved the prominence it has.

The passivity of the press is commonly—and mistakenly—called "objectivity," the ruling principle of American journalism ever since World War I put an end to the Progressive revolt against oligarchy, monopoly, and privilege. The code of "objective journalism" is simplicity itself. In writing a news story a reporter is forbidden to comment on his own, or draw inferences on his own, or arrange facts too suggestively on his own. Yet even in the most "objective" story, as Wicker notes, nothing can be said "unless some official-enough spokesman could be found to say so."

In 1984 the President and Congress were in agreement that a large voter turnout in El Salvador's presidential election would prove that "a step toward democracy" (as *The New York Times* would later characterize it) had been made, justifying massive aid to the ruling faction. The turnout proved large; the results were hailed and Congress voted increased military aid at once. In the vast farrago of El Salvador news one fact was missing: voting in El Salvador is compulsory. What rule of objectivity kept the American press from telling us the simple, salient, objective fact that gave the lie to the whole futile policy? None.

On February 25, 1986, *The New York Times* reported, a presidential panel investigating the crash of the space shuttle *Challenger* proved incapable of explaining "the cause of the National Aeronautics and Space Administration's apparent insistence that the liftoff proceed on Jan. 28." According to the *Times*, the panel was baffled by NASA's "changed philosophy" of launch safety and puzzled by its sudden decision to put engineers "in the position of proving it was unsafe [to launch], instead of the other way around." What went unmentioned in the *Times* story of official bafflement was a fact formerly known to all—that on the night of the ill-fated launch President Reagan had planned to deliver a State of the Union paean to "America moving ahead" (in the words of a Reagan aide explaining why the speech was postponed). What rule of objectivity required the *Times* to omit mention of this "coincidence" and so shield its readers from the blatant dithering of a presidential panel? None, of course.

There is no public information more objective than an official government document, yet "few Washington news operations have their own facilities for serious documents research," notes Hess. Even when there is time, there is a "shunning of documents research." What rule of objectivity accounts for the shunning of unimpeachably objective sources? None, yet even the most newsworthy documents disappear into journalistic oblivion at the mere behest of the powerful. On February 26, 1987, Reagan's "special review board," known as the Tower Commission, issued its long-awaited report on the Iran-Contra scandal. An hour's reading revealed a President obsessively concerned with, and intensely curious about, Iran-Contra matters, and determined to keep those matters in the hands of close personal advisers. To the press, however, the three members of the commission said exactly the opposite. In public statements, interviews, television appearances, and private meetings with leading editors, they insisted that Reagan was victimized by a "management style" that kept him in complete ignorance of everything blameworthy. That disgraceful lie, which in effect accused the President of his own defense, was endorsed at once by Democratic leaders and duly became the day's news, as if the report had never been written. When the Iran-Contra committees of Congress issued *their* report on the scandal, congressional leaders told the press at once that the whole sordid chapter was closed. The press did as instructed and closed the books at once on the most extraordinary abuse of power in presidential history. The report itself was ignored; a wealth of newsworthy information, impeccably "sourced," sank into journalistic limbo. The report termed Reagan's private war against Nicaragua "a flagrant violation of the Appropriations Clause of the Constitution," but that grave charge, worthy of blazing headlines, was scarcely noticed in the press and ignored entirely by the *Times*. What rule of journalism dictates such base servility to the powerful? No rule save the rule of the whip, which political power cracks over the press's head.

"Aggressive challenges to the official version of things" arouse what Wicker calls "Establishment disapproval" and bring down the Establishment lash: "lost access, complaints to editors and publishers, social penalties, leaks to competitors, a variety of responses no one wants." "To examine critically the institutions and mores of government," notes Leonard Downie, Jr., managing editor of *The Washington Post*, "might mean breaking friendships with trusted government contacts, missing the consensus front-page stories everyone else is after, or failing to be followed down a new path of inquiry." Punishments need not be draconian. "Manipulating access," says Wicker, "is the most standard means of stroking and threatening, and by all odds the most effective, even against bold and independent reporters." If draconian methods are needed, political leaders do not scruple to use them. When Halberstam's Vietnam reporting for the *Times* angered President Kennedy, his White House henchmen whispered to Wicker "the slander that Halberstam was a Saigon barhopper who had never been to the front." Twenty years later, Robert Parry's Central America reporting for the Associated Press ran afoul of Reagan's State Department, which launched a whisper campaign against him, accusing Parry of being a Sandinista sympathizer disguised as a journalist.

Self-serving politicians bully and threaten the publishers' employees, hinder their work, and weaken their stories, yet almost no audible protest comes from the "super-rich and powerful businessmen who ultimately controlled the U.S. news media." Slandered by State Department hatchet men, Parry discovered that, as he told Hertsgaard, "if you don't succumb to all that, you get the line from your editors that maybe they should take you off the story, since you seem to be pursuing a political agenda. When the government attacks you, even your colleagues begin to doubt your credibility." Assigned by the A.P. to the Pentagon beat in the 1960s, a young reporter named Seymour Hersh sidestepped its informational soup kitchen, found his own high-ranking official sources, and duly infuriated Assistant Secretary of Defense Arthur Sylvester, master of the soup kitchen at the time. Sylvester phoned Hersh's boss to complain about the "little ferret," as he was known in the Pentagon, and out went the inquisitive Hersh. The fact that his stories were impeccably "objective," that the A.P.'s member newspapers had been pleased to publish them, meant absolutely nothing. The Pentagon had spoken, and the A.P. obeyed. The obligation of a free press to "act as a check on the power of government" is checked instead by the power of government.

Fearful of losing access, "beat reporters must often practice self-censorship," notes Gans, "keeping their most sensational stories to themselves." Fearful of offending the masters of the soup kitchens, they "have little contact with an agency's adversaries." Servile by need, Washington reporters all too often become servile in spirit, like prisoners who come to side with their jailers. "You begin to understand," as I. F. Stone once put it, "that there are certain things the people ought not to know." For nearly twenty years reporters covered the FBI beat without reporting that the bureau was engaged in massive domestic spying under the transparent guise of "counterintelligence." For ten years reporters covered the CIA without reporting on the agency's own illicit domestic spying operation, although they surely had wind of it. For the "myopia of a Washington political beat," says Broder, "there is no sure antidote." Were the power of the media anything more than a shabby fiction, there might be some real hope. In fact, there is none.

The political whip that falls on reporters also falls on the media "powers that be." The publisher or broadcaster who allows his reporter to delve into the forbidden mores of government or to challenge the official version of things by making "controversial charges . . . quoting unidentified sources," says Wicker, "is likely to he denounced for 'irresponsibility.' " His patriotism may be questioned, his advertisers roused against him. He can be held up to public contumely as a prime example of unelected elitist power, with what effect on profits the "powers that be" do not wait to find out. "All too many of [them] are fundamentally businessmen," says Wicker, and nothing scares more easily than a billion dollars.

After President Nixon assailed the *Times* for publishing the Pentagon Papers, "the nation's most influential newspaper," as Rusher calls it, grew so frightened that "we bent over backwards trying to cultivate Nixon," in the words of Max Frankel, now the executive editor of the newspaper. After the Reagan White House publicly scolded CBS for its vivid prime-time documentary on the plight of the poor in 1982, "CBS News management," reports Hertsgaard, "began pressing journalists . . . to tone down criticism of President Reagan."

CBS was the protagonist, too, in one of the most telltale stories of political power and the national news media. On October 27, 1972, CBS News carried a fourteen-minute survey of the Watergate scandal as it stood after four months of brilliant investigative reporting by *The Washington Post,* which had dared treat the break-in as a crime to be solved, even *without official approval.* Elsewhere in the media, however, the story had been "bottled up," notes Halberstam in his account of the episode. The rest of the press treated it as mere partisan bickering; the *Times,* for its part, was still "bending over backwards." Now millions of CBS viewers heard Walter Cronkite describe in detail "charges of a high-level campaign of political sabotage and espionage apparently unparalleled in American history." A second installment on laundered money was scheduled to follow. At the White House, a coarse-minded scoundrel named Charles Colson was in charge of intimidating the press for the President. The day after the broadcast he telephoned the great power-that-be William S. Paley, board chairman of CBS, to hector and berate him. If Paley did not stop the second program, warned Colson, CBS would be stripped of the licenses to operate its five lucrative television stations. A frightened Paley tried his best to carry out the White House order. His newspeople, to their credit, resisted, and a compromise was reached: the second show was cut nearly in half and substantially weakened.

That was not compliant enough for the White House, however. A few days after Nixon's reelection, Colson called up Paley's longtime lieutenant, Frank Stanton, to issue a still more sweeping threat: If CBS persisted in broadcasting hostile news about the President, the White House would ruin CBS on Wall Street and Madison Avenue. "We'll break your network," said tyranny's little henchman. Stanton suppressed his rage. Paley, deeply ashamed, told no one of Colson's threats. Why didn't these two media magnates turn those threats into news? What else is a free press for if not to help a free people hold the powerful to account? Yet here was a President grossly abusing the power of his office (which was newsworthy in itself) in order to censor the news (which was doubly newsworthy) so that the electorate might not hold him accountable at the polls—which was newsworthy three times over.

In John Adams's thunderous words, a free people has "an indisputable, unalienable, indefeasible, divine right to that most dreaded and envied kind of knowledge, I mean, of the characters and conduct of their rulers." Now a ruler was subverting our inalienable right to dreaded knowledge of him. Surely that was newsworthy, yet it didn't become news. It rarely does. The news media in America do not tell the American people that a political whip hangs over their head. That is because a political whip hangs over their head.

"The Washington politician's view of what is going on in the United States has been substituted for what is actually happening in the country," former president of the A.P. Wes Gallagher pointed out in the mid-1970s, a time when the press enjoyed a brief hour of post-Watergate freeness. And why would Washington politicians want us to know that our knowledge of them comes from them? That is the kind of knowledge that awakens a sleeping people, that dissolves political myths and penetrates political disguises. To keep all such dreaded knowledge from the rest of us is the "information policy" of those who rule us. And so it is we hear, from the left as well as the right, the steady drone about media power.

From the "frightening information policy" to the impeachable offenses documented in the shunned Iran-Contra report, the private story behind every major non-story during the Reagan Administration was the Democrats' tacit alliance with Reagan. It is this complicity, and not the Reagan Administration's deft "management" of the news we hear so much about, that explains the press's supineness during the Reagan years. As usual, it was Congress that was managing the news.

"It was very hard to write stories raising questions about Reagan's policy, because the Democrats weren't playing the role of an opposition party," said the A.P.'s Parry, explaining to Hertsgaard why the press seemed to be "on bended knee" during the Reagan years. Congress, said Leslie Stahl of CBS News, "has not been a source for the press in the whole Reagan Administration. They don't want to criticize this beloved man." Even good stories fell flat, said Jonathan Kwitny, a *Wall Street Journal* reporter at the time, because "there is no opposition within the political system." When the *Times*, to its credit, reported on August 8, 1985, that White House aides were giving "direct military advice" to the President's private Contra army, Reagan replied at a press conference that "we're not violating any laws." Democratic leaders asked the President's national security adviser, Robert McFarlane (later convicted for his answer), whether the President was lying, after which they assured the press there was nothing to the report. And for many months one of the most momentous stories of our time "just went nowhere," as Larry Speakes, Reagan's press secretary, boasted to Hertsgaard.

Even stories with eminent sources "just went nowhere" during the Reagan Administration, because the political leadership in Congress, unwilling to challenge the President, refused to license them. For nearly six years New York's Senator Daniel Patrick Moynihan charged in numerous speeches and op-ed articles that our present paralyzing budget deficits were deliberately created by President Reagan and his faction. By slashing taxes (not to mention doubling military spending), they planned from the start to "create a fiscal crisis," Moynihan said, and use that crisis to force the country against its will to reduce "social spending" for years to come. The indictment was truly grave: an American President conspiring to deceive the American people in order to achieve goals he would never have dared avow. The would-be source was impeccable: a prominent senator, respected, reflective, and uncommonly eloquent. Yet Moynihan's indictment never became news, not even in the spring of 1986, when David Stockman's astonishing memoirs substantiated that indictment in dense and vivid detail. Instead of turning the former budget director's memoirs into momentous news, Washington's press corps attacked Stockman for writing them. "In all this torrent of comment about the book," noted James Reston of the *Times*, "there is very little analysis of his indictment of the methods and men who are still deciding the nation's policies." The press fled from the story, Moynihan said, because "the political class cannot handle this subject." Against a political establishment resolved to keep dreaded knowledge from the country, not even an eminent senator can make that knowledge news on his own.

For eight years the Democratic opposition had shielded from the public a feckless, lawless President with an appalling appetite for private power. That was *the* story of the Reagan years, and Washington journalists evidently knew it. Yet they never turned the collusive politics of the Democratic Party into news. Slavishly in thrall to the powerful, incapable of enlightening the ruled without the consent of the rulers, the working press, the "star" reporters, the pundits, the sages, the columnists passed on to us, instead, the Democrats' mendacious drivel about the President's "Teflon shield." For eight years we saw the effects of a bipartisan political class in action, but the press did not show us that political class acting, exercising its collective power, making things happen, contriving the appearances that were reported as news. It rarely does.

On May 8, 1969, the *Times* reported, none too conspicuously, that President Nixon was bombing a neutral country in Southeast Asia (Cambodia) and making elaborate efforts to conceal the fact from the American people. The Democratic Congress ignored the story completely, and without a congressional news license, perforce, it "dropped out of sight," as Wicker notes. The entire party establishment had tacitly rallied around a President who harbored dangerous ambitions. That was what had happened, but it wasn't news. Instead of revealing a would-be tyrant in the White House and his congressional allies, the news showed the American people nothing. Think of it: nothing. Our divine right to dreaded knowledge of our rulers, far from being indefeasible, could scarcely have been said to exist.

Three and a half years later, the same congressional leaders decided to delve into the Watergate scandal, almost certainly to check Nixon's careening ambitions. Yet how many Americans know that a bipartisan

political establishment had actually made such a decision, wise and prudent though it was? All too few. How many Americans believe that an "imperial press" had taken it upon itself to drive a President from office? All too many. And how many Americans have the faintest idea that "the earliest and most serious blow to Carter's credibility," as Broder recently recalled, "came from the way Democrats in Congress had described to reporters their early disillusionment with the President"? The *fact* of Democratic hostility would have been dreaded knowledge, indeed, in 1977: an "outsider" President, newly inaugurated, is assailed at once by his own party's "insiders." But that, too, never became news. Instead, the press reported the hostile jibes of Democratic leaders as if they were impartial judgments rather than blows struck in a political struggle. The "insiders" probably altered the course of our history, but thanks to a servile and subjugated press, we scarcely knew they existed.

So it has continued day after day, decade after decade. Our rulers make the news, but they do not appear in the news, not as they really are—not as a political class, a governing establishment, a body of leaders with great and pervasive powers, with deep, often dark, ambitions. In the American republic the fact of oligarchy is the most dreaded knowledge of all, and our news keeps that knowledge from us. By their subjugation of the press, the political powers in America have conferred on themselves the greatest of political blessings—Gyges' ring of invisibility. And they have left the American people more deeply baffled by their own country's politics than any people on earth. Our public realm lies steeped in twilight, and we call that twilight news.

BIBLIOGRAPHY

"The Two Americas" first appeared as "Republican Virtues" in the July 1979 issue of *Harper's Magazine.*

"The Radical Republic" first appeared as "The Constructs of a Conservative" in the November 1979 issue of *Harper's Magazine.*

"Reflections (After Watergate) on History" first appeared in the Winter 1974 issue of *Horizons* magazine.

"Thucydides in the Cold War" first appeared as "The Two Thousand Years' War" in the March 1981 issue of *Harper's Magazine.*

"Why Johnny Can't Think" first appeared in the June 1985 issue of *Harper's Magazine.*

"The New Social History" first appeared as "Textbook America" in the May 1980 issue of *Harper's Magazine.*

"How Republics Die" first appeared in the Spring 1975 issue of *Horizons* magazine.

"The Parliament of Fans I" first appeared as "The Soaps du Jour" in the July/August 1985 issue of *Channels* magazine.

"The Parliament of Fans II" first appeared as "Why the New Right Is All Wrong About Prime Time" in the September/October 1982 issue of *Channels* magazine.

"The Political History of Central Park" first appeared as "The Central Park" in the April/May 1981 issue of *American Heritage* magazine.

"The America That Was Free and Is Now Dead" first appeared in *The Politics of War,* published by Harper & Row, 1979.

"The Fallout-Shelter Craze of 1961" first appeared in the February 1980 issue of *American Heritage* magazine.

"The Enshrinement of Bobby Kennedy" first appeared as "RFK Enshrined" in the September 1978 issue of *Harper's Magazine.*

"The Hour of the Founders" first appeared in the June 1984 issue of *American Heritage* magazine.

"The Reagan Revolution and Its Democratic Friends" first appeared as "Playing Politics" in the July 1984 issue of *Harper's Magazine.*

"Liberty Under Siege" first appeared in the November 1985 issue of *Harper's Magazine.*

"All the Congressmen's Men" first appeared in the July 1989 issue of *Harper's Magazine.*

INDEX